*Social Welfare
Administration:
Managing Social Programs
in a
Developmental Context*

RINO J. PATTI

University of Washington

Social Welfare Administration: Managing Social Programs in a Developmental Context

PRENTICE-HALL, INC., Englewood Cliffs, New Jersey 07632

Library of Congress Cataloging in Publication Data

PATTI, RINO J.
  Social welfare administration.

  (Prentice-Hall series in social work practice)
  Includes bibliographical references and index.
  1. Social work administration.   2. Middle
managers.   I. Title.   II. Series.
HV41.P365   361′.0068   82-7617
ISBN 0-13-819458-0   AACR2

Editorial production/supervision
    and interior design: *Edith Riker*
Cover design: *Wanda Lubelska Design*
Manufacturing buyer: *John Hall*

Prentice-Hall Series in Social Work Practice
Neil Gilbert and Harry Specht, Editors

Printed in the United States of America

10 9 8 7 6 5 4 3 2 1

ISBN 0-13-819458-0

Prentice-Hall International, Inc., *London*
Prentice-Hall of Australia Pty. Limited, *Sydney*
Prentice-Hall Canada Inc., *Toronto*
Prentice-Hall of India Private Limited, *New Delhi*
Prentice-Hall of Japan, Inc., *Tokyo*
Prentice-Hall of Southeast Asia Pte. Ltd., *Singapore*
Whitehall Books Limited, *Wellington, New Zealand*

Contents

CHAPTER FIVE:
PROGRAM MANAGEMENT IN THE IMPLEMENTATION STAGE

Implementation Stage: Organizational Context, *106*
Developmental Goals, *112*
Management Tasks and Issues in the Implementation Stage, *113*
Summary, *149*
Notes, *149*

CHAPTER SIX:
PROGRAM MANAGEMENT IN THE STABILIZATION STAGE

Stabilization Stage: Organizational Context, *155*
Developmental Goals, *161*
Management Tasks and Issues in the Stabilization Stage, *162*
Summary, *202*
Notes, *203*

PART THREE: **PREPARING FOR THE FUTURE** (Conclusion

CHAPTER SEVEN:
FROM DIRECT SERVICE TO ADMINISTRATION: PROBLEMS AND PROSPECTS FOR SOCIAL WORKERS IN TRANSITION

The Clinician-Administrator and the Management Workforce in
  Social Welfare, *210*
From Direct Service to Management, *211*
Developing Clinician-Administrators: Some Workforce Strategies for
  Schools and Agencies, *221*
Summary, *229*
Notes, *229*

Preface

The quarter century between World War II and the 1970s was a period of unparalleled growth in the size and scope of the social welfare sector in this country. Government, building on a foundation laid by the New Deal, sought to establish a network of social programs that would ensure minimal health, welfare, and economic opportunity for the poor, disadvantaged, and disabled in our society. But even as this network was being created, many governmental leaders, reflecting the characteristic ambivalence of Americans toward social welfare, became restive about what had been committed and were concerned that this enterprise might be subverting the economic order and the traditional values on which this country had been based.

It was in this context in the late 1960s and 1970s, that the "management of social welfare" began to emerge as a central political preoccupation. Two broad and contrasting orientations to management arose from this milieu. The "advocates"—those basically sympathetic to the purposes of social welfare—saw management as an opportunity to strengthen the operation of social programs and to utilize more effectively the scarce resources available in the pursuit of social goals. These persons believed that improvements in management practice would maximize benefits for consumers of social welfare, and at the same time satisfy policy makers, resource controllers and their constituents, that social programs were being judiciously administered.

Others, whom we shall refer to as "antagonists," perceived management as a mechanism for bringing the social welfare enterprise in tow. For them, the purpose of management was to wrest control of this institutional sector away from in-house professional careerists, whose personal interests and philosophic orientation led them inexorably to push for expanded programs and liberalized benefits. The mission of social welfare management was to control these excesses, strip away frivolous and inefficient services, and reduce social welfare to those "essentials" that were required by the "truly needy."

At this writing, a tide of political reaction in this country is nurturing and legitimizing the antagonist's perspective on management in social welfare. Policy initiatives are being undertaken to significantly curtail the size and scope of the social welfare sector and to redirect the ideological foundation on which it rests. To what extent these initiatives will be successful in the 1980s is still a question, but there is little doubt that whatever cannot be obtained through legislative policy will almost certainly be attempted through administrative reforms and management practices.

This brings us to the intended audience of this book, the advocates of social welfare. In the years ahead, these persons will find themselves in an unhospitable environment, influenced by an ideology that seeks a drastically diminished role for social welfare. Such persons, among whom social workers will be prominent, will play a critical role in contesting this agenda and preserving the integrity of social programs. In the larger sense, we are concerned with how social welfare managers, particularly those at the middle levels of social agencies, can pursue this mission.

More concretely, we seek to formulate an approach to administration that grows out of, and is in the service of, the humane and progressive goals of social welfare and the values and ethics of the social work profession. We shall try to fashion a model of administration that is indigenous to social welfare and social work—one that seeks to tailor management practices to the problems, issues, and requirements of social service agencies and those they serve. For too long now, policy makers, administrative theoreticians, and others have sought to impose business and military management technologies on social welfare organizations as though the substance of the agency enterprise was inconsequential. Our view, however, is that we must develop social welfare management from the inside out: we should ask first what needs are to be addressed, what values and objectives are to be pursued, and finally, what management tools seem best suited to furthering these ends.

We also address several secondary though important issues. Much of the management of social agencies, particularly at the lower and middle levels, is in the hands of social workers and other human service professionals whose training and experience have been largely in direct service. Such persons seldom have had the benefit of formal management preparation before they have been thrust into the administrative arena. Moreover, such training and literature that has been available to them has been aimed at executive-level managers, whose problems and responsibilities, as we shall see, vary significantly from those of middle managers. One of our principle purposes in this book is to help human service professionals make the transition from direct service to management. We shall focus upon both the personal and professional adjustments that are required as they move into middle-level management and the unique contextual and organizational circumstances they will confront there.

This book is also concerned with the pervasive problem of failed program implementation. In recent years a substantial literature has emerged that addresses this problem,[1] but with few exceptions,[2] this material has focused on describing and analyzing political and institutional impediments to policy implementation rather than the roles of the actors engaged in this process. Here we will be concerned with one crucial but largely neglected set of actors in the implementation process: the program managers who are finally responsible for translating policy intent into social services. One critical reason some social programs fail to fully realize their potential is that managers are generally not prepared to recognize, and thus anticipate, the behavioral changes that are required of them as programs unfold. While there is a general appreciation of the notion that some managers are inherently more effective than others at certain points in the program developmental cycle, little attention has been given to the differential role and task requirements associated with stages of program growth. The result, too often, is that managers who have experienced success at one stage find that the style and technique previously employed are no longer functional in addressing emerging problems and issues. In some instances, a manager who is unable to make the transition is replaced by one who is better attuned to a program's current requirements. Perhaps more commonly, a manager attempts to modify his or her behavioral repertoire through trial and error. In either case, program performance is likely to suffer while the manager makes these adjustments. Our purpose, then, is to provide a framework that will help middle managers anticipate and thus prepare themselves for the tasks and responsibilities that arise as programs develop over time.

ORGANIZATION OF THE BOOK

This volume is organized in three parts. Part One provides a broad introduction to social welfare administration, in both historical and contemporary dimensions. Since social workers and the social work profession have played such a prominent role in administering social welfare, we have placed both the development and current nature of administrative practice in that professional context. Chapter 1 deals with the slow and torturous process by which administration ultimately came to be accepted as a legitimate form of social work practice and the implications of that history for current efforts to develop management in the profession. Chapter 2 outlines the salient aspects of modern administrative practice in social welfare, addressing, in particular, how the characteristics of social agencies serve to condition management and the tasks and activities that are performed by managers.

Part Two, which is the core of the book, presents a model of management practice, set in the context of stages of program development. The basic features of the model are set forth in Chapter 3; each of the following three chapters discusses management tasks and issues as they arise in the design, implementation, and stabilization stages, respectively. In each of these chapters we highlight the organizational processes that tend to characterize programs at particular stages, the goals sought by managers as they build program capability, and the tasks that must be accomplished to achieve these goals.

Part Three is concerned with the future of social welfare administration and the role of social work in advancing this area of practice. Chapter 7 focuses on the problems confronting social workers and other human service professionals who make the transition from direct service to middle management. Particular attention is given to what professional schools and social agencies might do to identify those front-line practitioners who may have administrative potential and prepare them for the assumption of these responsibilities. The final chapter sets forth several priority issues that must be addressed as social work seeks to enhance the state of social welfare administration and consolidate its leadership role in this field.

ACKNOWLEDGMENTS

I am particularly fortunate to work in an organization that has nurtured my interests and rewarded my work. I am especially blessed with an immediate circle of colleagues who share with me an intense desire to see that social welfare organizations are humane and effective instruments of social change, and who believe, as I do, that social work administrators have much to contribute in this regard. All have contributed, directly and indirectly, to the ideas that are ultimately reflected in this book, though none, of course, can be held responsible for its content. A special debt is owed Professors Herman Resnick and Michael Austin, collaborators and friends, who stimulated me to explore the idea of organizational development and its implications for administrative practice. I would also like to express my appreciation to Mitzi Vondrachek and Sandy Brown, both of whom laboriously typed the manuscript, often improving the text as they went along.

I am grateful to Davis McEntire, University of California–Berkeley, H. Wayne Johnson, University of Iowa, Dale F. Pearson, Brigham Young University, and George Brager, Columbia University School of Social Work for providing useful suggestions regarding the book at various stages in its development.

Finally, to Nadine, Chris, and Laura, who have given infinite patience and continued support to an often absent and distracted husband and father, my deepest love. I will spend a lifetime repaying the debt.

NOTES

[1]For example, see Jeffrey L. Pressman and Aaron Wildavsky, *Implementation* (Berkeley, Calif.: University of California Press, 1974); and Walter Williams and Richard Elmore, eds., *Social Program Implementation* (New York: Academic Press, 1976).

[2]Gordon Chase, "Implementing a Human Services Program: How Hard Will It Be?" *Public Policy,* 27, No. 4 (Fall, 1979), 385–435.

Rino J. Patti

CHAPTER ONE

The Emergence
of Administration
in Social Work

Although social workers have long been extensively involved in administering social welfare organizations, both public and private, the profession of social work has been slow—and for the most part reluctant—to recognize administration as a legitimate expression of professional practice. Since its earliest beginnings in the latter part of the nineteenth century, the profession has been called upon to provide administrative leadership and management expertise in the social welfare sector. Indeed, some of the profession's most luminous historical figures—Jane Addams, Harry Hopkins, Mary Richmond, and Julia Lathrop, to name a few—devoted much of their professional lives to developing and administering social programs. Though they and countless other social workers have carried out their responsibilities ably and often imaginatively, they have done so largely without any organized body of practice knowledge directly applicable to social welfare administration, and until recently, without benefit of formal educational preparation.

This situation began to change dramatically in the 1970s. Administration currently enjoys a much more prominent place in the constellation of social work methods; and efforts to conceptualize this form of practice, to formulate its test propositions, and to transmit this knowledge in educational programs are proceeding at an accelerated rate. Later in this chapter we shall explore these recent developments in greater depth; but before doing so we shall briefly examine the emergence of administration in social work, because in many ways the profession's historic posture toward this area of practice has left a legacy that continues to exert a significant influence on the nature and direction of social welfare administration today. We shall analyze developments in four periods: 1900–1935, 1935–1960, 1960–1970, and 1970–1975.

1900–1935: NOMINAL RECOGNITION

The period between 1900 and 1935 was decisive in molding the identity of social work as an occupation and confirming social casework as the dominant and distinctive method of this emerging profession. As social work emerged from the nineteenth century, it was at best a loosely knit network of volunteers, civic leaders, social reformers, paid workers, and agency administrators working in diverse settings such as charity organization societies, settlement houses, and child welfare organizations. Members of this network were joined together tenuously by a commitment to improving the social conditions of the poor and rationalizing the practices of charitable institutions.[1]

The several decades following the turn of the century witnessed an intensive period of professionalization. Social work was introduced in hospitals, courts, schools, and psychiatric settings; schools of social work were established; and professional associations were formed to set and monitor education and experience requirements for entry to the fledging profession.

The drive to develop a unified and coherent profession was difficult in the face of diverse specializations and interests. Leaders in the field sought to define a core technology, a "nuclear skill" in Lubove's terms, that would at once provide a model of practice for workers in various settings and serve as a basis for a distinctive professional expertise. Social casework, as is well known, became that nuclear skill, the focal point around which the profession would forge its identity.[2] By the 1920s social casework had become the most advanced and well-formulated field of practice in social work. Mary Richmond's systematic efforts to develop principles of practice in *Social Diagnosis* (1917) and *What is Social Case Work?* (1922) provided much of the theoretical underpinning that was later to be extended and elaborated with the introduction of Freudian psychology.[3] Schools of social work—closely linked with and reflecting the needs of agencies, particularly those under voluntary auspices—built their curricula around social casework and were almost singularly concerned with teaching skills and techniques that might be employed by front-line practitioners in resolving the problems of clients one by one.

Given the preeminent position of social casework, administration was afforded relatively little attention as a form of professional practice in the first third of the century. There were, of course, some leaders and educators in the field who argued that social casework was too narrow a focus for a profession that sought to affect the purpose, organization, and delivery of social services. Perhaps the most eminent of these critics was Edith Abbott, who along with her colleague at the Chicago School of Civics and Philanthropy, Sophonisba Breckinridge, urged the profession to adopt a much broader approach to social work education, an approach that would equip students not only for direct practice, but also for the eventual assumption of administrative and policy responsibilities. Speaking to the American Association of Social Workers in 1927, Abbott rejected the notion that professional education should consist exclusively of highly technical and specific courses focused on casework technique. Preparation in direct services was an important but insufficient basis for social work:

> The caseworkers of today should be prepared to become later the secretary of a state social welfare board or the secretary of a council of social agencies. . . . It should not be necessary . . . when such positions become available to look for a man who has been trained as a lawyer or as a university professor of economics instead of a person basically trained in the science of social welfare and promoted after experience competently earned in the ranks.[4]

And later in the same address: "The only difference between them [caseworkers] and the generals of the army should be differences of age and experience. Their basic education should be the same."[5]

It is important to note that the position of Abbott, and presumably the Chicago school, was not a dissent from social casework as the central professional function. Her argument, rather, was against making social work coterminous with social casework, against assuming that preparation for direct service was an adequate foundation for a later career transition from social casework to administration and other types of leadership responsibilities.

Abbott and her colleagues were not alone in arguing for a broader concept of social work practice. James Hagerty, who completed one of several studies on social work education conducted during the 1920s, also viewed the profession's preoccupation with social casework with alarm and maintained that the "most important task they [schools] should be engaged in" was "the education of the leaders, the organizers, and the administrators—in short, the executives in social work administration."[6]

These minority views notwithstanding, by 1930 social casework had become entrenched as the dominant method in social work, and caseworkers became the principal spokespersons for the field. It was difficult for the profession to disregard administration completely, since many social workers inevitably became involved in it. For the most part, however, it appears that Arthur Dunham was correct in concluding that in the early days of social work, "Administration was not ordinarily distinguished from direct practice, nor thought of as a separate function."[7] Knowledge and competence in social casework was assumed to be the foundation of all forms of professional practice. Having achieved this foundation, the social worker, aided by experience and an intimate familiarity with the social agency, could learn what was needed to administer effectively.[8]

Educational practices in social work during the early twentieth century both reflected and contributed to this prevailing assumption about administration. Courses in administration applied to specific agency settings (e.g., child welfare) were to be found in the curricula of many schools; and after 1914, a number of programs also offered courses in general social welfare administration. But since such courses were generally not treated as core requirements and were often taught by agency administrators who did not enjoy regular faculty status, we may assume that the content did not have high priority on the educational agenda.[9] Edith Abbott argued persuasively for basic curricula that would include public welfare administration so that all social workers would "understand the methods of organization, control, and administration of our public social services."[10] However, there is no evidence that this content was substantially addressed in the programs of any but a few schools. Indeed, when the American Association of Professional Schools of Social Work adopted its minimum curriculum for the first year of graduate programs in 1932, administration was consigned to a group of electives that students might or might not take in their course of study.[11]

The reluctant posture of social work education toward administration was perhaps best exemplified in the 1929 Milford conference at which leaders in the field met to define the nature of social work. After setting forth their conception of "generic casework," the conferees proposed a curriculum for professional training schools that would encompass the "fundamental techniques of social work" including social casework, group work, community organization, research, and administration.[12] A specific set of recommendations for casework training was included in this report, but little explicit attention was given to the content of training for the other practice methods. Interestingly, the report gave detailed attention to the framework and standards for the organization and structure of social agencies, but said little of the skills or processes that would be needed to bring about these conditions, nor the preparation managers would need to effectively practice in this arena.[13] Thus one of the era's most influential documents on education for practice on the one hand identified administration as fundamental to social work and the organizational context as critical to effective service delivery, and on the other, failed to specify what aspiring administrators should know and be able to do.

Research and scholarship in administration, as reflected in the literature of the era, fared little better. There were a sprinkling of articles on the subject to be found in journals like *Better Times* and *Survey*,[14] and in a few books, most notably those related to the administration of voluntary agencies.[15] However, the first broad statement of the philosophical and technical dimensions of social agency administration that might be applicable to various fields of service in both public and voluntary sectors, did not appear until 1931.[16]

Perhaps most revealing about the status of administration as a proper subject of professional study and practice was the fact that the first *Social Work Yearbook,* published in 1929, contained no article on this topic.[17] Administration was addressed in the *Social Work Yearbook* for 1933, but did not appear again as a regular feature until 1939. Interestingly, the 1935 *Yearbook* lists the "major divisions of social work" as social casework, group work, social planning, and research. Similarly, though articles on administration did appear from time to time in the proceedings of the National Conference of Social Work during this period, this subject was not routinely addressed by the conference until 1936. In short, a review of professional literature of that period indicates that there was no national forum in which the theory and practice of administration in social welfare could receive the sustained attention of the profession.

What then can be said of the status of administration as a method of practice in social work as the profession approached the Great Depression? Clearly, the social casework method had come to symbolize professionalism: it was considered the wellspring of practice in all its forms and settings. Mastery in this method was considered at least a necessary, if not a sufficient basis for achieving competency in the other methods, including administration. The profession gave nominal recognition to administration as a professional responsibility, but in fact attached low priority to its development as a coherent body of practice knowledge and techniques. Indeed, the profession seemed less concerned with *what* administrators did to manage agencies than it was with *when* they did it. So long as a social worker had served an apprenticeship in direct services and was well steeped in prevailing professional norms and values, he or she might then be safely given responsibility for managing an agency. The definition of administration as ancillary to casework seemed less a deliberate institutional strategy than a failure to understand and address the knowledge and skill requirements of administration in its own terms. This legacy was to plague administration as a field in social work for years to come.

1935–1960: THE STRUGGLE FOR LEGITIMACY

The Depression and the subsequent involvement of the federal government in providing economic assistance to millions of unemployed and economically dislocated people had important implications for the development of administration as a professional method of practice. The establishment of the Federal Emergency Relief Administration (FERA) in 1934, followed by the creation of a federal-state system of public assistance under the Social Security Act in 1935, stimulated an enormous demand for personnel in the public social services. Newly created or expanded state and local public welfare departments required large numbers of workers who could be quickly trained to plan, organize, administer, and supervise the delivery of social services mandated by these federal initiatives.[18] Though social work had until that time been most closely allied with the voluntary sector, government nonetheless looked to the profession to help shape the organization and delivery of services and provide educational direction.

The effects of this new association with public welfare for the profession were far reaching. Shortly after the FERA was established, grants were made available to the states to support intensive, short-term courses of study in schools of social work that would prepare personnel to work in public relief agencies.[19] The influx of students not only stretched the limited resources of these educational institutions, but also required them to reexamine their curricula, since for the most part schools of social work had been primarily concerned with preparing social workers for direct practice in voluntary settings. Though some of the content was apparently transferable to public welfare, it was also necessary for schools to recognize the distinctive elements of practice in these settings and to modify their curricula offerings accordingly. Among other things, schools were called upon to examine how casework and group work skills might be adapted to administrative and supervisory responsibilities in public welfare and to incorporate content on public social policy.[20] The impact on graduate programs was discernable. Street, commenting in 1940, noted about this period:

> Before the Depression very few of our schools of social work gave much, if any, attention to the problems of public welfare. There were some distinguished exceptions to this record. In general, however, the whole stress in social work training was on private agency service.... Now, however, the educational situation is entirely different. Nearly every school in the country gives one or more courses in public welfare administration, and social workers are given specialized training for professional life as public servants.[21]

Too much can be made of the influence of these developments in public welfare on social work education. In the last analysis, even though events in the Depression demanded that the profession incorporate new knowledge and perspectives, there remained an abiding commitment to casework as the fundamental method in social work. The greater bulk of the profession's energy was devoted to infusing these new public programs with principles and values that would make them receptive to casework as the major helping process.[22] Inevitably, however, it was necessary to contend with the public welfare system on its own terms, to understand the complexities of public policy development and the intricacies of program structure, finance, and personnel systems. Though this did not bring the profession headlong into a concern with administration as a method of practice, it did serve to alert the profession to the enormous complexity of administering public programs and the knowledge and skill that were required.[23]

It was in this context that social workers first began to look to the emerging field of public administration for a theoretical framework that could inform the practice of management in public welfare agencies. Particularly influential were the contributions of scholars such as Follett, Gulick, and Urwick. Dimock and White, theorists of the emerging school of administrative management, who provided, among other things, an orderly way of thinking about leadership, administrative processes, and principles for structuring organizations. Many of the formulations relating, for example to division of labor, span of control, line-staff responsibilities, coordination, personnel management, and managerial functions, were adapted to courses on social agency administration and reflected in the early literature on this subject.[24] Thus for the first time there began to emerge a set of principles and guidelines for administrative practice in social welfare that did not owe its intellectual inspiration to social casework.

While the involvement of social work in public welfare stimulated an increased interest in the organization and management of social services, administration continued to be perceived as a peripheral field of professional practice.[25] By the mid-1940s, a literature on administration had emerged that cataloged the duties and qualities of executives and the mechanics of administration in social agencies; but there persisted a tendency to characterize management as removed from the professional mainstream, as an adjunct to the main business of social work—albeit one that carried status and privilege. One of the principal textbooks of the period, for example, contained the following statement on the liabilities of administrative work:

> Not all social workers like administrative duty. First of all, it requires a willingness and a desire to get away from the routine of "practice." Physicians, like social workers, become habituated to their patient relationships. . . . If they are removed from the patient, most of them tend to lose the gripping interest that being face to face with a problem creates. As compared with the dramatic and tense situation of grappling with disease, executive positions in the medical field become mundane and uninteresting. Exactly the same position prevails in social work. *Practice of the profession is most interesting at firsthand, and the problems that arise with individuals and groups served.* [Emphasis mine.] There must be a willingness to leave this close relationship for the complications of executive control.[26]

One could hardly blame social workers of that period if they perceived administration to be something of a professional no-man's-land. If administration was to be included as a part of social work, it needed to be defined in terms that were less alien to professional practitioners.

Theoretical and conceptual developments in administration in the decade after World War II were purposefully directed at fashioning a method of practice that would be organically related to the core knowledge, values, and skills in social work. This effort to acculturate administration, to evolve a *social work administration,* was manifest in several ways.

First, social work administration was to be considered different—or at least a distinctive variant of—general administration. To be sure, elements of general administration were common to all organizational settings; but the unique character of social agencies and of social services conditioned the practice of administration to such an extent that it deserved attention as a subfield in its own right. The idea that a practice of administration existed that could be applied in diverse settings (if it had ever had currency in social work) was now being rejected in favor of the notion that administration in social work required specialized training and expertise. "This much we do know," wrote one prominent social work educator, "the greater bulk of content in social work administration is not common to other kinds of administration."[27] Among other things, the unique character of social work administration was thought to flow from its central preoccupation with quality of service, as reflected in the "adequacy of benefits and services, client-centeredness, professional competencies, effectiveness of programs, and efficiency of operation."[28] In addition, special problems confronted social agencies and social work administrators. Taxpayers and voluntary contributors were concerned that their money be spent on services to clients and not on "overhead" and "red tape." Social workers themselves resisted standardized procedures in administration. Measuring the effects of social services presented difficulties. These special problems were thought to require skills not commonly demanded of administrators in other types of settings.[29] It followed that social agency administration was a specialty which required an in-depth knowledge of the area that was to be administered.

Secondly, major theoreticians of that era sought to ally administration much more closely with the dominant values and methods of casework. The core function of administration was enabling individuals and groups in the agency to maximize their respective contributions through democratic processes.[30] Administration was not the unilateral exercise of authority by the executive, but rather a "cumulative responsibility" shared by all groups and interests, including staff, board, volunteers, members, and constituents.[31] Administrative authority, in this view, grew out of the reciprocal relations between the executive and those who worked in and received services from the agency. The vehicle for this collective authority was to be participation, wherein all salient groups had a real voice in determining a destiny of the agency. Ultimately, the executive's authority derived from "consensus and voluntary choice of action rather than fiat or decree."[32]

The philosophical orientation of this emerging social work administration was captured in the following comment by a leading social work educator:

> Modern administration must replace the hierarchical form of structure. . . . A new structure which unites rather than divides is called for. A new scheme of relationships which calls forth human energy rather than keeping it under control is essential. A belief that the agency exists for all and that administration must serve all can only be carried into action if we eliminate the false separation between "deciders," "doers," and "receivers."[33]

Third, the democratic, participatory nature of social work administration, and its attendant concern with interpersonal and group processes, necessarily made skill in human relations the very cornerstone of this emerging method. It simultaneously provided the bridge that was needed to bring this field of practice into the mainstream of the profession. If administration was a helping, enabling role, then there was, in fact, much that administrators could borrow from casework and group work. Thus could a leading educator and administrator assert:

> The professional service which the executive has to perform is similar in many ways to the function that is common to the caseworker, group worker, and community organization worker. His is essentially a helping role carried on by means of relationships which he has skill in developing between himself and others, between various groups that make up the agency and between all of them and the goal or purpose of the agency.[34]

Having drawn the essential parallel between casework, group work, and administration, it followed that the social work administrator should draw upon established principles and practices in these fields. Aspects of the group work method such as skill in group formation, facilitating movement and progress in groups, determining group objectives, discovering the interests and needs of individuals, and guiding interaction, could be employed by an administrator as he or she worked with boards, committees, staff, and community groups.[35] From casework, administrators could deepen their understanding of and relationships with individuals by applying such concepts as individualization and growth through relationships, and by understanding the dynamics of human behavior, including ambivalence, ego defenses, and the purposiveness of behavior.[36]

Efforts to define social work administration as a helping process largely focused on facilitating interpersonal relationships not only served to bring this method of practice into the ideological congruence with the profession, but also served to move social work administration away from the theoretical influence of the administrative management school and toward the emerging school of human relations. Herein lay a body of theory and empirical evidence which by the 1950s pointed strongly to the conclusion that morale, satisfaction, and productivity of subordinates was vitally affected by the social-psychological climate of the organization, and most especially, by the quality of relations between leaders and the led.[37] Effective leadership, as conceived by this school of thought, did not derive from one's ability to impose one's will on others, but rather on one's skill in promoting participation in the decision process and involving subordinates in the task of shaping their own environment. Though this concept had been developed in industrial and business settings, there were some social workers who did not miss its significance for social work administration. In the human relations school, one could find "scientific" confirmation of the efficacy of democratic administration. This happy confluence of science and practice was apparent to one social work academic who said in addressing the National Conference of Social Work in 1946:

> Happily, for those interested in "permissives" as well as in directives: who are seeking to develop power with rather than power over our employees; who try to get back of, rather than back at, persons who create difficulty; and who regard the administrative act as an educational act, that in the last analysis must square with laws of learning guidance in building a democratic work group is freshly available.[38]

By the 1950s then, it was apparent that administration was becoming "an inherent part of the whole social work process, rather than merely a tool, adjunct or facilitating device."[39] Though administration had gained a foothold, there continued to be an abiding resistance to recognizing it as a professional method of practice. Though many in the profession could recognize administration as an important contextual factor in the delivery of social services,[40] it was quite another thing to comit the profession to training neophyte social workers to become managers. A major study of social work education completed in the 1950s criticized the profession for its failure to adequately prepare social workers for administrative practice and noted:

> A substantial number of leaders in this field . . . doubt that social work administrators should be considered as members of the profession, and hence doubt that a professional school has any responsibility for their education. Instead, they believe administrators, other than supervisors, belong in a category similar to that used by the medical profession for administrators of hospitals and clinics.[41]

In the face of this resistance, schools of social work made relatively little progress in developing programs for training social workers for direct entry to administrative practice.[42] A few schools tailored special programs for selected, experienced students who would be immediately returning to administrative positions. However by the late 1950s, the dominant pattern was for schools to incorporate one introductory course in administration in curricula otherwise devoted to preparation for direct practice. Some students were also given structured exposure to administrative problems and practices in the course of their field placements,[43] but there is little indication that this aspect of field experience was given serious and systematic attention. The prevailing belief continued that where social workers became involved in administrative practice at all, they should do so only after a period of intensive training and experience in direct services.[44] The introductory content provided in graduate school was geared primarily to what direct services workers needed to know in order to handle the administrative aspects of their jobs. This, plus a program of study in casework or group work, was thought to provide much of the basic content for later entry to administration, supplemented by in-service and on-the-job training. Though there was as yet no widespread support for the idea that some social workers might be trained in administration per se, this recommendation was contained in two separate studies of social work education in the 1950s and received increasing support.[45]

In summary then, the period from 1930 to 1960 witnessed the emergence of administration as a bona fide method of social work practice. Though still a "minor" method, and the object of distrust in some circles, the widespread incorporation of introductory administration content in social work education signaled the fact that it had achieved some institutional acceptance. Much remained to be done before administrative practice would become an equal partner in the family of social work methods. The years that lay ahead seemed filled with promise.

1960–1970: PROMISE UNFULFILLED

In the early 1960s it appeared as though the profession was at long last ready to assume responsibility for preparing social workers for administrative leadership. Though most in the profession continued to look upon administrative practice less than enthusiastically, a significant community of opinion had emerged around the proposition that social work should move aggressively to develop theory and practice in administration and kindred areas.

Several developments symbolized this emerging conviction. The National Association of Social Workers (NASW) sponsored an institute in 1960 devoted to research in social work administration and community organization. The institute, attended by distinguished academics and practitioners, produced a document that both consolidated much of the then available theory and research on social welfare organizations and administration, and set forth an agenda for development that might have served as a road map for the profession in the 1960s.[46] The growing professional interest in administration was reflected also in the establishment of the

Council on Social Work Administration in NASW in 1963.[47] In 1960, the National Conference on Social Welfare, reflecting the increased attention being given to this area of practice, featured a number of papers on administration that had grown out of a conference-sponsored committee on common elements in administration.[48] One of these papers, summarizing the discussions of the committee, argued that specialized preparation in a profession was not necessarily desirable for managers of complex organizations, thereby challenging the assumption that casework training and experience were an essential prerequisite for social welfare administration.[49] Shortly thereafter, Eveline Burns, a leading social work educator, in a very influential paper delivered to the Council on Social Work Education in 1961, sharply criticized schools of social work for neglecting policy and administration content in their curricula. Among other things, she proposed specialized courses of study for practitioners who would enter the administrative arena.[50] Finally, in the following year, the Council on Social Work Education, the accrediting body for schools of social work, approved a curriculum policy that permitted individual schools to experiment with new approaches to education for practice, with prior Council approval.[51] Given the interest and resources, schools of social work could now initiate courses of specialized study in social work administration for significant numbers of students rather than be confined to individualized programs of study for a few experienced students as had previously been the case.

All indications pointed to the fact that administration in social work was on the threshold of a major developmental era. Unfortunately, this was not to be. By the end of the decade, some small strides had been made, but in the scheme of things they were insignificant. By 1971, for example, only 271 students were matriculated in administration programs in schools of social work, 2 percent of all graduate students. A number of schools had undertaken to expand their curricula in this area; but as of 1969, only seven schools had developed a full two-year specialization, and the median enrollment in these programs was only five students.[52]

On the face of it, the 1960s should have provided fertile soil for the strengthening of administrative theory and practice in social welfare. Throughout most of this decade there was a dramatic expansion of social services and a heightened demand for professionals to plan, manage, and evaluate new programs. How, then, can on explain why so little was being done to prepare a cadre of administrators to assume these responsibilities? Several speculative explanations can be offered.

From one perspective, the history of the 1960s can be characterized by the major changes that occurred in the way people—most notably youth, minorities, and disenfranchised groups—began to perceive and relate to social institutions. The change occurred partly because of the nation's inability to deal decisively with such massive problems as poverty, racism, and urban deterioration, even though the resources to make major gains in these areas were potentially available. The optimism that pervaded thinking and action in the early 1960s was due, in some measure at least, to the belief that political and economic institutions could, with some redirection and intensified effort, mount an effective attack on social problems that had persisted for so long. The frustration that occurred when social policy and program initiatives failed to yield needed changes became even more acute when the economic resources necessary to deal with these problems on the domestic front were increasingly diverted to the Vietnam War effort.

More specifically, it can be argued that the inability of these institutions to deal effectively with problems like poverty and racism gave rise to a profound disillusionment and cynicism about these arrangements and resulted in challenges to their legitimacy. Many people began to question the assumption that institutions represented the best interests of the people they were created to serve. Simultaneously, it became clear that the avowed purposes of institutions were sometimes less important than their latent and frequently self-serving objectives. Social welfare organizations, particularly those which were by now well established, were a central target in this broad social critique. Observers, both within and without the field, variously called attention to the fact that traditional agencies were neglecting their responsibilities to serve clients who were most in need.[53] Social agencies were widely criticized for being unresponsive to changing needs and conditions, and with being more preoccupied with organizational maintenance and security than with the provision of service. Worse yet, some analysts implicated social welfare organizations—particularly the public welfare system—in the political and economic processes that perpetuated inequality and denied the poor access to rights, services, and opportunities.[54]

These analyses, together with the experiences of an increasing number of activist groups around the country who sought to redress grievances and effect changes in the policies and practices of social agencies, exposed the functions and dysfunctions of such agencies in a way that had never before occurred. Inevitably, some agencies did not fare well under such close scrutiny. Students entering schools of social work, if they had not previously been aware of the failings of social welfare agencies, were very likely to be exposed to a literature that described and analyzed these problems in some detail. While for some, this may have suggested a career in administration as a vehicle for rectifying these difficulties, for most the critique appears to have reinforced the notion that organizations, especially large bureaucracies, were inherently flawed in ways that interfered with the provision of service and inevitably required professionals to compromise their values and competencies.[55]

What implications did this have for the development of administration in social work? The evidence is fragmentary, but observation would suggest that the growing distrust of and challenge to organizations during the 1960s ultimately tainted administration as a method and provoked disdain for administrators. In the last analysis, there is a tendency to personalize organizational dysfunction, so it was quite natural to attribute the shortcomings of social agencies to the professional and ideological deficiencies of those who managed them. Many students expressed fears of being "co-opted," of becoming part of the Establishment, of being part of the problem instead of the solution, and of betraying their social conscience; many students and academics as well assumed that administrative position, status, and authority were necessarily gained at the expense of professional integrity.

For the increasing number of students who were attracted to social work because of a desire to effect large-scale social change, community organization appeared to be a good alternative to administration. By the mid-1960s, community organization had become less closely tied to practice in community chests and welfare federations and had taken on a much more activist, reformist posture. Some students, academicians, and scholars found this method an attractive professional vehicle because it allowed for practice outside the mainstream of traditional social welfare agencies and was largely directed at changing how these agencies operated.[56] Community organization practice, at least as it was perceived at the time, afforded social workers an opportunity to use their professional skills and influence on behalf of the poor and disenfranchised and not against them.

In this context, it is understandable that community organization as a method of practice developed rapidly. Between 1960 and 1969, the number of students enrolled in community organization concentrations in schools of social work increased from 1.5 percent to 9 percent of the full-time graduate enrollment.[57] This growth in student interest was accompanied by a significant expansion in research and scholarship, including a major curriculum development project sponsored by the Council on Social Work Education.[58] By the end of the decade, community organization had achieved the status of a major method of social work practice.

Developments in community organization and those in administration were by no means mutually exclusive. Much of the theoretical work done in community organization was immediately applicable to administration and, indeed, significantly extended the knowledge base upon which social work administration might draw. There are, after all, substantial areas of overlap between the two methods, so that contributions in such areas as planning, citizen participation, work with boards and committees, and advocacy, were of direct benefit to administration theory and practice.[59] Moreover, the acceptance of community organization in social work helped to acculturate the idea that professional work with large systems was a central professional responsibility. Still, that core of theory and practice which is distinctive to administration remained largely untended during the 1960s. The full-scale emergence of administration, a prospect that had looked so promising at the break of the decade, remained more hope than reality.

1970–1980: CHALLENGE AND RESPONSE

Even in the midst of the excitement and expectation that attended the massive expansion of social welfare programs in the 1960s, there was evidence by mid-decade that policy makers in both executive and legislative branches were becoming increasingly concerned with how to effectively control and manage this vast enterprise.[60] To understand the reasons for this concern, and the subsequent demand for skilled administrators in social welfare that emerged so strongly in the early 70s, it is necessary to briefly examine the economic context of the times.

The decade of the 1960s witnessed a growth in social welfare expenditures unparalleled in this country's history. New programs, expanded eligibility, and increased benefits, while insufficient to meet rising expectations, nevertheless resulted in a mushrooming of governmental responsibility. Between 1960 and 1973, for example, social welfare expenditures encompassing income maintenance, health, housing, education, and social services at the federal, state, and local levels increased from $52.3 to $215 billion, an increase of over 300 percent. During roughly this same period, social welfare expenditures as a percentage of Gross National Product also increased dramatically, from 10.6 percent to 17.6 percent. Similarly, while federal, state, and local governments had expended 38 percent of their budgets for welfare purposes in 1960, this proportion had risen to 53 percent by 1973. Thus in both absolute and relative terms, the social welfare enterprise had expanded at a phenomenal rate. By the end of the decade it had become not only a major governmental activity, but a central preoccupation of the American people and their elected officials as well.

Throughout the 1960s a subtle but important phenomenon was occurring—namely, a gradual shrinking of the fiscal dividend. Early in the decade it had been assumed that a continued rate of economic growth would generate a fiscal dividend sufficient to support an expanding effort to combat social problems. However, the combined effect of several tax cuts, the Vietnam War, increased social welfare expenditures, and later, inflation and a reduced rate of economic growth served to erode the surplus that might have underwritten the continued expansion of social welfare programs. At the end of the 1960s it had become clear, as The Brookings Institution pointed out, that there would not be sufficient resources to support all the social welfare initiatives that seemed worthwhile on their face. This would be true, even if defense expenditures were substantially cut back.[61]

The net effect of these developments was to create a politics of scarcity where the emphasis was increasingly placed on choosing from among program alternatives those that produced the greatest increment of desired social and behavioral change for the dollar expended. In this context, decision makers, both executive and legislative, looked to experts who could provide them with hard information on which to base these difficult choices.

The politics of scarcity had a profound effect on management technology and social welfare organizations. Where once the administrators of these programs had the relatively simple task of advocating program expansion and justifying the need for additional allocations of money and resources, by the late 1960s they were being asked to provide detailed information about what was being done, at what cost, and with what results. Management was forced, in short, to shift from a preoccupation with program maintenance and expansion to a concern with program description, control, and evaluation. In making this shift, social welfare organizations found themselves confronted with a gigantic skill and knowledge vacuum. The pool of career professionals and program experts that had traditionally filled middle- and upper-management jobs did not, for the most part, possess the necessary technical know-how. Consequently, social welfare organizations began to look elsewhere for the management that was needed to respond to the demands of this new age.

The profession of social work was caught unprepared. The decades of inattention and then ambivalence toward administration as a method of social work practice had now come home to haunt the profession. The knowledge and skills, the research, and the trained personnel the profession needed to respond to the task of administering increasingly complex and costly social services were largely lacking. As if to make matters worse, the 1950s and 1960s had witnessed an explosion in management technology growing out of military and industrial settings—e.g., PPBS, cost-benefit analysis, and PERT—that was now being warmly received by policy makers who hoped to rationalize decision making in social welfare. Intellectual gatekeepers in the profession had simply not been attentive to these developments and thus had done little to incorporate them into social work administration. Moreover, a wave of political reaction in the country, rapidly escalating expenditures, and increasing conservatism in both the legislative and executive branches of government, generated an aura of distrust and anatagonism toward social welfare programs and social work professionals that made social workers in management positions all the more vulnerable. The threatening prospect that social work administrators would be replaced by generalist managers from business and public administration and others who had no substantive background in or demonstrated commitment to social welfare programs was, in many instances, becoming a reality in the 1970s.

Commenting on this crisis in one of the keynote addresses to the Annual Program Meeting of the Council on Social Work Education in 1973, Saari warned social work educators that:

> ... Unless the profession demonstrates that it can meet critical social needs ... and provide leadership in the design and delivery of social services, it will be relegated to roles as private practitioners and handmaidens to other professionals. There is no intent to deprecate private practice, ... but the evidence is ample to indicate that unless the profession is able to provide the leadership cadre ... it will lose control of its domain. Many leaders in social welfare today have stated that it is now woefully insufficient to be merely a social critic or lay advocate for social values and programs. Schools must prepare individuals to be able to enter the socio-political arena at all levels of government to succeed in the planning, design, implementation, and evaluation of effective social services.[62]

By the early 1970s Saari's urgent plea was being widely echoed in the profession, and there appeared for the first time a general sentiment that the training of social workers for administration deserved priority attention.[63] Social work would have to seriously address the task of preparing practitioners for administrative practice or risk a further erosion of influence in a field where it had historically provided leadership. At stake here was not simply the loss of status and jobs, important as these were, but more critically, the opportunity to purvey the values and objectives that social work had traditionally espoused.

The profession responded with alacrity to the threat and challenge that had emerged so clearly by the middle of the decade. Stimulated in part by national and regional training grants made available through the U.S. Department of Health, Education, and Welfare, there was a rapid expansion of administration curricula in schools of social work. By 1975, nineteen schools of social work (out of eighty-four) were providing for specialization in social welfare administration; and a number of others were preparing students for some combination of planning, organizing, and administration.[64] Barely two years later, the number of schools with specialized programs had increased to at least thirty-five.[65]

Predictably, the brisk expansion of education for social work administration stimulated (and was in turn reinforced by) increased scholarly attention to this method of practice. Professional conferences sponsored by CSWE, NASW, and the National Conference on Social Welfare, during the middle years of the decade prominently featured papers and forums on administrative practice. The number of journal articles on management and related subjects that appeared in *Social Work Abstracts* after 1973 increased dramatically; and in 1976, the journal *Administration in Social Work*, the first of its kind devoted exclusively to this area, was established. Finally, at this writing, an enriched literature on social welfare administration has begun to appear, which should help to consolidate and make more visible available practice knowledge and thereby facilitate professional discourse.[66] As yet there appear to be no clearly emerging paradigms or models of management practice in social welfare, but an era of significant scholarly development is in the making.

THE HISTORICAL LEGACY:
IMPLICATIONS FOR THE FUTURE

While administration appears well on its way to becoming a recognized and legitimate form of professional practice, on a par with social casework, group work and community organization, the long arm of history continues to exert its influence on theory and practice in this field. Indeed, many of the critical issues facing social work administrators, as well as scholars and academicians who attempt to inform this practice, grow out of the profession's failure to educate professionals for leadership in social welfare. How these issues are resolved in the next decade will determine, in large part, the shape and direction of administration in social work and ultimately its contribution to social welfare. Two issues of particular concern are the ability of the profession to define a distinctive field of administration and to prepare social workers for effective practice in this arena.

It is clear from the historical analysis that the dominant preoccupation of the profession for three-quarters of a century has been the development of direct services, most particularly social casework. Relatively little intellectual capital has been invested in administration as an area of practice and research, with the result that this field is still in an early stage of theoretical development; the theory of administration is marked by weak explanatory models, a paucity of empirical research that describes and evaluates practice, and even a lack of explicit ethical prescripts to guide practitioners. It does little good to bemoan this state of affairs, because history, after all, will not be undone. But this legacy does have some critical implications for current and future practice that should be recognized. First of all, it is increasingly clear that if social work is to provide organizational leadership in social welfare, its practitioners will have to be far more knowledgable about and skilled in administration than has heretofore been the case. Generalist administrators from other fields will continue to look upon social welfare as an attractive institutional arena and will no doubt compete with social workers for middle- and upper-level management positions in the field.[67]

Faced with the urgent necessity to rapidly upgrade administrative skills, social work practitioners and academicians alike have looked eagerly to the established management professions and related disciplines for theory and technology. The interest in joint and dual degrees between schools of social work and business or public administration is one example of this trend.[68] Yet recent experience suggests that there is a tendency to adapt knowledge and technology from other fields without sufficient attention to its utility or consequences for social agencies, or its consonance with the mission and values of social work.[69]

Some may read this criticism as an argument against interdisciplinary collaboration and for professional parochialism. No such message is intended. Rather, the issue that confronts social work is whether it will take responsibility for defining the parameters of professional administrative practice in social welfare and for developing a framework that enables it to deliberately select those theories, concepts, and technologies which further its purposes and those of the institution it serves. The failure to do this in the years ahead will render social work a supplicant in the field of administration and blur the distinctive contribution its practitioners can make to furthering the effectiveness of social welfare organizations. Though leaders in the profession have long claimed the distinctive nature of social work administration, there has yet to be a convincing case made for how this specialty differs from general administrative practice. That will be the task of the profession in the 1980s and one that will be addressed in forthcoming chapters.

A second issue confronting the profession, and one that is very much an artifact of its history, concerns the manner in which social workers are best prepared for management roles in social agencies. For some years, as we have seen, there was a general acceptance of the notion that training and experience in direct services was a necessary, if not sufficient, background for practice. Interpersonal skills and knowledge of human growth and behavior were thought to provide a generic foundation for subsequent administrative practice. But aside from the utilitarian value of clinical education, there was also a belief that identification with the values of the profession was best nurtured in the context of direct service practice. Having demonstrated this professional identification, the social agency might then safely promote the caseworker or group workers to supervisory or management positions and be reasonably assured that such persons would be responsible stewards of the profession's values and technology.

To be sure, many social workers over the years have used their direct service backgrounds to good advantage in administrative roles. But recent analyses have suggested that the translation of direct service skills to management is by no means as straightforward as has been assumed and that, in fact, certain skills may be dysfunctional to good administration.[70] There is also growing support for the notion that professional identity can be cultivated as effectively in the course of training for administration as in programs of clinical training.

In any case, there is no substantial evidence to indicate that the direct service pathway to administration is inherently more desirable than others. The growth of two-year graduate programs for social welfare administration will offer an opportunity to look at the question of preparation as an empirical matter rather than as an article of faith. Perhaps even more important than the comparative efficacy of various pathways to administration is the issue of how best to prepare clinicians for an eventual transition to management. Even if schools of social work begin to graduate significant numbers of administrative specialists in the years ahead, it seems likely that agencies will continue to draw the bulk of their management personnel from the ranks of direct practice. How best to introduce these clinicians to administrative content early in their careers; how to identify and cultivate the managerial potential of such persons while they are still in direct practice; how to support and facilitate direct services workers who make the transition to administrative roles: these are questions that will require systematic attention in years ahead, and we will return to these issues in Chapters 7 and 8.

NOTES

[1] Roy Lubove, *The Professional Altruist: The Emergence of Social Work As a Career, 1880–1930* (Cambridge, Mass.: Harvard University Press, 1965), p. 22–54.

[2] *Ibid.*, pp. 119.

[3] Mary E. Richmond, *Social Diagnosis* (New York: Russell Sage Foundation, 1917); *What Is Social Case Work?* (New York: Russell Sage Foundation, 1922).

[4] Edith Abbott, *Social Welfare and Professional Education* (Chicago: University of Chicago Press, 1931), p. 37.

[5] *Ibid.*

[6] James E. Hagarty, *The Training of Social Workers* (New York: McGraw-Hill, 1931), p. 99.

[7] Arthur Dunham, "The Administration of Social Agencies," *Social Work Yearbook* (New York: Russell Sage Foundation, 1939), p. 16.

[8] *Ibid.*

[9] Pierce Atwater, *Problems of Administration in Social Work* (Minneapolis: University of Minnesota Press, 1940), p. 294.

[10] Abbott, *Social Welfare*, p. 30.

[11] Lubove, *Professional Altruist*, p. 152.

[12] *Social Casework: Generic and Specific* (New York: American Association of Social Workers, 1929), p. 78.

[13] *Ibid.*, pp. 35–73.

[14] Dunham, "Administration of Social Agencies," pp. 16–17.

[15] F. H. McClean, *The Family Society: Joint Responsibilities of Board, Staff, and Membership* (New York: American Association for Organizing Social Work, 1927); Ada Sheffield, *The Charity Director: A Brief Study of His Responsibilities* (New York: Russell Sage Foundation, 1913).

[16] Elwood Street, *Social Work Administration* (New York: Harper & Brothers, 1931). In fairness, it is important to note that both administrative and organizational theory were still in their infancy. There were, in fact, few external stimuli for

the development of social work administration. See Fremont Kast and James Rosenweig, *Organization and Management: A Systems Approach* (New York: McGraw-Hill, 1970), pp. 57–62.

[17]*Social Work Year Book* (New York: Russell Sage Foundation, 1929).

[18]Josephine C. Brown, *Public Relief: 1929–1939* (New York: Henry Holt and Co., 1940), pp. 273–98.

[19]*Ibid.*, pp. 280–89.

[20]*Ibid.*, pp. 290–91.

[21]Elwood Street, *The Public Welfare Administration* (New York: McGraw-Hill Book Co., Inc., 1940), p. 6.

[22]Elizabeth de Schweinitz and Karl de Schweinitz, "The Contribution of Social Work to the Administration of Public Assistance," *Social Work Journal*, 29, No. 4 (October, 1948), 153–62, 177.

[23]Arthur Dunham, "Administration of Social Agencies," *Social Work Year Book* (New York: Russell Sage Foundation, 1941), pp. 20–22.

[24]See, for example, Monetta Stevenson, *Public Welfare Administration* (New York: Macmillan, 1938); Clyde R. White, *Administration of Public Welfare* (New York: American Book Co., 1940), pp. 327–37; and Street, *Public Welfare Administrator*.

[25]For example, the Curriculum Policy Statement of the American Association of Schools of Social Work, issued in 1944, recognized administration as one of the eight areas of study to be included in curricula of graduate social work programs. See Ernest V. Hollis and Alice L. Taylor, *Social Work Education in the United States* (New York: Columbia University Press, 1951), p. 47.

[26]Atwater, *Problems of Administration*, p. 9.

[27]John C. Kidneigh, "Social Work Administration: An Area of Social Work Practice?" *Social Work Journal*, 31, No. 2 (April, 1950), 57–61, 79.

[28]*Ibid.*, p. 57.

[29]Arlien Johnson, "The Administrative Process in Social Work," *Proceedings of the National Conference of Social Work* (New York: Columbia University Press, 1947), p. 253.

[30]Harleigh B. Trecker, *Group Process in Administration* (New York: The Woman's Press, 1946), p. 25.

[31]Johnson, "Administrative Process," p. 257.

[32]Trecker, *Group Process*, p. 18.

[33]*Ibid.*, p. 21. This egalitarian view was not shared uniformly by leading writers. Johnson, for example, recognized that in larger agencies, particularly those under public auspices, the "hierarchical arrangement of functions and persons" became important. Johnson, "Administrative Process," p. 254.

[34]Johnson, "Administrative Process," p. 257; see also Trecker, *Group Process*, p. 32, for a similar view.

[35]Trecker, *Group Process*, pp. 32–59.

[36]Kidneigh, "Social Work Administration," p. 59.

[37]Charles Hendry, "The Dynamics of Leadership," *Proceedings of the National Conference of Social Work* (New York: Columbia University Press, 1947), pp. 259–68. For a brief overview of the human relations school, see Kast and Rosenweig, *Organization and Management*, pp. 78–86.

[38]Hendry, "Dynamics of Leadership," p. 268.

[39] Trecker, *Group Process,* p. 16.

[40] Sue Spencer, *The Administration Method in Social Work Education: Volume III, A Report of the Curriculum Study* (New York: Council on Social Work Education, 1959), p. 9.

[41] Ernest Hollis and Alice Taylor, *Social Work Education in the United States* (New York: Columbia University Press, 1951), p. 254.

[42] As late as 1958, for example, there were only twenty-one social work graduate students involved in training for administration. Spencer, *Administration Method,* p. 46.

[43] *Ibid.,* p. 15.

[44] *Ibid.,* p. 18.

[45] Hollis and Taylor, *Social Work Education,* p. 227; and Spencer, *Administration Method,* p. 20.

[46] David Fanshel, ed., *Research in Social Welfare Administration* (New York: National Association of Social Workers, 1962).

[47] Harleigh B. Trecker, *Social Work Administration: Principles and Practices,* rev. ed. (New York: Association Press, 1977), p. 17.

[48] Ella Reed, ed., *Social Welfare Administration* (New York: Columbia University Press, 1961).

[49] James D. Thompson, "Common Elements in Administration," in *Social Welfare Administration,* ed. Ella Reed (New York: Columbia University Press, 1961), pp. 27-29.

[50] Eveline Burns, "Social Policy: Step-Child of the Curriculum," *Education for Social Work,* Proceedings of the Annual Program Meeting (New York: Council on Social Work Education, 1961).

[51] Council on Social Work Education, *Manual of Accrediting Standards* (New York: Council on Social Work Education, 1965) pp. 73-75.

[52] Rosemary Saari, "Effective Social Work Intervention in Administration and Planning Roles: Implications for Education," *Facing the Challenge* (New York: Council on Social Work Education, 1973), p. 37.

[53] See, for example, Richard Cloward and Irwin Epstein, "Private Social Welfare's Disengagement from the Poor: The Case of the Family Adjustment Agencies," in *Social Welfare Institutions: A Sociological Reader* ed. Mayer Zald (New York: John Wiley & Sons, 1965), pp. 623-44; S. M. Miller and Frank Reissman, *Social Class and Social Policy* (New York: Basic Books, 1968); Peter Morris and Martin Rein, *Dilemmas of Social Reform* (New York: Atherton Press, 1967), pp. 40-55.

[54] Frances Piven and Richard Cloward, *Regulating the Poor: The Functions of Public Welfare* (New York: Pantheon, 1971).

[55] Irving Piliaven, "Restructuring the Provision of Social Services," *Social Work,* 13, No. 1 (January, 1968), 34-41.

[56] See, for example, Rothman's formulations of C.O. practice. Two of the models he posited, social action and locality development, were located in settings that were outside large, established, welfare agencies. Jack Rothman, "Three Models of Community Organization Practice," in *Strategies of Community Organization,* 2nd ed., Fred M. Cox et al., eds. (Itasca, Ill.: F. E. Peacock Publishers), pp. 22-38.

[57] Fred Cox and Charles Garvin, "Community Organization Practice: 1865-1973," in *Ibid.,* p. 57.

⁵⁸Arnold Gurin, *Community Organization Curriculum in Graduate Social Work Education: Report and Recommendations* (New York: Council on Social Work Education, 1970).

⁵⁹See, for example, Ralph Kramer and Harry Specht, eds., *Readings in Community Organization Practice*, 3rd ed. (Englewood Cliffs, N.J.: Prentice-Hall, Inc., 1983).

⁶⁰Rino Patti, "The New Scientific Management: Systems Management for Social Welfare," *Public Welfare*, 33, No. 2 (Spring, 1975), 23. Portions of this section are drawn from this article.

⁶¹*Ibid.*, p. 25.

⁶²Saari, "Effective Social Work Intervention," pp. 31–32.

⁶³Bernard Neugeboren, "Developing Specialized Programs in Social Work Administration in the Masters Degree Program: Field Practice Component," *Journal of Education for Social Work*, 7, No. 3 (Fall, 1971), 35–48; Monica Shapira, "Reflections on the Preparation of Social Workers for Executive Positions," *Journal of Education for Social Work*, 7, No. 1 (Winter, 1971), 55–68; Jerry Turem, "The Call for a Management Stance," *Social Work*, 19, No. 5 (September, 1974), 616.

⁶⁴Kenneth Kazmerski and David Macarov, *Administration in the Social Work Curriculum* (New York: Council on Social Work Education, 1976), p. 18.

⁶⁵James R. Dumpson, Edward J. Mullen, and Richard J. First, *Toward Education for Effective Social Welfare Administrative Practice* (New York: Council on Social Work Education, 1978), p. 19.

⁶⁶Richard Steiner, *Managing the Human Service Organizations: From Survival to Achievement* (Beverly Hills, Calif.: Sage Publications, 1977); Simon Slavin, ed., *Social Administration* (New York: Haworth Press, 1978); Marc L. Miringoff, *Management in Human Service Organizations* (New York: Macmillan, 1980); Rosemary C. Saari and Yeheskel Hasenfeld, eds., *The Management of Human Services* (New York: Columbia University Press, 1978); Felice D. Perlmutter and Simon Slavin, eds., *Leadership in Social Administration* (Philadelphia: Temple University Press, 1980); Michael Austin, *Supervisory Management in the Human Services* (Englewood Cliffs, N.J.: Prentice-Hall, Inc., 1981).

⁶⁷Rino Patti and Charles Maynard, "Qualifying for Management Jobs in Public Welfare," *Social Work*, 23, No. 4 (July, 1978), 288–94.

⁶⁸Brian W. Klepinger, "Interdisciplinary Education for Social Work Administration: Promises and Problems," *Administration in Social Work*, 2, No. 2 (Summer, 1978), 143–44; and George Brager and Megan McLaughlin, eds., *Training Social Welfare Managers* (New York: Columbia University, School of Social Work, 1978), pp. 16–21.

⁶⁹Patti, "New Scientific Management," pp. 23–31; also Murray Gruber, "Total Administration," *Social Work*, 19, No. 5 (September, 1974), 23–31. By permission of The Haworth Press, Inc.

⁷⁰Rino Patti and Michael Austin, "Socializing the Direct Service Practitioner in the Ways of Supervisory Management," *Administration in Social Work*, 1, No. 3 (Fall, 1977), 273–80; and Rino Patti, Elenore Diedreck, Dennis Olson, and Jill Crowell, "From Direct Service to Administration," Part I, *Administration in Social Work*, 3, No. 2 (Summer, 1979), 131–51. By permission of The Haworth Press, Inc.

CHAPTER TWO

The Dimensions of Social Welfare Management

The purpose of this chapter is to set out the major dimensions of social welfare administration. Our intention is to map the salient characteristics of this field of practice and provide a context within which to place the more specific discussion on program management that will follow in subsequent chapters. We begin with a definition of social welfare administration and a brief treatment of the words "management" and "administration." Next, since we assume that management in social agencies has distinctive properties, we examine several selected features of social welfare organizations and how they act to condition administrative practice. We then proceed to look in more detail at the tasks and activities associated with management, and then, finally, to know the configuration of practice varies at several organizational levels.

DEFINING "ADMINISTRATION"

Social welfare administration has typically been defined in two different but overlapping ways. The broad and inclusive definition characterizes administration as a cooperative and coordinated endeavor, involving all members of an organization, each of whom contributes variously to the

24

processes of goal formulation, planning, implementation, change, and evaluation. In this sense, "administration" includes the totality of activities in a social welfare organization that are necessary to "transforming social policy into social services."[1] This conceptualization would include such diverse elements as the contributions made by direct service workers to program development, recordkeeping and service evaluation, the participation of consumers in advisory committees, and policy-making efforts of boards and legislative bodies, the educational and personnel development work conducted by supervisors and trainers, and the like. This definition underscores the fact that responsibility for achieving the objectives in an organization does not rest exclusively with those in executive or subexecutive positions, but is broadly shared by participants in the agency. It democratizes the concept of administration by emphasizing a notion of organizational citizenship, wherein each person (i.e., role), every functional entity in the agency, plays a vital part in the administrative process.[2]

The more restrictive definition of social welfare administration, and the one employed in this book, conceives it as a method of practice. Viewed in this way, administration refers to a systematic, interventive process, consisting of interdependent tasks and functions and associated activities employed by management personnel to facilitate the achievement of selected organizational goals and objectives. It denotes the purposeful application of knowledge, skills, and values to such tasks as defining objectives and planning programs, mobilizing and maintaining resources, and evaluating outcomes.[3]

As a method of practice, social welfare administration is informed by general organization and administrative theory, the management sciences, and conditioned by the specific purposes and characteristics of social welfare agencies. We shall discuss the impact of these contextual variables on social welfare administration more fully in a moment.

Throughout this text we shall use the terms "administration" and "management" interchangeably. Until quite recently, the term "administration" enjoyed much wider usage in the literature. The reasons for this are somewhat obscure, but may derive from the historic tendency in social work to identify "administration" with public, not-for-profit endeavors, and "management" with the business sector.[4] In addition, the word "administer," in one of its meanings at least, conveys the idea of tending to or taking care of—as in "administering to the needs of the poor or sick."[5] In this sense, administration can be interpreted as a helping, nurturing, or enabling function—one, as we saw in the last chapter, that is compatible with the philosophic orientation of a service profession like social work. Management on the other hand, conveys notions of control, direction, and dominance.[6] In a professional culture that values democratic processes, participation and collaboration, the image of a central figure dominating an organization and manipulating it to a personal end is likely to be alien.

Notwithstanding the distinctions that have sometimes been made between administration and management in social work, these terms are increasingly employed as synonyms, as they will be here. In so doing, we acknowledge that authority is inherent to the administrative or management process. The manager does indeed direct and control, and there is nothing to be gained by clouding this reality. On the other hand, in its contemporary meaning, the concept "management" incorporates a concern with participatory decision making, and the delegation and, where necessary, the decentralization of authority. Whether we talk of administration or management, the critical issue is how authority is exercised, and in the service of what values. We will return to this issue in subsequent chapters.

DISTINCTIVE ELEMENTS
OF SOCIAL WELFARE
ADMINISTRATION

Does social welfare administration differ in significant ways from general administration? This has been a matter of some discussion, and one that will no doubt continue to be debated.[7] In general, there are two major positions. Some argue that administrative functions are generic to all types of organizations. Variations in goals, structure, technology, and clientele, which so readily appear to differentiate classes of organizations, tend, in this view, to obscure the essential similarities among organizations and the management processes that are necessary to make them function effectively. Although this position takes cognizance of contextual factors, such variables are not considered to fundamentally alter managerial responsibilities. The phrase, "social services is an industry that must produce a product like any other," is a popular phrase which reflects the belief that administration is a generic process, transferable from setting to setting with only minor adaptations. The governor of a western state recently appointed an executive from a large business corporation to direct the state welfare agency despite the fact that he had no prior experience in social welfare, and by his own admission little knowledge of social service programs. When questions were raised about the appointment, the governor responded that what the state agency needed was the "management" expertise the incumbent had demonstrated in his previous position. Clearly the governor (and many others one might add) subscribed to the notion that the knowledge and skill required of managers is the same regardless of setting.

The position taken here, and one that seems to enjoy increasing currency in both the general literature on administration and that relating to social welfare management,[8] is that the nature of the organization has a significant impact on management practice, including, for example, the relative emphasis given to certain values, objectives, tasks, and activities. In other words, this view contends that the characteristics of organizations are important contingencies that appear to condition the way in which managers order their priorities, the strategies and tactics they employ to achieve their purposes, and how they allocate their time and energy. Empirical studies comparing the practice of administrators in social welfare with that of practitioners in other types of organizations are as yet quite sparse.[9] In what follows we focus on selected characteristics of social welfare organizations and their implications for management practice. The four areas discussed—advocacy, eliciting cooperation in the task environment, building internal consensus, and management control—by no means exhaust those that might be addressed.[10] Our intent here is simply to illustrate how the attributes of social agencies condition management practice.

Societal Ambivalence and the Need for Administrative Advocacy

Many of the administrative problems confronting social welfare organizations can be attributed to the relative lack of societal support for the goals they pursue and/or the stigma attached to the clientele they serve. While this is not uniformly true in all areas of social welfare and for all client groups, it is fair to say that society and those who represent it are ambivalent and often divided about what should be done for such groups as the poor, the mentally ill, delinquents, unmarried mothers, and so on. Although the policy mandate under which an agency operates at any given time may permit progressive and humane treatment of these groups, such support is frequently tenuous and easily eroded when political sentiments change or funds become scarce.[11] One needn't look far for evidence of this ambivalence. Administrators of welfare agencies are continually called before legislature to explain why recipients of financial aid are not required to work. Efforts to create community-based facilities to permit the deinstitutionalization of the mentally ill or delinquent are frequently resisted by community groups who fear the impact such persons may have on their neighborhoods. Programs providing services to runaways and youth in conflict with their families are often accused of undermining parental authority. These and similar examples suggest the extent to which society is often divided about the aims of social programs.

What are the consequences of this inhospitable social climate for administrative practice? There appear to be at least three. First, since the administrator cannot assume a stable, continuing base of social and political support, he or she must ordinarily devote considerable attention to winning support for the organization's goals. This is done in various ways, including promoting an image of efficiency in the community, explaining what the agency does and how it contributes to community welfare, and cultivating powerful patrons or supporters who may use their influence to protect or maintain the agency in times of attack or reaction. Second, in order to create receptivity to program expansion and refinement, administrators must often work to modify community attitudes regarding the client groups they serve and alter the popular stereotypes about how such clients should be dealt with. Efforts to change public perceptions regarding the motivations of welfare clients, to reassure the community about the behavior of mental patients and prison inmates, and to persuade the public that abusive parents should be helped rather than punished are some of the things managers do to generate favorable public sentiment for the objectives of their agencies.[12] Finally, the social welfare administrator must take care that the program objectives and activities of the agency do not consistently violate or threaten widely held community values and norms. The management task here is to see that the agency's efforts to extend or liberalize services, or to experiment with promising but controversial innovations do not exceed the community's definition of reasonableness. In sum, the social welfare administrator is likely to spend a good deal of energy seeking legitimacy for agency goals and sensitizing the public and their representatives to the plight of client groups and their need for services. The fact that clients themselves seek and benefit from the agency's services, while important, does not by itself legitimate agency goals. The general community, and most particularly those who act in their behalf (e.g., legislatures), must also be persuaded that the agency's programs serve what they consider to be worthwhile social values.

Building Support and Cooperation in a Task Environment with Diverse Expectations

Social welfare agencies typically operate in a task environment consisting of groups and organizations that hold multiple and often conflicting expectations regarding who should be served, to what ends, and in what manner.[13] There is likely to be little natural consensus as to goals and objectives among such diverse groups as funding and policy-making bodies, other agencies that provide services to the same clientele, professional associations, labor unions, client or consumer associations, and so on. For example, a state legislative body may emphasize the treatment of chronically disabled mentally ill patients in allocating funds for community mental health centers. Mental health groups in the community while recognizing this need, may also decry the failure of such centers to provide education and prevention services aimed at the general populace. Yet others, like family and child welfare agencies, may feel it is important for mental health centers to provide intensive, specialized therapeutic services to persons with acute and emergent emotional disorders. Reconciling these expectations, if indeed they can be reconciled, is no mean accomplishment. To be sure, some of these constituencies will be more influential than others and may, indeed, have the power to compel an agency to comply with their expectations. But an agency that is consistently inattentive to the preferences and values of other constituencies in the task environment, even those with relatively little influence, runs the risk of provoking counteractions that can disrupt its operations or damage its credibility. Strikes, organized protests by consumer groups, or the withdrawal of support and cooperation by other agencies are some of the consequences incurred by organizations when they fail to respond to the values and interests of significant constituencies. This is not to say that an agency builds consensus and support for its operations merely by reflecting these diverse expectations, because doing so would inevitably bring other problems. The point is that in order to build support and cooperation, the social agency must seek some level of reciprocity and exchange that simultaneously responds to the interests of these parties and maintains the resources and cooperation the agency needs in order to operate effectively.

The social welfare manager is at the center of this complex network of relationships. Thus an important feature of the manager's responsibility is to maintain contact with these diverse constituencies, keep abreast of their changing needs and circumstances, keep them in turn informed of developments within the agency that may have direct implications for their operations, and negotiate both formal and informal agreements regarding exchanges of resources and services. In carrying out these functions the administrator is inevitably confronted with the conflicting expectations mentioned earlier. Prioritizing these in terms that are consonant with the agency's primary mission, attempting where possible to reduce or reconcile discrepant expectations, and managing the discordance that occurs when one or more constituencies feels their interests are not being well served: these and related responsibilities loom importantly in the social welfare administrator's work.

Reconciling the Perspectives of Various Organizational Members

Just as the value preferences and expectations among significant external groups in the task environment will vary, so too will those of participants within the organization. There are many sources of this diversity. Clients, individually and in organized associations, often hold and express views about the objectives an agency should pursue that are quite distinct from those who manage the organization or provide its services.[14] For example, clients may come to an agency seeking tangible services to relieve problems like the lack of housing, unemployment, or income loss, while the agency may see its role as helping clients to deal with social-psychological dysfunctions that give rise to these problems. Professional workers, as has been frequently observed, are sometimes committed to values and norms that contrast sharply with those implied in organizational policies and procedures.[15] Often, for example, they place high value on intensive services to clients and press for lower caseloads in order to make this possible. Managers, on the other hand, faced with legislative mandates and budgetary constraints, may find it desirable to provide less intensive services, thereby serving a greater number of clients at lower per unit cost. Likewise, board members often come to their responsibilities with an ideological perspective on the role of social welfare organizations that differs markedly from that of the paid staff.[16] Differences on such matters as clients' rights and entitlements, professional automony, and advocacy for social change can often be observed. These and other groups are likely to pursue courses of action in the agency that are intended to maximize their value preferences; and since there is seldom an objective standard (e.g., profitability) against which to measure the efficacy of these competing conceptions of agency purpose and performance, some mechanisms must be found to mediate the differences.

Some of the most critical of these mechanisms are the procedures used to recruit and select various organizational members—i.e., clients, staff, and board members—whose values and expectations are not widely disparate. Orientation, training, and supervision are also ways in which agencies seek to reduce ideological dispersion in their own ranks. In the last analysis, however, such efforts are usually only partially effective in forging a uniform commitment for the goals and objectives of the agency. The day-to-day task of reconciling these divergent views and bringing some internal coherence to the organization devolves principally on the administrator. In part, this task can be achieved through centralized direction and control in which the manager prescribes the boundaries of acceptable behavior (and implicitly values), and uses the authority of the office to enforce them. While such a strategy may bring about short-term compliance, exclusive reliance on this approach can have long-term negative consequences. Staff may respond to this approach with lowered morale, informal resistance, and high turnover. Under certain circumstances, clients, as individuals or in groups, can refuse to cooperate or actively oppose such directives. Members of boards and advisory committees, for their part, often have access to external resources that they can use to oppose managerial initiatives that are contrary to their value preferences.

The inherent limitations of centralized management, together with the generally positive valence toward democratic processes in social welfare, often incline social welfare administrators to rely heavily on participatory management. This strategy seeks to build voluntary consensus and commitment through a process in which clients, staff, and other groups contribute variously to agency decision making. Of course, a great many contingencies will influence when participatory management is used, with whom, and on what issues.[17] Suffice it to say that, in general, social welfare managers probably use a participatory strategy more consistently and on a broader range of administrative issues than is true of their counterparts in other types of organizations. Some observers have interpreted this as evidence of administrative indecision, and others have criticized the time-consuming and often ritualized nature of this approach to decision making.[18] No doubt these criticisms are sometimes justified. Nevertheless, the value diversity that typically characterizes the membership of a social welfare organization must somehow be internally reconciled if there is to be a modicum of agreement regarding means and ends. Failure to achieve a degree of consensus among various membership groups can result in fragmentation and stalemate. Whatever its imperfections then, participatory management appears to be a necessary administrative strategy for addressing this internal political reality.

Social Service Technology and Management Controls

Information, it is said, is the lifeblood of management. Certainly the manager must know, or be able to find out, what is being done in an organization in order to intelligently allocate resources, assign staff, monitor progress toward goals, and so forth. However, in social welfare organizations, the process of monitoring and controlling organizational activities is complicated by the fact that both service technology and service outcomes are frequently variable and thus difficult to specify and measure. If clients presented similar problems and reacted similarly to the services provided, if desired outcomes could be specifically defined and easily evaluated, and if the agency knew with some certainty that the application of selected procedures would result in predictable outcomes, then the administrative task of monitoring and controlling agency operations would not be too unlike that in many other types of organizations. Clearly, however, these conditions are seldom obtained in social welfare organizations. On the contrary, clients usually present an array of quite different problems and capabilities, and are likely to have their own ideas about how to ameliorate these difficulties. The outcomes to be sought, even if they can be readily defined, cannot normally be imposed on the client, but rather must grow out of a process of mutual goal setting. Direct services workers thus often find it necessary to fashion treatments that are tailored to the unique problems, desires, and capabilities of the clients they serve, because unlike inanimate "raw materials," their active cooperation is a necessary ingredient to effective service.[19]

In short, front-line workers in many social welfare organizations deal with largely nonroutine service events that require a good deal of ad hoc problem solving and the exercise of discretionary judgment. Not only does this process occur in private interactions with clients, but the terms of the treatment relationship (i.e., treatment objectives and techniques) are likely in any individual case to change over time. Finally, in the case of professionally oriented workers who value the norms of autonomy and confidentiality in their work, transactions with clients tend to be private and largely inaccessible to direct scrutiny by supervisors.[20]

This characterization of the service delivery process, oversimplified though it may be, illustrates the special problems of monitoring and controlling agency operations. First, the fluid, nonuniform, and private nature of service delivery usually makes it difficult to design information systems that are sensitive to what is actually being done by subordinates. Elaborate, sophisticated schemes can be developed, but the time, energy, and costs necessary to implement and maintain them frequently make them unfeasible. A recent conversation between a consultant and a hospital social worker, illustrates some of the difficulties encountered in trying to obtain accurate information about service delivery. A new information system had just been installed in the social service department.

CONSULTANT: What do you think about the new system that's being used?
WORKER: It's O.K. The director [of social service] needs the information for administrative purposes, I guess.
CONSULTANT: Do you find the monthly reports on your caseload useful?
WORKER: Not really. Every now and then I see something of interest, but the forms I fill out don't really reflect what I do with my patients. Its hard to push what you do into those categories.
CONSULTANT: Have you discussed your reactions with the director?
WORKER: Yea, he knows we're not too enthusiastic about the paperwork. I've decided just to cut my losses. I save all the forms to do when I'm tired and then just get it out as fast as I can. Frankly, I don't know how accurate it all is, but that's not really my problem.

To deal with these and related problems in formal information systems, agency managers must often collect supplementary data through other means such as supervisory conferences, staff meetings, case recordings, and ad hoc consultations. These mechanisms, costly and time consuming in their own right,[21] are often more sensitive to nuances, subtleties, and variations in the service experience, than more standardized and quantitatively oriented systems. Thus it should come as no surprise that social agencies invest a good deal of time in maintaining communications between superiors and subordinates. Some have argued that the persistence of informal monitoring methods in these organizations reflects a resistance to more uniform and systematic data collection procedures. Though there may be some basis for this assertion, the inherent nature of social service technology clearly requires a flexible, intensive approach to monitoring. Without this, managers would find it difficult to discern whether the myriad of discretionary judgments inevitably made by subordinates are collectively consistent with agency program objectives and procedures.

One final note on the implications of social service technology for management practice. Because technical processes are difficult to standardize, managers in social welfare agencies must often interpret the meaning of the information they receive from subordinates. The sometimes vague and inchoate information about treatment procedures, relationships, and client responses may seem impenetrable to one who has not been intimately involved in service delivery. Managers can choose to avoid this apparent thicket, but it is important to bear in mind that this is the stuff around which the workers' daily existence revolves. Understanding these difficulties in handling information about practice is essential. When front-line workers perceive their superiors as insensitive or uninformed about the realities they encounter, they are likely to be guarded and defensive about sharing information. The adverse effects of this on manager's ability to monitor and control the activities of subordinates should be readily apparent.

MANAGEMENT TASKS AND ACTIVITIES IN SOCIAL WELFARE

Social welfare administration, as we noted earlier, is a systematic process of intervention employed by managers in the service of achieving selected organizational objectives. This process has been the subject of extensive discussion in the literature, and a number of formulations have been presented.[22] In this section we focus on two aspects of managerial practice: *tasks* that managers must accomplish, or cause to be accomplished, in order to create and sustain an organization's capability for effective and efficient service delivery; and *activities* they must engage in in order to achieve these tasks. In what follows, tasks and activities are presented as discrete, independent, and sequenced elements in the process, but the reader should bear in mind that in the reality of practice these elements are seldom so neatly separable. Moreover a failure to achieve one task is very likely to affect the manager's ability to accomplish all others. Similarly, activities are interdependent, so that inadequate performance in one area will usually detract from performance in others.

Management Tasks

The principal tasks of social welfare administration are as follows:

1. Planning and developing the program. The social agency operates under a mandate contained in public law and administrative regulations, articles of incorporation and board policy, or some combination thereof. These mandates are seldom specific enough to provide detailed guidance for agency action, and so it falls to the administrator and staff to clarify and interpret these directives and ultimately see that they are translated into goals and objectives that provide guidelines for agency operations. In constructing these goals and directives, the administrator must at once see that they are responsive to the policy mandate and capable of accomplishment, given the resources available to the organization. Inherent in this task is the responsibility for advocating changes and modifications in policy that may make it more sensitive to organizational realities and local circumstances. Thus the administrator is not merely a passive recipient and implementor of external mandates, but also seeks to influence the shape of policy based on the agency's experience.

Programs are the instrument through which the social agency accomplishes its goals and objectives. The administrator's task is to assess the needs of potential consumer populations that fall within the purview or jurisdiction of the agency, determine (often with the assistance of consumer or citizen groups) which of these needs will be addressed, and design programs to reduce or ameliorate the identified conditions. The program plan is a model for action that includes intended outcomes, the nature of the services to be provided, the recipients to be served, and the resources required. Since discrepancies inevitably exist between the program plan and subsequent implementation, however, planning is a continuous activity involving incremental adjustments and modifications on the initial design. In addition, changes in community needs and conditions, altered funding arrangements, and the ideas and interests of agency staff frequently require that programs be updated and refined to reflect current realities.

2. Acquiring financial resources and support. A critical task of social agency administration is obtaining the inputs required to sustain the organization's programs and services. Perhaps the most important facet of this task is obtaining funds, which may be available through legislative appropriation, federated funding arrangements (e.g., United Way), or competitive fundraising (e.g., grants, contracts, and donations). To acquire financial resources, the agency administrator must represent the needs and accomplishments of the agency and justify its claim on the "public purse." No small part of this responsibility is identifying and, where possible, responding to the priorities of funding sources.

Although the acquisition of funds is essential to agency survival, so too is the support and cooperation of groups and organizations in the task environment. To acquire this support, the administrator maintains a wide array of contacts, spends a good deal of time explaining and justifying agency purposes and activities, answering critics, cultivating advocates and spokespersons for the agency, and arranging mutually beneficial exchanges.

3. Designing organizational structures and processes. Organizational structure is the formal specification of authority, responsibility, and expectations. The administrator's task is to create and maintain a framework that permits a degree of constancy and predictability in relations between organizational participants and yet permits them sufficient flexibility to respond creatively to nonroutine and unanticipated events. Thus, among other things, the manager determines the division of labor in the agency, how authority is to be distributed among actors in the system, the nature and number of job specialties, rules to govern behavior in a wide variety of situations, procedures regarding work flow and relationships between work units, and so on. Organizational structure and processes will ordinarily be codified in the organizational chart, the manual of operations, and in job descriptions. Though these instruments provide only a partial picture of the "living" organization, they may be likened to a skeletal structure that creates the possibility, if not the certainty, of organizational coherence and concerted action.

4. Developing and maintaining staff capability. The quality of services provided by a social agency is largely dependent on the intelligence, skill, and commitment of its staff. In the first instance, this task requires that the administrator define the skills and capabilities necessary to implement program plans. Next, he or she must be clear about the personal, experiential, and educational characteristics necessary for successful performance in the various jobs; he or she must develop criteria against which to assess employee behavior. Having selected appropriate staff, the administrator is then responsible for providing developmental opportunities to employees, professionals and nonprofessionals alike. These opportunities are generally made available through on-the-job supervision, in-service training and continuing education, but may also take other forms, such as constructive performance evaluations, job rotation, special assignments, and so on. In addition to individual staff development efforts, the administrator also plays a vital role in creating an agency climate that is conducive to job satisfaction and effective performance. Clear agency goals and policies, effective communication up and down the hierarchy, opportunities for workers to exercise some discretion in the performance of their responsibilities, supportive and expert supervision, are among the environmental qualities that appear to stimulate employee growth, morale, and performance.[23]

5. *Assessing agency programs.* The task of assessment is multifaceted. It variously entails assessing program efforts, (what was done), program efficiency (what was done at what cost), and program effectiveness (to what extent were program objectives achieved).[24] Program evaluation is increasingly important, both to account to policy-making and funding bodies, but also as a source of information for internal planning and decision-making purposes.

The increased emphasis on evaluation in social welfare has necessitated the development of more elaborate management information systems that can generate data on activities, costs, outcomes, and a variety of other aspects of agency performance. Designing and maintaining such systems can be quite costly, but if they are designed to service specific decisional purposes, they can be useful aids in the management process. There is an expanding pool of techniques and approaches the manager can draw upon for evaluative purposes, including experimental and quasi-experimental research, benefit-cost and cost-effectiveness analyses. Understanding the similarities and differences in these techniques and selecting the approach that suits the manager's decision needs becomes an important and increasingly complex responsibility.

A second facet of evaluation is the assessment of individual worker performance. The manager's task is to devise ways of assessing and monitoring the job performance of employees. This information can be variously useful for providing corrective feedback, identifying skills and attitudes that need improvement, supporting and rewarding effective performance, and justifying promotions and pay raises.

6. *Changing agency programs.* Organizations are open systems that must adapt to changing environmental conditions if they are to remain relevant and effective. But even when events in the external world do not require change, conditions and processes within the agency will, from time to time, create problems or suggest the need for improvements that must be addressed by the administrator. Managers are, consequently, central actors in efforts to modify policies, programs, and procedures in agencies. The change efforts of managers are among their most consequential acts, since the alteration of existing practices is likely to require not only substantial outlays of time and energy, but inevitably touches upon the critical interests and sentiments of agency members and consumers. The manner in which the change task is carried out, therefore, is not only important to the adoption and implementation of new practices, but is also likely to have significant implications for the quality of the agency's work environment.

Management Activities

The six managerial tasks outlined above suggest something of the administrator's responsibility in developing and maintaining an effective social agency. They may be viewed as the immediate or proximate objectives of administrative practice: those conditions that the administrator must create, or cause to happen, if the organization is to achieve its purposes. But what of day-to-day practice itself? What does the manager do to accomplish these tasks?

Although there has been a good deal of research on managerial activity in business and governmental settings,[25] until recently little or no attention was given to studying administrative practice in social welfare organizations. A recent study conducted by the author examined the activities of ninety managers who were purposefully selected to represent several administrative levels in public, quasi-public, and voluntary agencies providing social services.[26]

The purpose of this study was to determine what social welfare managers did during the course of the typical work week, the amount of time they devoted to these activities, and which of the activities they considered most significant to the performance of their jobs. Activity data were obtained in interviews with managers in which an effort was made to reconstruct the respondents' work activities during the preceding week in as much detail as the managers' recall, aided by their calendars, would allow. This information was then classified into thirteen functional categories and analyzed to determine how much time managers devoted to activities in each of the categories.

1. Planning. Activities were classified as *planning* when the manager was engaged in determining goals, policies, and courses of action. Strategy setting, work scheduling for the entire staff or major units, grant development, and writing are examples.

2. Information processing. This category consists of information-processing and communicating activities where the manager or the interviewer was unable to specify the specific functions being filled. Reading and writing correspondence, reports, memoranda; dictation; filling out, reviewing, and signing forms; "telephoning," "paperwork," and "clearing my desk" are examples of items assigned to this category.

3. Controlling. Activities that served the function of "keeping on top of the job" were classified in this category. *Controlling* consists of collecting and analyzing information as to how the total operation or major segments of it are going. It is traditionally defined as studying records, reports, and accounts and preparing summary reports for superiors. However, the dominant mode of "keeping on top of the job" in our sample of managers appeared to be information sharing between subordinates and superiors during administrative staff meetings and conferences. When it was possible to specify that the controlling function was being filled during such meetings, the time spent was classified as controlling.

4. Coordinating.   Time spent in exchanging information with persons within or outside the agency, other than the managers' subordinates or superiors, in order to relate and adjust programs was classified as *coordinating*. Attending a meeting of agency department heads where one department reports changes in its procedures that affect other agency departments is an example of an activity that would be classified as coordinating.

5. Evaluating.   Activities were classified as *evaluating* when they entailed the assessment of proposals and reported or observed performance. Appraising individual employee performance, program performance, and evaluating suggestions and proposals were included in this category. Also included were any research-related activities conducted for evaluation purposes.

6. Negotiating.   Time spent conferring, bargaining, or discussing with a view to reaching an agreement with another party was classified as *negotiating*. Management-union negotiations, handling employee grievances, or setting up contractual arrangements are examples.

7. Representing.   Those activities the managers engaged in to advance the interests of their agencies through contacts with individuals, groups, or constituencies outside of their organizations were classified as *representing*. Speaking before groups, contacts with the press, and legislative testimony are examples.

8. Staffing.   *Staffing* consisted of those activities engaged in to maintain and build the effectiveness of the agency's staff. It included recruiting and interviewing prospective employees and placing, promoting, and transferring employees. Recruiting volunteers was included in this category.

9. Supervising.   This category included leading, directing, training, and reviewing the work of subordinates. Explaining assignments and work rules, answering questions from subordinates concerning procedures, taking disciplinary action, delegating responsibilities, staff training, and case consultation were included in this category. Obviously the specific activities involved in fulfilling the supervising function vary a great deal with management levels.

10. Supplying. Time spent planning for and obtaining space, equipment, supplies, and other nonfinancial resources required for accomplishing the agency's work was classified as *supplying*.

11. Extracurricular. Activities done during the work week or job-related activities that would not be part of a job description were assigned to this category. Representing the profession, rather than the agency, at a meeting of a professional association, partisan political activity, union organizing, and attending school are examples.

12. Direct service. Giving counseling, treatment, or advice directly to a client and directly intervening for or performing services on behalf of a client was classified as providing *direct services*. Seeing a client for the purpose of providing therapy, making phone calls in order to arrange for transportation for a client (as opposed to making arrangements for the transportation of agency clients) are examples.

13. Budgeting. Time spent planning expenditures and allocating resources among items and programs in the budget was classified as *budgeting*. Monitoring of line-item expenditures and accounting was classified not as budgeting but as controlling.

Table 2–1 shows the mean number of hours spent by all ninety respondents in the sample week for each of the activity categories. Perhaps

TABLE 2–1   Mean Hours Spent in Each Activity by Managers

Activity	Mean Hours
Supervising	6.7
Information processing	6.2
Controlling	5.4
Direct practice	4.1
Planning	3.9
Coordinating	3.8
Extracurricular	1.9
Representing	1.8
Evaluating	1.5
Budgeting	1.0
Staffing	.9
Negotiating	.8
Supplying	.3

the most significant finding that emerged here was the fact that, in the aggregate, managers engaged in a wide array of activities. Respondents devoted at least one hour a week to ten different types of activities, six of which consumed nearly four or more hours of their time. These data suggest the diverse and complex structure of management responsibility, although as we shall see later, the distribution of activities varies substantially by management level.

The mean number of hours devoted to various activities compares quite well with conventional knowledge regarding how managers spend their time. As might be expected, substantial portions of the work week were spent in supervising, information processing, controlling, planning, and coordinating. The large amount of time given to information processing may seem unusual, but it should be noted that this category encompassed all of those activities concerned with reading reports and other job-related materials, making telephone calls, filling out reports, and writing memos and letters. Interestingly, direct practice with clients occupied an average of over four hours a week, though much of this time was accounted for by managers in small agencies operating under voluntary auspices. The other finding that may appear somewhat unusual at first glance is the relatively small amount of time given to budgeting, since the activities associated with this function are so common in management practice. This finding may be explained by the temporal character of the budgeting process and by the fact that this category included only those activities directly related to budget preparation. In addition, a large number of respondents in the sample were in lower-level management positions, where responsibility for developing budgets per se was not a central element of the job. In the last analysis, however, this finding may reflect the reality that little time is spent in actual budget preparation by most managers. This of course does not diminish its importance, nor does it adequately reflect the extensive analytic work that must precede the construction of budgets or the importance of budgeting to sound planning.

Table 2-2 shows how the managers ranked the significance of each activity to the effective performance of their job. Several findings are worth noting. Over two-thirds of the managers in this sample judged activities subsumed under controlling, supervising, and planning as the most important ones they had performed during the prior week. Somewhat less than one-half of the respondents ranked coordinating as significant, while one-quarter or less of the managers felt that activities associated with representing, information processing, direct practice, and evaluating were important to effective job performance.

In order to compare the amount of time given to each kind of activity with managers' judgments regarding the significance of these activities, the data were converted to ranks as presented in Table 2-3. An examination of

TABLE 2–2   Number and Percentage of Managers Who Ranked Activities Among the Five Most Significant to Effective Job Performance

Activity	Number of Times Ranked Significant	Percentage of Managers Who Ranked Activity Significant
Controlling	67	74.4
Planning	61	67.7
Supervising	61	67.7
Coordinating	40	44.4
Representing	25	27.7
Information processing	24	26.6
Direct practice	20	22.2
Evaluating	18	20.0
Negotiating	13	14.4
Budgeting	10	11.1
Extracurricular	4	4.4
Staffing	12	3.4
Supplying	2	2.2

this table reveals that, for the most part, there was a correspondence between the amount of time given to an activity and the importance that managers attached to it. But there are several exceptions. Information processing and direct practice were not considered as important to effective job performance as the amount of time spent on these activities would

TABLE 2–3   Ranking of Activities by Time Spent and Significance of Activity to Effective Job Performance

Activity	Time Spent[a]	Significance[b]
Supervising	1	2 (tie)●
Information processing	2	6
Controlling	3	1
Direct practice	4	2 (tie)
Planning	5	7
Coordinating	6	4
Extracurricular	7	11
Representing	8	5
Evaluating	9	8
Budgeting	10	10
Staffing	11	12
Negotiating	12	9
Supplying	13	13

[a] 1 = largest amount of time spent.
[b] 1 = most significant.

suggest. Conversely, planning, representing, and negotiating were generally considered somewhat more significant than the time given to these activities would indicate.

This study suggests that activities associated with supervising, controlling, planning, and coordinating are the most important management tasks as judged by both the amount of time they consume in a representative work week and the significance that managers attach to them. Information processing and direct practice are among the most time-consuming activities, but are viewed as less important to effective performance. While relatively little time was spent on representing and negotiating, a disproportionate number of managers judged these to be among the most significant activities they performed. This suggests that although a relatively small number of managers are engaged in these activities, those who are consider them essential to effective job performance. Managers spent relatively little time in activities relating to evaluating, budgeting, staffing, and supplying, and generally did not consider these tasks centrally important to their functioning.

Descriptive research on administrative practice in social welfare is still sparse, but existing studies generally support the findings reported above. Studies by Kaeser and Frey and Cashman,[27] focusing on how managers allocate their time, though using somewhat different schemes for classifying activity, nevertheless support the finding that managerial work in social welfare agencies is characterized by great variety. Not only do managers attend to a diverse array of interpersonal, analytic, and evaluation responsibilities, they relate to a variety of interest groups, including subordinates, other managers operating related units or departments, superiors, and varied external constituencies. These studies also support the finding that activities relating to planning, program development, staff supervision, and monitoring and controlling program operations, consume a major portion of the managers' time, while activities devoted to budgeting and evaluation are, in general, less time consuming. Research by Kruzich supports the rank order significance data reported earlier. The 323 public welfare administrators surveyed in her study rated activity categories such as staff supervision, planning and program development, and internal operations (similar to what we refer to as "controlling") as the most important aspects of their jobs.[28] Thus the fragmentary evidence available points to patterns of significant activity that are similar to those that appeared in the author's research.

The manager is indeed an administrative generalist, but formulating plans, deciding what is to be done and how, directing, supporting and facilitating the performance of subordinates (i.e., supervision), and overseeing what is done to ensure that it is in conformity with expectations (i.e., controlling), seem to be the core activities.

VARIATIONS IN MANAGEMENT PRACTICE

So far we have focused upon common elements of management practice in social welfare organizations: the tasks and activities that are performed in some degree by all managers regardless of their location in the administrative hierarchy. Yet, while there are essential similarities, this should not obscure the fact that the relative emphasis given to tasks, and thus the activity configuration of management practice, varies significantly with the organizational level in which that practice occurs. The nature of these variations are briefly discussed in this section.

For the purposes of this discussion we suggest three levels of administrative organization and corresponding management functions.[29] The *executive management level* comprises those persons who carry the overall responsibility for directing the organization or a major portion thereof. Directors, assistant directors, heads of major divisions in large agencies, and others comprise the personnel at this level. These administrators carry the major responsibility for interpreting policy mandates and translating them into organization-wide goals and objectives and obtaining the necessary financial and political support. They will ordinarily be heavily involved with policy and funding bodies, variously accounting for their agency's performance, justifying requests for funds, seeking authorization for new agency initiatives, negotiating agreements, and generally attempting to get favorable consideration for the organization's needs and accomplishments. But in addition to representing the agency's interests, the managers at this level also play a vital role in identifying emerging changes and opportunities in the environment that may have important long-range implications for their agencies. By sensing these changes, assessing their likely consequences, and translating them into potential courses of future action, the executive-level managers help to keep their organizations in tune with external realities. Finally, these managers provide overall leadership and direction to the agency. Major allocation and program decisions, issues concerning organizational structure, and questions of agency priority are generally decided at this level.

The *program management level* includes those persons who are directly responsible for departments, bureaus, programs, and other major operational units. Sometimes referred to as the mid-level management, this cadre is responsible for devising the means the organization will use to accomplish its goals and objectives. Such persons convert the directives of executive-level management into specific program objectives, choose among alternative program strategies for achieving these objectives, procure and assign staff and materials to various program elements, develop internal operating procedures, and monitor, coordinate, and assess program activities. But other critical responsibilities are borne at this level as well. Since program managers are a major link between technical front-line personnel and top management, they play a major role in mediating between these levels. On the one hand, they explain, interpret, and convey the wishes of those at upper levels to their subordinates; on the other hand, they serve as spokespersons and advocates for the ideas, requests, concerns, and needs of front-line personnel. Where the interests and aspirations of subordinates conflict with those of top management, the program administrator seeks to reconcile the differences. Second, the middle manager carries responsibility for representing and negotiating the interests of the program not only with superiors, but with heads of other units at the same organizational level. Maintaining lateral relationships with other parts of the agency—no easy task when there is competition for resources—is a significant aspect of this management level. Finally, the program manager is a critical actor in the task of developing and maintaining conditions conducive to worker morale, efficiency, and effectiveness. Facilitating the flow of communication vertically and horizontally within and between departments, resolving interpersonal and intergroup conflicts, maintaining a normative system that rewards risk, innovation, and problem solving, and encouraging growth and development are responsibilities that fall largely, though certainly not exclusively, to the program manager. In subsequent chapters we shall examine the roles and functions of program management in some depth.

The *supervisory management* level includes those administrative personnel who have direct day-to-day contact with front-line staff. They are responsible for overseeing program implementation, maintaining work flow, delegating and assigning work, and seeing that the services are provided in a manner consistent with policies and procedures. They will ordinarily carry primary responsibility for consulting front-line workers on case-level decisions. Unit supervisor, coordinator, and team leader are some titles commonly given to managers at this level. A distinctive feature of supervisory management is the relatively intense relationship with technical and professional workers on a day-to-day basis. In this context, the manager provides advice and instruction on technical aspects of work, identifies areas of knowledge and skill deficiencies and provides opportunities for upgrading them, and evaluates individual performance. To perform these responsibilities, the supervisory manager must usually have some firsthand knowledge of methods and techniques employed by subordinates. Indeed, such managers are often recruited from the ranks of technical and professional employees because they have shown expertise and proficiency in an area of direct practice. Where this has occurred, the manager may serve as a kind of senior practitioner and role model. Like those at the program level, supervisory managers also serve as linking agents, advocating and representing the interests of subordinates to supervisors, and also communicating, clarifying, and enforcing the directives of their superiors. Because of the close relationship and often intense loyalties that develop with staff, supervisory managers sometimes experience conflict when they are required to gain compliance with organizational policies that subordinates oppose.

The limited research evidence available supports the notion that the configuration of tasks and activities in social welfare management practice varies significantly with organizational level. Patti in the study referred to earlier, found that executive-level managers spent considerably more of their work week representing the agency in the community and negotiating with groups and organizations, than persons at either the program or supervisory levels.[30] Planning activities, directed at such things as setting goals and objectives and designing program structures and processes, also played a prominent part in the work of executives and of program managers, but not of supervisory managers. Similarly, budgeting activities were much more common in the jobs of executives, less so for program managers, and virtually absent in the jobs of supervisory managers. On the other hand, the amount of time given to supervising subordinates was inversely related to management level. As the formulation above would suggest, lower-level managers spent a major portion of their work week in directing, advising, and reviewing the work of subordinates. Program-level managers spent much less of their time in this activity than supervisors, and executives even less.

In summary, we have suggested that the tasks and activities of managers at three organizational levels differ in some important respects. The executive-level manager is concerned with the overall direction of the organizational enterprise and with maintaining relationships with external groups and organizations that provide important sources of support. The program manager is more narrowly focused on a single portion of the organization. His or her responsibility is to create and maintain the capability that will turn plans into operational realities. Within the context of a program, the supervisory manager is primarily involved with developing and facilitating technical and professional processes.

One final note on levels of management: Variations in management practice tend to become much more visible in large organizations. As the number of administrative levels between the first-line supervisor and top executive become greater, their functions become more specialized. Indeed, in some very large social agencies, significant variations may occur even within levels of management. Conversely, in very small social agencies, it is not uncommon to see one manager perform the functions associated with all three levels of management practice. On a particular day, for example, the director of a small agency may have individual conferences with several caseworkers to review case progress or discuss treatment strategies (supervisory management), work on a proposal for a new system of client intake (program management), and then meet with the board of the agency to consider some revision in the agency's priorities or objectives for the coming fiscal year (executive management). We mention this only to indicate that variable functions may be performed by one person rather than several, as has been implied in the preceding discussion.

SUMMARY

This chapter has been concerned with defining social welfare administration as a field of practice. First we provided a broad conceptual definition of social welfare administration and then identified aspects of this practice that distinguish it from general administration. Six major tasks that must be accomplished by social welfare managers were discussed: planning and developing programs, acquiring financial resources and support, designing organizational structure, developing and maintaining staff capability, assessing program performance, and changing programs. Activities engaged in by managers to accomplish these tasks were discussed; it was pointed out that practitioners engage in a wide variety of activities, the most critical of which are planning, supervising, and controlling. The chapter concluded with a brief discussion regarding levels of management, with particular attention to the varied configuration of tasks and activities that characterize management practice at executive, program, and supervisory levels.

NOTES

[1] John C. Kidneigh, "Social Work Administration: An Area of Social Work Practice," *Social Work Journal*, 31, No. 2 (April, 1950), 58.

[2] Schwartz defines this as "administrative process" to distinguish it from "administrative management." See Edward Schwartz, "Some Views of the Study of Social Welfare Administration," in David Fansel, ed., *Research in Social Welfare Administration* (New York: National Association of Social Workers, 1962), pp. 42–43.

[3] This definition corresponds generally to that used by Saari. See Rosemary Saari, "Administration in Social Welfare," *Encyclopedia of Social Work*, John B. Turner, ed. (New York: National Association of Social Workers, 1977), I: 42–46.

[4] Chauncey Alexander, "Management of Human Service Organizations," *Encyclopedia of Social Work*, John B. Turner, ed. (New York: National Association of Social Workers, 1977), II: 845.

[5] *Random House Dictionary*, unabridged ed., 1967, p. 9.

[6] *Random House Dictionary*, pp. 869–70.

[7] See, for example, Schwartz, "Some Views"; James D. Thompson, "Common Elements in Administration," *Social Welfare Administration*, Ella Reed, ed. (New York: Columbia University Press, 1961), pp. 27–29; Saari, "Administration,"

pp. 46–47; Harold Lewis, "Management in the Non-Profit Social Service Organization," in *Social Administration,* Simon Slavin, ed. (New York: Haworth Press, 1978), pp. 7–14.

[8]See, for example, Fremont Kast and James Rosenweig, *Organization and Management: A Systems Approach* (New York: McGraw-Hill, 1974), pp. 497–519; Henry Mintzberg, *The Nature of Managerial Work* (New York: Harper & Row, 1973), pp. 103–9; Yeheskel Hasenfeld and James English (eds.), *Human Service Organizations* (Ann Arbor, Mich.: University of Michigan Press, 1974), pp. 8–22; and Richard Steiner, *Managing the Human Service Organization* (Beverly Hills, Calif.: Sage Publications, 1977), pp. 18–30.

[9]There have been some studies comparing management practice in public and business sectors. See Mintzberg, *The Nature of Managerial Work,* pp. 259–68 and 107–9.

[10]Other features of social welfare organizations with implications for management are the nature of labor force, the special problems of evaluating effectiveness, and the intensity of client-staff interactions. See Hasenfeld and English (eds.), *Human Service Organizations,* pp. 8–21.

[11]Sidney E. Bernard, "Why Service Delivery Programs Fail," *Social Work,* 20, No. 3 (May, 1975), 206–212.

[12]A good case example can be found in Willard C. Richan, "The Administrator as Advocate," *Leadership in Social Administration,* Felice O. Perlmutter and Simon Slavin, eds. (Philadelphia: Temple University Press, 1980), pp. 72–85.

[13]Hasenfeld and English, eds. *Human Service Organizations,* pp. 9–12; and Simon Slavin, "A Theoretical Framework for Social Administration," *Leadership,* Perlmutter and Slavin, eds., pp. 7–18.

[14]Hasenfeld and English (eds.), *Human Service Organizations,* pp. 8–9.

[15]Wilbur Finch, "Social Workers Versus Bureaucracy," *Social Work,* 21, No. 5 (September, 1976), 370–75.

[16]Ralph Kramer, "Ideology, Status, and Power in Board Executive Relationships," *Social Work,* 10, No. 4 (October, 1965), 108–114.

[17]Herman D. Stein, "Administrative Leadership in Complex Service Organizations," in *Social Work Administration,* Harry A. Schatz, ed. (New York: Council on Social Work Education, 1970), pp. 288–98.

[18]Steiner, *Managing,* p. 25.

[19]Hasenfeld and English, eds., *Human Service Organizations,* pp. 8–9, 12–14.

[20]Lewis, "Management," pp. 9–10.

[21]Alan R. Gruber, "The High Cost of Delivering Services," *Social Work,* 18, No. 4 (July 1973), 33–40.

[22]See, for example, Harleigh Trecker, *Social Work Administration* (New York: Association Press, 1971); Walter Ehlers, Michael Austin, and Jon Prothero, *Administration for the Human Services* (New York: Harper & Row, 1976); Marc Miringoff, *Management in Human Service Organizations* (New York: Macmillan, 1980).

[23]Rino J. Patti, "Social Work Practice: Organizational Environment," *Encyclopedia of Social Work,* John B. Turner, ed. (New York: National Association of Social Workers, 1977), II: 1534–41.

[24]Tony Tripodi, Phillip Fellin, and Irwin Epstein, *Social Program Evaluation* (Itasca, Ill.: F. E. Peacock Publishers, 1971), pp. 41–60.

[25]For a review of some of these studies, see Mintzberg, *Nature of Managerial Work,* pp. 7-27.

[26]Rino J. Patti, "Patterns of Management Activity in Social Welfare Agencies," *Administration in Social Work,* 1, No. 1 (Spring, 1977), 5-18. The material in this section draws heavily from this article.

[27]Linda Kaeser and Gerald Frey, *Educating for Management* (mimeo), School of Social Work, Portland State University (June, 1975), pp. 22-29; and James Cashman, "Training Social Welfare Administrators: The Activity Dilemma," *Administration in Social Work,* 2, No. 3 (Fall, 1978), 347-58.

[28]Jean Kruzich, *Working Paper No. 4: Analysis of Social Welfare Administrator Questionnaire* (mimeo), Social Welfare Administration Project, School of Social Work, University of Minnesota (March, 1976), pp. 4-5.

[29]This formulation draws upon Saari, "Social Welfare Administration," pp. 47-48, and Thompson, "Common Elements," pp. 17-29.

[30]Patti, "Patterns of Management Activity," pp. 12-15.

CHAPTER THREE

A Model of Program Management in the Social Services

In the two preceding chapters we set forth a broad picture of social welfare administration, in both historical and cross-sectional dimensions. One can liken this to an aerial view that has defined the boundaries and mapped the general terrain of social welfare administration. In this chapter we will take a closer look at one part of this larger terrain called *program management.* More specifically, our purpose in this discussion shall be to define the principal conceptual components of a model of program management and the assumptions that underlie it. The model is built on the notion that what a manager does is, or should be, largely dictated by the structural charac- teristics and developmental goals associated with the various stages of de- velopment. In Chapters 4, 5, and 6, we examine the relationship of these components to one another. Before proceeding, however, let us focus on the elements of the general model: the program, the program develop- ment cycle, the program manager, developmental goals, and management tasks.

SOCIAL SERVICE PROGRAMS

A social service program shall be defined as a formal administrative system of an organization concerned with delivering rehabilitative, access, or per- sonal care services to clients.[1] Programs are the locus of specialized activities where the service technologies of an agency are brought directly to bear on the client population. They are the point at which policy planning, resources, and expertise find expression in the form of services.[2] In an important sense, everything that happens in an organization is ancillary to, and supportive of, program activity; for it is here that the organization seeks to fulfill its mission.

Operationally, programs may be identified as projects, sections, bureaus, departments, or divisions. Because terminology varies from organization to organization, function is a far better way of defining a program entity than title. Some examples of the types of social service programs we will refer to are: the social service department of a general hospital, the day treatment program of a community mental health center, the foster care division of a voluntary social agency, the employee assistance program in a business firm, and a group home program for juvenile offenders.

A program is formally responsible for pursuing a relatively specific and limited subset of objectives that are derived from, and in the service of, the parent organization's overall goals and objectives. Its objectives may be central to the host agency's purpose (e.g., the counseling program in a family service agency), or marginal to it (e.g., an employee assistance program in an industrial firm). In any case, as an instrument of the larger organization, its claim to continued support rests heavily, though often not exclusively,[3] on the extent to which it serves the purpose of the host agency. It is also important to note that a program is likely to be both dependent upon and in competition with other programs and functions in the organization. Dependent in the sense that its objectives cannot be achieved without the support and cooperation of other units: competitive in the sense that, except in times of expansion, it is likely to be contending with other programs for its share of the agency's resources. These elements of centrality to agency purpose, interdependence, and competition do much to define the program's relationship to the organizational environment. We shall return to this in subsequent chapters.

The structural characteristics of programs vary considerably, depending on their size and geographic dispersion. A public, statewide program of child protective services may have several hundred employees in numerous geographic locations. In such an instance, there may be five administrative levels corresponding to direct services, supervisors, office director, assistant program administrator, and program administrator. A program of this size may have a significant component of support staff such as planners and trainers. At the other extreme may be an adult outpatient treatment program in a community mental health center, with perhaps eight direct service workers and a program director. Unlike the example above, this program has only two administrative levels. The director will be in face-to-face interaction with subordinates and will ordinarily be intimately familiar with, if not personally involved in, the delivery of services. Support services will ordinarily be provided by other units in the organization not administratively responsible to the program director. These two entities, though quite different structurally, are both components of a larger organization responsible for delivering a specific type of social service to a defined client population. In this sense they are both programs as we define that term here.

A program's location in the administrative hierarchy appears to be primarily related to the size (i.e., number of employees) and complexity (i.e., number of discrete programs) of the parent organization. In general, it seems that the greater the size and complexity of an agency, the greater will be the number of administrative levels between the executive director and the program head. There are two frequent exceptions to this general rule. Where the program consumes a disproportionate share of the organization's resources, or is a major instrument for carrying out the agency's purpose, it will often be placed at a level closer to the top. Second, when a program is established for experimental or demonstration reasons and has major implications for the future direction of the agency, it may be placed at a higher level in the administrative hierarchy so that the chief executive can give it closer attention.

THE PROGRAM DEVELOPMENT CYCLE

Social service programs typically evolve through several stages over time, each of which is characterized by a set of structural characteristics and developmental goals that collectively set it off from all others. Each stage, as we shall argue, poses different problems and dilemmas for the program manager, and thus demands differential attention to certain administrative tasks and techniques. We shall return to the relationship between program development and managerial behavior, but let us first describe the development cycle in more detail.

The notion that formal organizations move through a predictable cycle of development has been the subject of considerable commentary and analysis in the social science and management literatures. Though models of development differ in their emphasis and level of descriptive detail, there appears to be some agreement among theorists that organizations have a natural tendency to grow, elaborate, and become more formalized with age. This view, which is variously referred to as the *biological,* or *metamorphic, model,* contends that

> ... growth is not a smooth or continuous process, but is marked by abrupt and discrete changes in the conditions for organizational persistence and the structures appropriate to these changes.[4]

This process of growth and change has been postulated for organizations in general[5] and for specific types of organizations as diverse as voluntary associations,[6] governmental agencies,[7] business concerns,[8] and human service programs.[9] While there is little understanding of the factors that account for the rate of progress through the developmental cycle, or the time it takes to pass through different stages, the process does appear to be ordered and sequential. Moreover, students of this phenomenon have observed that transitions from one stage to another are likely to be experienced as crises involving a heightened sense of discontinuity, disorganization, and conflict.[10]

Following this line of analysis, we propose that social service programs typically evolve through three stages of development that we shall refer to as *design, implementation,* and *stabilization.* Each of these is described briefly below. More detailed profiles of the structural characteristics and processes associated with each stage of development are presented in subsequent chapters.

1. Program design.   *Program design* is the initial stage of development; it usually commences after a program has been authorized and funds have been allocated for its operation. This initial period is usually marked by preoccupation with translating the authorizing policy, generally stated in broad terms, into a more concrete plan that will at once win the support of the parent organization's leaders and simultaneously provide guidance and direction to those with responsibility for program implementation.

2. Implementation stage.   The *implementation stage* commences as the program swings into full operation. The program plan, which until this point has been a set of untested assumptions and hypotheses, is now elaborated and refined in order to better fit the realities and unanticipated problems encountered. Frequently marked by trial, error, instability, and change, this stage usually witnesses efforts to bring greater coherence and rationality to program operations and attempts to consolidate relations between the program and its external environment.

3. Stabilization stage.   In the *stabilization stage,* concern shifts from program development to program maintenance. Attention and energy are directed to replicating, marginally improving, and institutionalizing policies and practices. The evaluation of efficiency and effectiveness tend to become central preoccupations as program personnel seek to maximize productivity and impact. At the same time, these evaluation processes are likely to generate feedback and suggest needed changes. Where such changes require a significant departure from existing modes of operation, the program enters a new developmental cycle.

The developmental scheme presented above is compared in Table

3–1 with several others that have been proposed. The reader will note that it parallels the Hage and Aiken scheme, but with several modifications.[11] Their model starts with an evaluation phase, wherein organizational decision makers determine whether to initiate a new program. Our model begins with the design of a new program and presupposes that the decision has already been made. We have chosen to start here since this is likely to be the point at which the program manager arrives on the scene. In some instances the manager will have been involved in proposing a new program, but will not be responsible for the decision to initiate a program. The initiation stage proposed by Hage and Aiken corresponds roughly to the design and implementation stages in our model. Finally, their routinization stage parallels our stabilization stage.

For purposes of this discussion we shall focus on the *initial* developmental cycle that begins when a new program is established by the parent organization and ends when the objectives and/or means employed by a *stable* program are modified in a way that requires a significant departure from existing modes of operation. When a developmental cycle ends is a matter of some definitional difficulty, since changes in program ends and means are occurring at each stage. The design and implementation stages, particularly, are inherently oriented to change as the program adapts to emerging internal and external realities. At some point, however, the change curve begins to flatten. The program achieves a degree of equilibrium, and continuity and routine become the prominent features of day-to-day operations. This is the stage of development we shall refer to as *stabilization*. The initial developmental cycle is completed when this stabilized arrangement, as noted above, is substantially modified.

Subsequent developmental cycles will seldom involve all aspects of the program. Even with major change, programs are likely to carry forth many of the policies, procedures, and personnel previously employed. Thus, as

TABLE 3–1   Comparison of Stages of Development

Stages of Program Development	Hage and Aiken[a]	Perlmutter[b]	Katz and Kahn[c]
Design	Evaluation Initiation	Self-interest	Primitive system
Implementation	Implementation	Professionalism	Stable organization
Stabilization	Routinization	Social interest	Elaboration of structure

[a] Jerald Hage and Michael Aiken, *Social Change in Complex Organizations,* (New York: Random House, 1969).
[b] Felice D. Perlmutter, "A Theoretical Model of Social Agency Development," *Social Casework,* 50, No. 8 (October, 1969), 467–73.
[c] Daniel Katz and Robert L. Kahn, *The Social Psychology of Organizations,* (New York: John Wiley & Sons, Inc. 1966), p. 78.

suggested in Figure 3-1, succeeding cycles of development tend to involve components of programs and not entire programs themselves. A new mode of service delivery, a departmental reorganization, the opening of a new branch office; these are examples of program components that may be changed as the program emerges from its initial developmental cycle.

How long does it take for a program to complete this initial developmental cycle? At this point there is little basis for anything more than speculation. Observation suggests a period of perhaps three to five years, but a number of variables may shorten or extend this period. Some of the most salient are:

1. The period of anticipated funding for a program.   A program faced with a short funding cycle of three years, and the necessity of engaging in a competitive renewal, will likely proceed through the developmental cycle more quickly.

2. The stability of the parent organization.   An organization that experiences frequent policy changes, leadership turnover, loss of funding, and so on, is likely to be ambiguous and inconsistent in its expectations and thus retard a program's development.

3. The specificity of the authorizing policy.   If the mandate is clearly articulated and relatively easy to translate into operational terms, a program may move more quickly through the design and implementation phases toward stabilization.

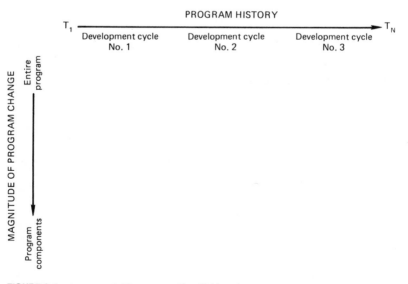

FIGURE 3-1   A program's history as an identifiable unit.

4. The degree of program innovativeness. The extent to which a program approximates, or diverges from, prior practice will likely affect the amount of uncertainty it faces and therefore, the period of trial and error that will be required before stability can be achieved.

5. The extent to which constituents and supporters agree about the purposes and objectives of the program. Since a program lies at the intersection between those who consume its services and those who provide its resources, sharp disagreements between these groups and the attendant necessity to mediate and reconcile these conflicts can divert energy that might otherwise be devoted to internal program development.

6. The nature of the program's work force. Programs employing people who are unfamiliar with the problems the program is supposed to address, or unskilled in the technologies to be used, will likely move through the design and implementation phases more slowly.

This list is only suggestive of the many variables that no doubt impact the rate of program development. It is intended here only to stimulate discussion and, hopefully, systematic investigation. Further understanding of how these and other variables interact to slow or facilitate the program developmental cycle will ultimately be critical to a model of program management.

THE PROGRAM MANAGER

Program managers are those persons who are directly responsible for social service programs. They are accountable to their superiors for the operations and outcomes of the program unit. Often referred to generically as middle-level managers, these persons carry a variety of titles such as chief, administrator, supervisor, service coordinator, director, and so on. For purposes of this book we shall use the designations program manager, director, and administrator interchangeably when referring to personnel at this level.

Program managers are often recruited from within the organization or from other social welfare organizations after a period of service in direct practice and first-line supervisory positions. A recent study of social service managers in a variety of social agency settings, for example, revealed that 80 percent of persons in second-line supervisory positions had prior experience as both direct service workers and first-line supervisors before assuming their current posts. Among department and project heads in this study, over 60 percent had had both direct practice and supervisory experience before moving into their present jobs.[12] Additional evidence suggesting this pattern of upward mobility for program managers is available from another study, which examined the educational and experience requirements for administrative jobs in state public welfare agencies. Here it was found that an average of two or more years' direct practice experience was required to qualify for supervisory positions in social services, mental health, and correctional programs.[13]

Given this pattern of upward mobility from direct service, to supervisory, to program management responsibility, it seems reasonable to assume that most program administrators come to their jobs with little or no formal academic preparation in management. In most cases such persons receive their basic professional preparation in direct services and, based on competence in this arena, program knowledge, and job experience, ascend to higher levels of administrative responsiblity.

The problems associated with this career pattern are receiving increased attention in the literature. In Chapter 7 we give this matter careful attention. For now it is sufficient to note that although there is widespread concern about the lack of management preparation among those in the middle echelons, there is a prevalent, though by no means uniform, belief that direct practice experience and program knowledge gained in the ranks are important prerequisites for program management. This tendency was reflected in a recent study of job-hiring preferences of directors of large urban, county, and regional public welfare departments. When asked to choose among hypothetical job applicants for program management positions—e.g., director of a halfway house, service delivery coordinator for a medical assistance program, and so on—respondents disproportionately favored applicants with direct service backgrounds and program knowledge in areas for which they would be responsible. Such applicants were generally preferred over those with more formal management training, but less service and program experience.[14]

The career pathway to program administration and the policies and preferences that support it may be called into question as the management skills required of persons in these jobs become increasingly more sophisticated and specialized. For the present, however, a major manpower issue confronting human service professions is how to adequately prepare persons whose past performance and experience in social service programs has propelled them toward management.

The difficulties inherent in making the transition from direct service to administration are accentuated for program managers because of the complex role requirements associated with these positions.[15] Perhaps the most critical aspect of this role, implied in the term *middle manager*, is the responsibility for mediating between the expectations of top agency administration, on the one hand, and those of supervisory and direct service staff on the other.[16] The program manager is at the intersection between the highest and lowest organizational levels and must respond to the needs, interests, and expectations of persons operating in these quite distinct and distant administrative sectors. The demands imposed from above and below are often disparate, frequently conflicting, and sometimes irreconcilable. Because of their location, program managers are likely to understand the realities confronting both superiors and subordinates and thus appreciate the factors that give rise to their various perspectives. The imperative of fiscal austerity must be balanced against the urgency for strengthened services. The need for control and accountability must be weighed against the importance of discretion and autonomy for practitioners. Access to, and involvement in, both of these realities is likely to create a situation of recurring role strain for the program manager.

The following case example suggested by Michael Austin & Susanne Devich, reflects something of the cross-pressures to which middle managers are exposed:

Daniel was a supervisor in a court correction agency and was managing an experimental program that had recently been funded by the state legislature. A problem came up in regard to the service contract for the state. The contract required that professional workers complete an application on every person they investigate and feed it into a computer. The staff refused to do it. Daniel and the county administrators also felt that it was inappropriate and violated client confidentiality. The matter was in the process of being negotiated with state and federal officials, and the county officials were confident that they would win. Simultaneously, the county executive had agreed with the state while negotiations were going on that the staff would collect this information, that it would be held internally, and if it was not needed for the computer, it would be destroyed. The staff refused to collect the information even on a temporary basis. Daniel wrote a memo to the staff explaining that it was necessary to collect the information. Three staff members refused to comply, hired a lawyer, and had a press conference. Daniel was getting close to the point of firing the staff for insubordination. With that possibility being one day away, a waiver came through from federal officials that exempted the county from collecting the information. The whole problem built up ugly feelings between the administration and the mental health professionals. It was a very unpleasant and unfortunate experience for all. Trust was lost between Daniel and some of the workers, and morale was at an all-time low.

The complexity of the program manager's role is further reflected in the multiple lateral relationships that must be maintained with the heads of other operating units in the host organization and with representatives of groups and organizations in the community. The manager not only has to weigh and prioritize their demands and requests, but must do so with a view to eliciting the cooperation, support and resources that are inevitably needed if the program is to function effectively. On any given day, for example, the manager of a day treatment program in a mental health center may meet with the head of the vocational training department in the agency to consult on patients served by both programs, visit with a director of social services at a nearby state mental hospital to develop procedures for referring patients to the day treatment program, and then confer with members of a program advisory committee to discuss what might be done to lobby against proposed legislation that would reduce funds for the chronically mentally ill. More will be said later of this network of lateral relationships. Suffice it to say now that the program manager operates in a complicated web of contrasting and sometimes conflicting expectations: a web that influences and is influenced by the manager's behavior.

The complexity of the program administrator's role is also manifest in the necessity to be informed about and proficient in the technical aspects of the units of work. While the executive-level administrator is likely to be removed from day-to-day operations and concerned about aggregate performance, the program manager must know enough about the program's inner workings to make informed decisions about day-to-day operations. He or she must have some familiarity, if not firsthand experience, with the substantive issues and technical processes involved in service delivery. If program managers become removed from this operating reality, or fail to keep current with the latest technical developments in a program area, their credibility with subordinates will not only be damaged, but their ability to effectively oversee and evaluate program performance will be impaired. In short, program managers must combine both administrative skills and substantive expertise.

Finally, it is often observed that program managers' authority is seldom equal to their responsibility.[17] Ultimately, they are held to account for the performance of their units, but the formal power and resources at their command to affect outcomes is frequently insufficient. One consequence of this is that program managers must rely variously on tactics such as persuasion, education, pressure, exchange, and negotiation in order to elicit cooperation and compliance. This is certainly the case in relations with other program heads in the organization and agencies in the community, but also, in varying degrees, with superiors and subordinates as well. In the last analysis, the political skill necessary to develop and maintain these agreements may be the most demanding aspect of the program manager's role.

DEVELOPMENTAL GOALS
AND MANAGEMENT TASKS

Developmental goals, as used in this discussion, are future desirable conditions, processes, or modes of operation within the program, or between the program and elements of its task environment. They are basically concerned with the way in which an organizational unit functions in order to attain service outcomes, *not the service outcomes themselves.* As such, developmental goals may be seen as intermediate steps that are sought in order to generate and support a program's service capability. Developmental goals resemble the system goals that Perrow refers to, except in his formulation such goals may be independent of the organization's formal ends. Organizational states such as growth, stability, and change may, in Perrow's view, be ends in themselves that have no specific relationship to the production of an organization's goods and services.[18] In the model presented here, developmental goals are considered to be means; they are necessary, if not sufficient conditions, for the delivery of effective social services. The systems model of organizational analysis, described variously by Etzioni,[19] Georgopolous and Tannenbaum,[20] and Levinson,[21] comes closest to our notion of developmental goals since it focuses on the conditions and processes in an organization that are likely to make it most effective in pursuit of its formal goals.

In the next three chapters we shall argue that at each stage of program development certain critical goals must be substantially achieved if the program is to actualize its performance potential at that point in its history. Moreover, a failure to establish the modes of operation appropriate at one stage usually means that these unfulfilled goals will persist as issues and serve as obstacles to the actualization of a program's potential at subsequent stages. At the very least, this legacy of unresolved issues will require the continuing attention of the program manager and thus divert time and energy away from the pursuit of goals that are essential at successive stages. Finally, we shall contend that the realization of all the developmental goals is necessary before a program can become fully effective in achieving its ultimate purposes.

The six tasks outlined in Chapter 2 are ongoing responsibilities of management. They must be continuously addressed throughout a program's history and are never fully achieved. In the chapters that follow, however, we will not be concerned with all management tasks in all stages of development. Rather, our intent will be to highlight selected tasks that take on particular importance as the manager confronts varying configurations of structural characteristics and developmental goals. This approach follows the contingency view of management, which is based on the notion that organizations are changing, complex, multivariate entities that are not amenable to monolithic explanatory or intervention models. Accordingly, it is argued that there is no unvarying prescription for administrative behavior, but that the configuration of management activities must vary to suit the specific characteristics of the organization and the environment in which it operates. Blau summarizes the broad outlines of this approach:

> The contingency view seeks to understand the relationships between subsystems as well as between the organization and its environment. . . . It . . . attempts to understand how organizations operate under varying circumstances and in specific situations. Contingency views are ultimately directed

toward suggesting organizational designs and managerial actions most appropriate for specific situations.[22]

The model of management presented here draws from and builds upon this notion. It is directed to enhancing managers' ability to understand developmental contingencies that emerge over time and to selecting and implementing administrative strategies that are responsive to these realities. Table 3–2 reflects the major variables that will be discussed in the next three chapters. In each, we shall first discuss some of the characteristics commonly associated with programs in various stages of development, suggest goals that are likely to be the central concern of the manager at each point, and the tasks that must be accomplished if the program is to achieve these goals.

SUMMARY

This chapter has set forth the elements of a model of program management in the social services that is to be elaborated in the succeeding three chapters. The central premise of this model is that social service programs typically evolve through several stages which we refer to as design, implementation, and stabilization. Each stage of development is characterized by certain structural characteristics and developmental goals that call forth a configuration of management tasks. Thus, for example, in order to achieve the developmental goals associated with the design stage, managers usually find it necessary to give special attention to the planning and re-

TABLE 3–2 Components of the Program Management Model

Stages of Program Development	Developmental Goals	Management Tasks
Design	Establishinmg credibility in the parent organization Demonstrating program potential	Program planning Resource acquisition
Implementation	Increasing certainty in relations with the task environment Establishing a service domain Building internal capacity for competent program performance	Resource acquisition Structuring the organizational unit Staff development and maintenance
Stabilization	Creating a positive organizational climate Creating a capacity for program evaluation Developing a capacity for change	Staff development and maintenance Assessment Change

source acquisition tasks. A failure to address the management tasks appropriate to the developmental goals at any stage will undermine a program's capability at that point in its history and retard its ability to address developmental goals at subsequent stages of development.

NOTES

[1] Alfred K. Kahn, *Social Policy and Social Services* (New York: Random House, 1973), pp. 27–33.

[2] Other kinds of programs in organizations do not fall within our definition. For example, programs to train personnel, conduct research, or raise funds are not addressed here since they are not directly engaged in service delivery.

[3] There are instances, for example, when a program has enjoyed such widespread community support that the parent agency has little choice but to continue providing support.

[4] William Starbuck, "Organizational Growth and Development," in *Handbook of Organizations,* James March, ed. (Chicago: Rand-McNally, 1965).

[5] Daniel Katz and Robert L. Kahn, *The Social Psychology of Organizations* (New York: John Wiley & Sons, 1966), pp. 77–83; and John R. Kimberly and Robert H. Miles, *The Organizational Life Cycle* (San Francisco: Jossey-Bass, 1980).

[6] Theodore J. Lowi, *The Politics of Disorder* (New York: Basic Books, 1971), pp. 37–51; and Sheldon Messenger, "Organizational Transformation: A Case Study of a Declining Social Movement," *American Sociological Review,* 20 (February, 1955), 3–10.

[7] Anthony Downs, *Inside Bureaucracy* (Boston: Little, Brown, 1967); and Fremont Lyden, George Shipman, and Morton Kroll, eds., *Policies, Decisions, and Organization* (New York: Appleton-Century-Crofts, 1969).

[8] Larry E. Greiner, "Evolution and Revolution as Organizations Grow," *Harvard Business Review,* 50, No. 4 (July–August, 1972), 37–46; Gordon L. Lippitt and Warren H. Schmidt, "Crises in a Developing Organization," *Harvard Business Review,* 45, No. 6 (November–December, 1967), 102–12; Henry Mintzberg, *The Nature of Managerial Work* (New York: Harper & Row, 1973), pp. 122–26.

[9] Jerald Hage and Michael Aiken, *Social Change in Complex Organizations* (New York: Random House, 1969); Felice Perlmutter, "A Theoretical Model of Social Agency Development," *Social Casework,* 50, No. 8 (October, 1969), 467–73; Melvin Mugolof, "A Developmental Approach to the Community Action Idea," *Social Work,* 12, No. 2 (April, 1967), 12–20; William Rosengren, "The Careers of Clients and Organizations," in *Organizations and Clients,* William Rosengren and Mark Lefton, eds. (Columbus, Ohio: Charles E. Merrill, 1970); Tony Tripodi, Phillip Fellin, and Irwin Epstein, *Social Program Evaluation* (Itasca, Ill.: F. E. Peacock Publishers, 1971).

[10] Lowi, *Politics of Disorder,* p. 40; and Greiner, "Evolution and Revolution," pp. 37–46.

[11] Hage and Aiken, *Social Change,* pp. 93–106.

[12] Rino J. Patti et al., *Educating for Management in Social Welfare* (mimeo), Schools of Social Work and Business Administration, University of Washington (1976), II: 22–28.

[13]Rino J. Patti and Charles Maynard, "Qualifying for Managerial Jobs in Public Welfare," *Social Work*, 23, No. 4 (July, 1978), 292-93.

[14]Rino J. Patti and Ronald Rauch, "Social Work Administration Graduates in the Job Market: An Analysis of Managers' Hiring Preferences," *Social Service Review*, 52, No. 4 (December, 1978), 567-83.

[15]Hugo E. R. Uyterhoeven, "General Managers in the Middle," in *Developing an Effective Organization*, Harvard Business Review Reprint Series, 5-15; and Thomas A. Petit, *Fundamentals of Management Coordination* (New York: John Wiley & Sons, 1975), pp. 317-37.

[16]Raymond Bissonette and Jack Zusman, "Mental Health Training for the Middle Manager," *Administration in Mental Health*, 3, No. 2 (Spring, 1976), 193-99.

[17]Uyterhoeven, "General Managers," p. 9.

[18]Charles Perrow, *Organizational Analysis: A Sociological View* (Belmont, Calif.: Brooks-Cole Publishing Co., 1970), pp. 144-58.

[19]Amitai Etzioni, "Two Approaches to Organizational Analysis: A Critique and a Suggestion," *Administrative Science Quarterly*, 5, No. 2 (September, 1960), 257-278.

[20]Basil S. Georgopolous and Arnold S. Tannenbaum, "A Study of Organizational Effectiveness," *American Sociological Review*, 22, No. 5 (October, 1957), 534-40.

[21]Perry Levinson, "Goal-Model and System-Model Criteria of Effectiveness," in *Planning, Programming, Budgeting*, 2nd ed., Fremont Lyden and Ernest Miller, eds. (Chicago: Markham Publishing Co., 1973), pp. 285-96.

[22]Peter Blau as quoted in Fremont Kast and James Rosenweig, *Organization and Management* (New York: McGraw-Hill, 1974), p. 505.

CHAPTER FOUR

Program Management in the Design Stage

This chapter begins with a discussion of the characteristics commonly associated with programs in the design stage of development in order to set the organizational context that serves as both a source of constraint and opportunity for the manager. In this context, the program manager confronts the challenge of converting what is still an assemblage of ideas and resources into a functional entity with the potential for delivering social services. The goals sought in building this potential, the critical tasks and issues that must be confronted in realizing these goals, and selected strategies and techniques useful for this purpose constitute the remainder of the chapter.

DESIGN STAGE: ORGANIZATIONAL CONTEXT

The impetus for the creation of programs can emanate from a number of sources, but let us suggest three that are commonly observed. Perhaps the most frequent impetus comes from *sources external to the organization* in which the program is ultimately located. Legislative or executive initiatives at federal, state, or local government levels, often specified and interpreted by planning and regulatory bodies, frequently provide the authorization and incentive for the creation of new programs. In recent years, for example, federal statutes have been passed to stimulate the development of services to victims of rape and child abuse, to substance abusers, and to the elderly. In some instances, laws have required public agencies to provide services, thus leaving them little discretion regarding the adoption of programs.[1]

Although the formal authorization for programs may be provided by legislative or executive mandate, the stimulus for such action is frequently provided by the advocacy efforts of groups or associations closely identified with, or speaking on behalf of, the population that stands to gain by the initiative. For example, groups such as the mental health lobby, civil rights, minority and women's groups, labor unions, and client-based organizations like welfare rights and Parents Anonymous are often instrumental in articulating needs, promoting awareness in the general population, mobilizing a political constituency, and lobbying legislators.[2] At a local level, citizen groups and associations may appeal directly to social welfare organizations to create new social service programs. An organized campaign to acquire funds from a local United Way or a proposal to an agency to establish a program for heretofore unserved client groups are illustrations. In yet other cases, such community groups establish their own programs independent of existing organizations. In these instances local interest groups incorporate and form organizations that will provide the auspices for the program or programs they believe are needed.

New programs may also be initiated by *organizational leaders*—e.g., executives or boards of directors. The decision to do so may result from a variety of factors including, for example: a perception of an unmet need in the community, the availability of new funds which allows organizational growth or stabilization, a desire to alter the direction or goals of an agency, or an interest in experimenting with a service innovation or new technology. What Mintzberg refers to as "improvement projects" fall into this category.[3] Organizational leaders, based on some reading of the external environment and the needs of the organization, decide that a new program is desirable.

Finally, there are cases in which new programs result from the efforts of *persons in lower levels* of the organization. Although authorization must be obtained from organizational leaders or external policy groups, the perception of need, the source of ideas, and the energy come primarily from persons or groups at subexecutive levels. The impetus often derives from firsthand experience with inadequacies in current agency operations; or the impetus may come from those who are strongly influenced by values or ideologies that are not reflected in current programs. In some instances new programs may be seen as an opportunity for increased power or upward mobility, or they may be prompted by the desire for a vehicle that will enable the expression or development of professional interests or techniques.

Whatever the source of initiation, a new program commences when an agency policy or directive has been formulated authorizing its establishment and setting its broad goals and purposes. Ordinarily this mandate will recognize the need for a new service, indicate the population to be served, and the outcomes expected. It remains for the program staff to elaborate this intent and bring it to expression.

During the design phase, the organizational and external environments are likely to exert a profound influence on the character of the program.[4] Among this array of forces, perhaps none will be more important than the leadership of the parent organization itself. Program staff, particularly the manager, are likely to be heavily dependent upon superiors for information, support, and legitimacy.[5] If the manager and staff have been recruited from within the organization, their dependence on superiors may not be as pervasive. Yet even under these circumstances they will probably rely heavily on organizational leaders for contacts with and access to funding sources, community influentials, and policy-making bodies. At the very least, they will ordinarily turn to superiors for clarification regarding policy intent, needed resources, and direction regarding the permissible parameters of program operation.

Agency elites exercise a disproportionate influence at this early stage of development. Their knowledge of community expectations, their prestige, and their ability to acquire and allocate funds are important resources for a developing program.[6] Moreover, to the extent that a new program signals some change in the character of the parent agency, their role as stewards assumes critical importance. Zald notes, for example, that the power and involvement of boards of directors increases considerably when the organization is undergoing a major transformation:

> Pressures to change aspects of [organizational] character almost inevitably become issues for the board of directors. First, both legal requirements and the standard functions of boards in policy settings become obviously implicated when the major dimensions of the organization are subjected to change. Second, if these aspects of character have developed qualities of the sacred and traditional, changing them is likely to develop conflict. Managers will be forced . . . to bring such matters to the board.[7]

The program's dependence on organizational elites in the design phase is thus a function of both its need for support and resources and the superior's need for control. Until the program has been fully integrated into the organization, leaders are likely to play a critical role in its formulation.

Relationships with other units of the host organization (e.g., other departments or programs) will be affected by whether the new program is perceived as a rival for resources, jurisdiction, or both.[8] To the extent that established units anticipate a threat to their service domain, foresee a potential loss of power or status in the organization, or anticipate competition for scarce resources, they may withhold full cooperation until the effects of the new program on their operations are clear. For example, the director of an alcoholism treatment program may suspect that a new program for drug abusers will dilute the agency's commitment to serving alcoholics. Likewise the manager of a homemaker program in an agency serving the elderly may resist the introduction of a new chore services program out of a concern that if chore services prove a less expensive alternative to preventing institutionalization, the program will be reduced. If, on the other hand, a new program is perceived as augmenting or complementing existing functions, the reception is likely to be more positive. For example, the head of a counseling program in an institution for juvenile offenders that is controlled by a custody-oriented staff, may see a new community release unit in the institution as a potential ally in the struggle to obtain more resources for rehabilitative services. Another factor that may figure prominently in relations with existing organizational units is the extent to which the new program disrupts routine patterns of behavior or calls for additional energy or resource expenditures from others. All other things being equal, it appears that new programs are more favorably received if their staff is known and respected and if organizational leaders are unequivocably supportive of the initiative.

The impact of the external (extraorganizational) environment during the design phase is likely to vary depending on how the program was initially brought into existence. Where the program was initiated largely as a result of the efforts (influence) of community groups, their influence on the program will normally be greater, especially immediately after the program has been initiated. Such groups will usually have a sense of proprietorship and seek to imprint their values on the new venture. Since they may also have some significant influence in molding public perceptions, program staff often find it necessary to consider seriously, if not accommodate, their expectations in order to gain credibility in the community. In recent years, for example, community action groups advocating for the developmentally disabled, physically disabled, women, and the aged, have played a substantial role in molding the policies and practices of programs they helped bring into existence. If advocates find new programs pursuing unacceptable policies, they may attempt to undermine these programs or establish others that will be more responsive.

The influence exerted by external groups in the design phase may also be determined by the presence or absence of a statutory provision for citizen participation in program planning. Programs that must be formally reviewed by citizens or governmental agencies frequently find it necessary to modify their designs in order to obtain the concurrences required by law. Citizen participation in social program development, thought by many observers to be on the decline after the 1960s, has been incorporated into much current legislation. The State and Local Assistance Act of 1972 and the Housing and Community Development Act of 1974 are examples of how citizen involvement has become institutionalized in the program development process.[9] In recent years the requirements for public participation in the development of social service plans under Title XX of the Social Security Act have afforded many groups an opportunity to influence the direction of new programs. The impact of public participation varies in different states, but experience suggests that the influence of well-organized constituencies can be considerable.

The internal climate of programs during the design stage tends to be characterized by greater spontaneity, informality, and voluntary compliance than is likely to be true at later stages. The program staff will generally consist of a relatively small group of persons who have either been self-selected because of their role in bringing the program into existence, or chosen by agency leadership because of their prior interest in, or commitment to, the program form envisioned.[10]

Given this commonality, interpersonal relationships among the initial cadre of staff tend to be marked by relatively high levels of agreement regarding purpose and, accordingly, some willingness to temporarily submerge individual differences and idiosyncratic needs in the interest of dealing with a commonly perceived problem.[11] In this context, the program director is likely to rely heavily on *normative power* in personal dealings with subordinates. Normative power, in contrast to power based on coercion or the use of material incentive, derives from the shared commitments of both superior and subordinate to the program's purpose. Thus the program director is likely to elicit cooperation from staff by appealing to the cause which they both consider right and good.[12] Subordinates, for their part, though not always in agreement with administrative directives, tend generally to accept the program director's authority as a legitimate means for attaining the program's purpose. Moreover, because the staff group is usually small enough to permit frequent interaction between manager and subordinates, the sense of commonality often grows and becomes more intense during the design stage.

Reliance on normative power in relations with subordinates is, in addition, often necessitated by the fact that many of the work problems confronting the program at this stage are novel ones for which there are no ready solutions. While the manager may be more expert in the program area, his or her past experience is not likely to provide a sufficient guide for how to solve problems in this new setting. Under these circumstances, it becomes necessary to rely on subordinates for information and ideas in the decision-making process and to allow them considerable discretion in carrying out directives. Managers will vary in the amount of centralized decision making and control they consider important, but efforts to establish a sharply differentiated authority hierarchy at this point are usually difficult because of the need for flexibility and spontaneity in the face of uncertainty. Commonly at this stage, therefore, programs are marked by relatively fluid, informal relationships between superiors and subordinates; participatory decision making is the prevailing mode, and roles are situationally defined by problem-specific expertise rather than formal authority.

Finally, during the design stage, the program is not likely to have yet developed an elaborate set of rules, procedures, or job descriptions. Consequently, performance criteria and clear definitions of responsibility are often lacking. This situation allows for some of the flexibility and creativity mentioned earlier, but it can also, over time, generate interpersonal strain, poor coordination, and a lack of accountability.[13] In addition, such informality often requires a very high time and energy investment in interpersonal problem solving that may divert the staff from its program development tasks. Ironically then, the very conditions that allow for creativity and innovation may, after a period, impair the staff's effectiveness. Where this occurs, formalization and standardization take on added importance. Efforts to move in this direction may undermine the sense of common purpose referred to earlier.

DEVELOPMENTAL GOALS

"Organizations [and, we would add, programs] are born in a climate of excitement and hope: they must survive in a world of test and challenge.[14] Originally written about business organizations, this comment applies as well to human service agencies. In the face of increasingly tighter accountability and competition for resources, new programs especially have uncertain futures. Shifting political sentiments, funding cutbacks, and changes in organizational leadership—events that seem to occur with increasing regularity—further increase the probability that new programs will fail or be significantly curtailed before they have had an opportunity to realize their full potential. The initial stage of program development, then, is a time of vulnerability as much as it is a time of hope and expectation. It follows that an overriding concern of the program manager at this point is to ensure that there will be a future: to see, in short, that the new venture survives its founding.

Two developmental goals that grow out of this concern are: (1) to establish credibility with major constituencies, both within and without the organization, and thereby develop the support and resources necessary for survival and program integrity; and (2) to establish a capability that shows promise of realizing the intent (purpose) set forth in the authorizing policy. These goals are interactive. Realizing one without the other is not likely to provide a sufficient foundation for future program development.

What must be done to move a program toward these developmental goals? We must at the outset acknowledge that what a program manager and staff do in this regard is only one of a host of factors that influence these outcomes. As we suggested earlier, such things as changing political sentiments, economic circumstances, and turnover in organizational leadership, developments over which the manager has little control, may have a determinative impact on the program, especially during the initial phase. We confine ourselves in the following discussion to those conditions on which the manager may reasonably be expected to exercise some influence.

MANAGEMENT TASKS AND ISSUES IN THE DESIGN STAGE

In Chapter 2 we outlined the tasks that social welfare managers must accomplish, or cause to be accomplished, in order to create and sustain the performance of the unit for which they are responsible. While these tasks are persistent aspects of management practice, we will argue that certain tasks take on greater significance in response to the organizational characteristics and developmental goals that typically arise at successive stages of development. Two management tasks assume critical importance in the design stage of development: planning and resource acquisition. To be sure, these are not the only tasks the manager must address at this stage. Others, such as designing organizational structures and processes, developing and maintaining staff capability, and program assessment, will also require the manager's attention in varying degrees. While these tasks cannot be neglected, the manager's principal concern must be directed at planning and resource acquisition, since these are the principal means for establishing the credibility and potential capability that serve as the foundations for later program implementation.

THE PLANNING TASK

In the simplest sense a plan is "any detailed method, formulated beforehand for doing or making something."[15] A *program plan,* as we define it, is an attempt to set forth future desirable conditions to be achieved in a specific time period by the program staff using specified means and resources. In contrast to *strategic plans,* which are ordinarily formulated at executive or policy-making levels and are concerned with general courses of action aimed at broad goals, program plans focus on near-term, concrete objectives and means.[16] Plans at this organizational level, also referred to in the literature as operating or tactical plans, are intended to provide fairly specific direction in the day-to-day implementation of the program.[17]

The planning task in the design stage basically involves translating the authorizing policy or strategic plan into a working model that is sufficiently detailed to guide implementation and provide a basis for assessing subsequent performance. Though the manager is likely to become periodically engaged in program planning throughout the developmental cycle as experience and unforeseen contingencies require the program to be modified, it is perhaps during the design phase that this managerial task consumes the greatest time and energy.

A well-formulated plan serves several important purposes in the development of new programs. First, although the initial plan is likely to be only a rough approximation of the program that will eventually evolve, this formulation provides an essential framework within which to make a series of secondary decisions such as which funding sources to pursue, what qualifications should be required of staff, what kind of service delivery technologies are to be employed, and the like. Deciding upon these questions in the absence of a program framework can set the program on a course that was never intended. Second, the program plan sets forth explicit objectives and standards against which to monitor and assess the actual performance of the program. Since new programs are particularly subject to external review, it is crucial that the manager be able to assess whether it is being implemented as intended, and ultimately, to evaluate whether the objectives have been achieved. Third, until a program begins to take on shape and substance, organizational elites, as we mentioned earlier, are likely to be hesitant to commit the resources and support the program needs to buffer its initial vulnerability. A board or agency executive may endorse the general purpose and thrust of a new program, but the support will usually be provisional until there is clarity regarding such matters as the objectives to be sought, the clientele to be served, the services provided, and so on. Fourth, not until the program has been specified can potential clients, other units in the organization, and agencies in the community, begin to determine whether the new venture will serve their interests and what they must do (or give in return) for services and cooperation. In order to develop exchange relationships with the outside world, the program must acquire some stability and continuity in its policy and procedure. The ambiguity and inconsistency that comes from poorly planned programs is likely to undermine attempts at establishing such reciprocity.

Finally, the program plan can serve the function of rallying staff commitment. The process of search and exploration involved in formulating a plan is often marked by excitement and optimism in which staff are bound together by a sense of cause and anticipation. At some point, however, the ambiguity and uncertainty that characterizes the search process gives rise to a need for priorities, direction, stability, and routine. The closure that comes with the formulation of a program plan and its approval by superiors marks an important transition during which the staff begin to transfer their energy from what they hoped the program would be, to what, in the light of compromise and constraint, it is likely to become. As these expectations are adjusted and workers become clear about their responsibility and authority in the new undertaking, the manager, in turn, learns whether the commitment and expertise needed to implement the program are, in fact, available.[18]

Having argued the importance of the planning task in the design stage, it is necessary to observe that the development of a quite specific, detailed plan is not only very difficult at this point, but may be undesirable as well. The new program operates in an uncertain environment. Information regarding opportunities, threats, the preferences of organizational elites, and external constituencies is very likely to be incomplete. Managers of new programs will often find it necessary to experiment and change in response to new information, or to accommodate the ideas and values of persons and groups whose cooperation is needed in order for the program to operate effectively. Committing the program to a precise course of action at this point carries the danger of promoting inflexibility and diminishing the program's capacity to adapt to these changing circumstances.[19]

Program plans vary considerably in specific detail, but they are generally comprised of four generic, interrelated elements: needs assessments, objectives, intervention strategies, and resources. In what follows we shall address each of these elements and then turn to a discussion of Management by Objectives (MBO) and Program Evaluation Review Technique (PERT) as planning strategies.

Assessing Community Needs

What are community needs? On the face of it this would seem to be a relatively straightforward question. In practice it is elusive and complex. Bradshaw, for example, has suggested that need can be defined in at least four ways, each of which may yield a somewhat different estimate of deficits in the community.[20] *Normative need* is the need that is determined by experts who judge that some group in the community falls below a standard considered desirable or appropriate. *Felt need* is the need that is reflected by what community members themselves say they want in order to improve some aspect of their lives. *Expressed need* is felt need converted into a demand for service. People may feel the necessity for homemaker or day care services, but take no action to formally request or apply for these services. When they do so, their need, in Bradshaw's terms, is expressed. Finally, *comparative need* is determined by analyzing the service utilization rates of two or more similar population groups in the community. Where the two groups are comparable, but one has less access to, or lower utilization of, the service in question, comparative need is established.

Using these definitions may produce quite different estimates of community need. Moreover, within each category two dimensions of need should be kept separate. *Diagnostic need* refers to problems experienced by members of the community. Thus, it may be found that x number of persons are without sufficient income to acquire the basic necessities. *Prescriptive need,* on the other hand, refers to the services that may be required to alleviate the problem.[21] These services might be in the form of direct financial assistance, vocational training, employment counseling, job finding, or some combination thereof.

By combining these components of need, we derive an eight-fold matrix that permits a more refined analysis (see Table 4–1). Each of the cells contains indicators that might be used by program personnel to determine needs in a particular community. There are two points that should be made in connection with this matrix. As one proceeds down the columns, it becomes clear that each of these perspectives may provide the basis for different conclusions about the extent, nature, and severity of needs, and thus the kinds of services that should be offered. Second, by treating diagnostic and prescriptive needs as distinct phenomena, the program manager is more likely to avoid the problem of confusing problems and solutions.

Needs assessments potentially serve several important functions. First, in the absence of good information about the problems confronting potential clients, there is frequently a tendency among human service professionals to foreclose on the types of services that will be provided. Thus services become the focal point of program design; while outcomes—or more specifically, the relationship between services and outcomes—are relegated to secondary importance. When this occurs the opportunity to consider a variety of alternatives to meeting needs, an opportunity most pronounced in the design stage, is often lost in a premature preoccupation

TABLE 4–1 Need Matrix

	Dimension of Need	
Type of Need	Diagnostic	Prescriptive
Normative	Expert judgments regarding an unmet need	Expert judgments regarding the type of service that will best meet need
Felt	Potential clients indicate a need, problem, or deficit in living conditions	Potential clients indicate a type of service they need or want
Expressed	Not applicable	Inability of existing service system to meet client demand indicates need for expansion or establishment of new program
Comparative	Incidence or prevalence of problem among a group in the community indicates need	Service utilization rate of one group indicates need for more service or better access

with implementing solutions. In the process, client needs often come to be defined in terms of the services provided, rather than the reverse.[22]

Needs assessments can also serve as a valuable source of baseline information that can at some later point be used to assess program impact. Program objectives derived from a sophisticated understanding of the nature and magnitude of the problems to be addressed serve as realistic criteria against which program performance can be later evaluated.

Information regarding client needs can also be used in the service of program advocacy. Over time organizational elites become inurred to the requests for more: more workers, more money, more facilities, and so on. Such requests invariably have a self-serving quality unless they are tied to some evidence regarding need.[23] Armed with systematic information regarding the extent and severity of problems in the community and the potential demand for services, the program manager is in a much stronger position to argue for resources, jurisdiction, increased authority, and the like.

Finally, needs assessments can be important to the dynamic process of "mutual adaptation," wherein program operators seek modifications in policy that reflect local circumstances and experience. This corrective feedback from the front line has been found to be an important ingredient in the implementation of program changes, since it enables staff to gain some control over their sphere of operation and fosters a commitment to successful program implementation.[24]

Numerous techniques are available to assess community needs, be they diagnostic or prescriptive. The following is an overview of the range of techniques available and the potential limitations and benefits of each. Faced with the task of determining the needs a program might address, the manager is likely to weigh at least four factors: the time required; the cost, both direct (e.g., cash outlay) and indirect (e.g., staff time); the availability of staff expertise; and informational utility. Following Moroney,[25] we will examine four general approaches in terms of these criteria.

1. Using available research. Potentially the quickest and least costly manner of determining the needs of a potential client population, this approach relies on existing studies and surveys. Some of this material is available in published form, but even what is not can usually be obtained from authors or agencies at little or no cost. However, though much of this information is technically available, discovering what is in existence is often a formidable task. The mass of periodicals, books, and government reports, many of which are quite obscure, often poses a real obstacle to the manager and staff. Consultation with program specialists, researchers, or academics working in a problem or service area, will often provide leads regarding pertinent sources or generate suggestions about where to begin the search. In addition, various indices to periodical literature (e.g., *Social Work Re-*

search and Abstracts, Poverty and Human Resources Abstracts, Psychological Abstracts), computerized bibliographic services, and guides to government reports can also help direct the search.

Having located prior research that addresses the needs of the problem population in question, program personnel often find them of only partial utility. In the case of empirical studies, for example, problems of limited or nonrepresentative samples, lack of sufficient detail, and analytic or interpretative bias often make findings difficult to apply to local circumstances. With regard to large national surveys, Moroney points to related problems; for example the data are often not specific to a particular geographic area or may employ operational problem definitions that vary from those used by the program.[26] Some of these problems are intrinsic to the original research, while others may be dealt with if the staff has sufficient expertise (or access to it) to understand and interpret the information available and weigh its relevance to local needs.

2. Service providers as an information source.   This approach to needs assessment relies on information provided by agencies who are currently serving the population of interest. The program director and staff look to existing providers, variously, for perspectives on client needs, patterns of service utilization, characteristics of service users, the adequacy and sufficiency of service delivery systems, and related matters. There are several techniques for obtaining such information. The program staff may interview selected key informants in the service delivery system who, by virtue of reputation, experience, or position, are likely to have a broad and informed view of client needs and services in a particular area. This is a relatively low-cost and quick method; it also has the advantage of allowing for in-depth, flexible explorations that may sensitize the staff to subtle and sometimes complex issues involved in providing service to a population.[27] It is, on the other hand, a technique that yields inherently biased information (not necessarily wrong) because of the selection criteria. To the extent that key informants are busy and occupy politically sensitive positions, moreover, it is sometimes difficult to obtain the trust and candor necessary to make such contacts meaningful.

A somewhat more ambitious technique for assessing need is the *systematic resource survey,* or *inventory.* Here the program staff attempts to collect information from agencies currently serving the population of interest. This may be done through questionnaires or in-person interviews. In either case, the intent is to obtain a reasonably comprehensive view of the nature and distribution of services available, the number and characteristics of clients served, and estimates of unmet need or underserved geographic areas. In communities of any size, resource inventories can be expensive to conduct. The construction of questionnaires, time spent conducting interviews, mailing costs, follow-up inquiries, analysis of the data collected—these and other activities consume valuable resources. For smaller programs, therefore, it may be necessary to rely on survey information obtained by local planning bodies. Where such information is available, it can be most useful in assisting the program manager to determine the potential demand for services, where and to whom services should be targeted, and to avoid duplicating efforts that are already in existence.

The major limitation of data obtained from service providers, as Moroney points out, is that they give no indication of the nature and prevalence of the needs of persons who are not in contact with the service delivery system. Thus, when using this information as a basis for program planning, the manager and staff of a new program must entertain the possibility that the users of service represent a distinctive subset of the population at risk whose needs may vary from those of nonusers.[28] The manager must also contend with the possibility that the needs information generated by providers may be colored by their investments in existing service arrangements.

3. Potential clients as an information source. This approach to needs assessment, unlike those previously discussed, directly taps the opinions and perceptions of those who may ultimately utilize the services offered by a new program. Its purpose may variously be to determine what the population at risk considers its needs to be, the types of services that would satisfy the needs identified, or the extent to which such services would be utilized, if available. The two most common techniques for obtaining need information directly from potential users are *surveys* and *public meetings*. Surveys are considered to be perhaps the best method of assessing client need, provided the purposes of the survey are clear, the sample representative of a population, and the instrument properly constructed and consistently administered. Under these circumstances, the community survey can yield specific, reliable information regarding client need. (See Figure 4–1 for an example of a needs assessment questionnaire.)

The major disadvantage of the survey is the time and cost required. The process of conceptualizing the purpose of the survey, constructing and pretesting the instruments, and identifying and contacting informants often takes several months and substantial resources. In the case of small programs, virtually the entire staff may be preoccupied with little else. Mailed questionnaires of telephone interviews, as opposed to in-person interviews, can be less costly, but the tradeoffs are frequently a lower response rate and a loss of information.[29] The time required to complete surveys may also result in data obsolescence. Between the time a survey is initiated and completed, circumstances sometimes change sufficiently so as to raise questions about the relevance of the findings.[30] In the face of these limitations, the survey, despite its value as a primary data source, is sometimes not a viable option for the program director. If one adds to this the possible effects of surveys in raising unrealistic community expectations, it is clear that they should not be undertaken without careful forethought.

Dear _____

We are trying to find out whether you could use help with child care and if so, what kinds of day care services would be most useful to you.

Please complete this brief questionnaire and return it to your social worker. Your answers will be kept confidential. They will not affect your eligibility for public welfare or the level of your benefits.

Thank you for your cooperation.

Sincerely,

1. How many children do you have living with you? (check one)
   0_____ 1_____ 2_____ 3_____ 4_____ 5 or more_____

2. How many of the children living with you are between 2 and 6 years old? (check one)
   0_____ 1_____ 2_____ 3_____ 4_____ 5 or more_____

3. Have your children attended a day care center before? (check one)
   Yes_____ No_____

4. If your children have attended a day care center before, was it in your present community? (check one)
   Yes_____ No_____

5. What current child care arrangements do you have? (check the one which you use most often)
   _____a. None
   _____b. Day care center in community
   _____c. Day care center outside the community
   _____d. Older children babysit
   _____e. Outside babysitter
   _____f. Leave children with friends outside the house
   _____g. Other (please write in) _____
   _____
   _____

6. If a day care center were available to you, how many days a week would you use it for your children? (check one)
   0_____ 1_____ 2_____ 3_____ 4_____ 5_____ 6_____ 7_____

7. At what times would you be most likely to use day care services? (check one)
   Mornings_____ Afternoons_____ Mornings and Afternoons_____

8. For each of the statements listed below, indicate the extent to which you agree or disagree by checking whether you Strongly Agree, Mildly Agree, Mildly Disagree, or Strongly Disagree.
   a. Day care centers should provide educational instruction as well as babysitting for the children.   SA_____ MA_____ MD_____ SD_____

b. Day care centers should provide for nighttime babysitting.   SA_____ MA_____ MD_____ SD_____
c. Parents should participate in day care center activities.   SA_____ MA_____ MD_____ SD_____

9. If your children attended a day care center, how interested would you be in going back to school? (check one)
   Very Interested_____ Somewhat Interested_____
   Not Interested_____

10. If your children attended a day care center, how interested would you be in going back to work? (check one)
    Very Interested_____ Somewhat Interested_____
    Not Interested_____

11. If your children attended a day care center, how interested would you be in getting some additional job training? (check one)
    Very Interested_____ Somewhat Interested_____
    Not Interested_____

Finally, we'd like to ask a few questions about yourself: (check one response for each question)

12. Age: 18 or below_____ 19–25_____ 26–35_____ 36–45_____
    Over 46_____

13. Race: White_____ Black_____ Chicano_____ Other_____

14. Marital Status: Married_____ Divorced_____ Separated_____
    Never married_____

FIGURE 4-1 An example of a needs assessment questionnaire. *Source:* Irwin Epstein and Tony Tripodi, *Research Techniques for Program Planning, Monitoring, and Evaluating* (New York: Columbia University Press, 1977), pp. 16–18.

Public meetings are generally a less expensive technique for obtaining needs assessment data. Staff time for preparation, outreach, summarizing and analyzing input, and for conducting meetings themselves can be significant, but it is usually less than that required to implement a survey. Moreover, it often happens that meetings generate a dimension of community attitude and feeling that is not reflected in individual interviews or questions. As a basis for collecting systematic data on needs, however, public meetings are seldom sufficient. Even with outreach and advance advertising, the group attending may not be broadly representative of the potential user population. The constraints on time, the fortuities of group process, the presence of particularly vocal or assertive community members—these and other factors may result in certain needs being highlighted while others, equally urgent, receive little or no attention.

The nominal group process developed by Delbecq and his colleagues, when properly employed, can mitigate some of the limitations noted above.[31] Basically, this process allows for the systematic collection of information regarding community perceptions of need, while controlling for the distortions that sometimes occur when spontaneous testimony or group interaction are allowed to take their own course. Figure 4–2 contains an outline for a meeting with consumers to obtain information on needs. In the last analysis, however, nominal group process as a means for generating needs information is only as effective as the manager's ability to select and involve a reasonably representative cross-section of the community to be served.

If the manager and staff recognize the inherent limitations of public meetings, they can provide a useful, if only partial view of community need. In the bargain, public meetings may serve as a vehicle for alerting potential clients to new programs, as well as identifying leaders and spokespersons whose influence may later be useful in gaining visibility for the program and cooperation in the community.

Setting Objectives

What is to be accomplished by this program? The director appointed to head a new program invariably confronts this question in some form shortly after, if not before, he or she assumes the post. Though the policy authorizing the establishment of the program will generally set forth the parameters of choice, and may even in some instances impose quite specific expectations, the job of specifying objectives most often falls to the manager. This second element of the program plan may well be the most critical aspect of the manager's planning task, because in the absence of a clear statement regarding the program's outcomes, there is little rational basis for choosing intervention strategies or deciding upon the resources necessary to implement them.

For purposes of this discussion, *goals* shall be defined as statements that express a program's long-range intent to eliminate, reduce, or ameliorate a problem or need in the community. They reflect values and conditions to which we aspire, and thus provide a sense of purpose and direction, but they are seldom specified at a level of concreteness or within a time frame that permits evaluation. Such statements as the "prevention of child neglect," the "promotion of self-sufficiency," or the "enhancement of opportunities for growth and self-actualization" are typical examples of how program goals are stated.

In contrast to goals, *objectives* are operationalized statements of program intent that express in specific, observable, preferably measurable terms, those changes (outcomes) the program seeks to produce within some designated time period.[32] For example, a foster care program may have as

I. Selection of client or consumer sample
(Divided according to age, geography, technical application, or other appropriate categories)

II. Meeting with clients or consumer groups to explore problem dimensions

   A. Introduction (10 minutes)
      1. Welcome
      2. Expression of organization(s)' interest in clients' problems
      3. Indication that focus is on problems, not solutions
      4. Explanation of "personal" vs. "organizational" problems

   B. Directions for small-group participation
      1. Assign clients to small groups of 6 to 9
      2. Instruct them in nominal group format
         a. Listing "personal" problem dimensions on 5" × 7" cards (15 minutes)
         b. Listing "organizational" problem dimensions on 5" × 7" cards (15 minutes)
      3. Provide flip chart and recorder for round-robin sharing of individually noted items
         a. Items from individual cards (first organizational, then personal)
         b. New items suggested by process

   C. Fifteen-minute break

   D. Interacting group discussion of each item on flip chart in serial fashion for clarification, elaboration, and/or defense, but not for collapsing or condensing items.

   E. Nominal group voting on 3" × 5" cards for top five priority items on both "personal" and "organizational" lists

   F. General Session—discussion of tabulated votes from each small group

   G. Explanation of PPM and election of representative(s) for Phase II

FIGURE 4-2 An outline of Phase I meeting –program planning model. *Source:* André L. Delbecq and Andrew H. Van Den Ven, "A Group Process Model for Problem Identification and Program Planning," in Neil Gilbert and Harry Specht, eds. *Planning for Social Welfare* (Englewood Cliffs, N.J.: Prentice-Hall, Inc., 1977), p. 337. Reproduced by special permission from *The Journal of Applied Behavioral Science*, 7, No. 4, pp. 466–92, copyright 1971, NTL Institute.

a policy objective returning some percentage of its children in foster homes to their natural parents within a specified time period; a program serving delinquent youth may set the objective of reducing recidivism among its clientele; a senior center's program may have the objective of reducing the incidence of institutionalization among the elderly its serves, and so on. In some instances, where it has been possible to establish a baseline for the condition or problem the program seeks to change, an objective may include the magnitude of change from current levels that is anticipated as a result of program activity. Thus in the case of the senior center's program mentioned above, a program objective might indicate the percentage of reduction in institutional placements among its clientele (below current levels) that is anticipated in the next fiscal year.

Although defining goals and objectives may seem a relatively straightforward task, there are, in fact, a number of important issues to be considered in arriving at these decisions. Among these are: the nature of the evidence regarding community need; the extent to which program objectives are consistent with the policy mandate; the extent to which program objectives are supported by the host organization; and the degree of agreement regarding objectives that exists among the major program constituents and the staff.

Intervention Strategies

Program objectives indicate what is to changed, but not how. A third important element of the plan, then, is a determination of the service strategies that will be employed to achieve the desired outcomes. Frequently the relationship between objectives and service strategies—that is, the rationale for why an intervention is likely to produce the desired change—is left vague. What is called for here is an *impact model,* which sets forth the logical or empirical connection between the service strategy and the program objective.[33] Decisions regarding intervention strategies may be influenced by factors that have little to do with the intrinsic value of the service. Among these may be the biases or skill limitations of the staff, pressures from community groups, inducements or constraints imposed by policy, and so forth. It is, nevertheless, important for the manager and staff to explicate the impact model in order to lay bare any logical gaps or unrealistic expectations in the plan. This frequently results in a reassessment of the feasibility of achieving the desired objectives, the adequacy of the interventions envisioned, or both.

Intervention strategies may be variously conceptualized, but for purposes of discussion the taxonomy proposed by Schoenberger and Williamson can serve as an illustration.[34]

1. Education.
2. Prevention.
3. Individual treatment.
4. Rehabilitation.
5. Regulation.
6. Supporting or strengthening existing programs.
7. Generating institutional change.

The selection of one or more of these intervention strategies will require the further specification of technique. If the strategy of choice for the program is individual treatment, the manager and staff will have to decide upon such questions as the duration and frequency of treatment contacts, the theoretical orientation to be employed (e.g., behavioral, ego-psychological, and so on), and the eligibility criteria to be used in client selection (e.g., age, sex, income, severity of need). (Figure 4–3 illustrates the highlights of a plan for a vocational rehabilitation program containing goal, objective, and service components.

Determining Resources

The final element of the program plan concerns the resources necessary to support and implement the intervention strategy chosen. Finances and personnel are obviously major resources in social welfare programs, but facilities, equipment, and supplies are vital as well.[35] Where program services involve in-kind (e.g., meals on wheels), or income (e.g., financial aid) distributions, or the purchase of services (e.g., medical care or sheltered workshops), the funds necessary for these purposes will also constitute a major resource. This aspect of program planning requires that the manager calculate the amount of each of these resources necessary to provide the projected service to a given number of clients. In the personnel category, for example, the manager must determine the functions and activities necessary to implement a service strategy, the number of people needed to perform these functions, the knowledge and skill they should have to perform their responsibilities adequately, and the salaries and fringe benefits for positions in each job class.

At some point, usually quite early in the planning process, costs of resources necessary for program implementation during a given period must be estimated, and these estimates compared with anticipated revenues during the same period. The resulting budget is, in the simplest sense, a tool for determining whether expenditures and resources will balance. In this sense, it provides the manager with a means for determining whether the program's objectives and service strategies can realistically be achieved with the funds available. If this does not appear possible, the manager is faced with modifying the scope of the program or requesting additional funds to meet the shortfall.[36]

Several budget formats can be used to display and communicate information to organization superiors or to external decision makers who will make the final decisions regarding allocations to the programs. The *line item budget* is a statement that lists the objects of anticipated program expenditures for the coming fiscal year, often presenting them on a comparative basis with similar expenditures for the previous year. Commonly, line item budgets include categories of expenditures such as salaries and

GOAL I: Achieving or maintaining economic *self-support*

OBJECTIVE

Vocational rehabilitation counselors will provide services to establish and implement rehabilitation plans for 1,658 clients in sheltered workshops during July 1, 1976, to June 30, 1977. The objectives of these plans will be to provide evaluation and training services for approximately 745 clients to assist them in achieving self-support.

Of the 745 clients in evaluation and training, the objective will be to achieve 150 job placements directly into competitive employment, and to assist an additional 405 clients progress to Extended Sheltered Employment.

SERVICE

The Vocational Rehabilitation agency provides counseling and guidance services in developing and implementing a sheltered workshop rehabilitation plan for new clients. The handicapped person receives a diagnosis and evaluation of his or her mental and physical limitations. A variety of physical and mental restorative services such as surgery, psychiatric treatment, prosthetic devices, speech or hearing therapy, eye glasses, visual services, and dental care, are provided when not otherwise available.

Training programs, including those in sheltered workshops, will be used to prepare clients for a job. Payments for maintenance of the client or his family may be necessary to sustain him or her while receiving services.

Payment for transportation costs of commuting to and from the workshop facility may be necessary. Certain tools, equipment, hot lunches, and other services may also be necessary. When the client is placed in competitive or self-supporting employment, certain additional follow-up services may be necessary to retain employment.

Monthly conferences are scheduled by vocational rehabilitation counselors to review progress, revise plans, and to authorize continued services to increase employability.

FIGURE 4-3   A plan for a vocational rehabilitation program containing goal, objective, and service statements.

fringe benefits, staff travel, telephone, supplies, office equipment, and so on. Each category or line may simply have an aggregate figure (i.e., $100,000 for salaries), or it may be broken down into sub components (e.g., $30,000 for three full-time secretaries, $70,000 for three professional social workers).[37]

The line item budget, though widely employed in human services agencies, has in recent years been criticized as an insufficient tool for decision making and accountability because it does not relate expenditures to program activities, performance, or objectives.[38] In other words, this format tends to focus attention on expenditures themselves rather than the cost of delivering services or achieving objectives. To address these deficiencies, two additional approaches, referred to respectively as performance (or functional) and program budgeting, have emerged. *Performance budgeting,* in its simplest application, relates line item expenditures to program activities. Thus, if a program has foster care, adoption, and counseling components, the expenditure items (e.g., salaries and travel) are listed separately for each service component.[39] Further refinements in performance budgeting may involve developing productivity or output measures for each service delivery component (e.g., number of hours of counseling, completed foster care placements) and determining the costs involved in producing each unit of service.

Conceptually akin to the performance budget, the *program budget* also relates expenditures to ends; but rather than focus on activities or outputs, it uses the more ambitious criterion of program objectives. Thus, as Lohman suggests, this format links expenditures to the outcomes that are the purpose of the program's activities by "essentially pricing the various organizational objectives."[40] Stated differently, the program budget takes as its point of departure the anticipated effects of the program and then seeks to determine the costs associated with all the activities, direct and indirect, that are involved in achieving these objectives.

Performance and program budgets are not easily implemented in human services organizations because of the difficulty involved in conceptualizing and measuring both service activities and outcomes, and the time, energy, and skill necessary to implement these systems. Still, there seems to be some agreement that these approaches are useful to managers and decision makers in making more informed choices about where to allocate resources and why. Unlike the line item budget approach, performance and program budgeting have the potential for keeping the manager's attention squarely focused on program performance and outcome, of insuring that resources are used in the service of objectives rather than seen as an end in themselves.[41]

Planning Tools

Since it was first formulated by Drucker in 1954, Management by Objectives (MBO) has been widely advocated and utilized in business and industry. In more recent years it has found increasing popularity in the not-for-profit sector, including social welfare. MBO is a multifaceted concept of management which, according to Raia, is at once a philosophy (proactive, results oriented, participatory), a process that systematically links objectives, plans, monitoring, and evaluation, and a system that facilitates and integrates planning, decision making, staff development, and a host of other organizational activities.[42] It is not our purpose here to address all these dimensions of MBO, nor to suggest its unqualified utility as a management approach for social welfare agencies. Too little is yet known about the feasibility or implications of introducing a full-blown MBO approach in social agencies to suggest its wholesale adoption.[43] Rather, in this discussion, we will be interested in that aspect of MBO which concerns designing a program—i.e., specifying a relationship between objectives, activities, and resources. Raia refers to this as the *action plan,* or "what is to be done, how, when, where, and by whom, and how much is required to reach the stated objectives.[44] The process of developing an action plan involves the following general steps.[45]

1. Specifying objectives—i.e., outcomes.   Objectives should be expressed as concrete, observable outcomes to be accomplished within a specific time period. Where possible, they should be measurable so that the program personnel will later have the ability to determine if, in fact, objectives were achieved. Objectives may be stated in terms of number of clients who have achieved some status or condition (e.g., returned to school or become gainfully employed), the presence or absence of behaviors (e.g., absence of delinquent acts, regular attendance or participation in some activity, frequency of self-critical comments), or the presence or absence of affective, cognitive, or attitudinal states. The difficulty of specifying, and therefore measuring objectives, usually becomes greater as one moves from status, to behavior, to internal psychological states as program outcomes.

In specifying program objectives, there are several points to be kept in mind. First, as Raider indicates, it may not always be possible to meaningfully formulate program objectives in quantifiable terms.[46] This may force the manager to utilize intermediate objectives or surrogate indicators of outcome to measure program achievement (e.g., client self-reports). Second, the staff of agencies, if not the manager, may need direction in how to formulate objectives. The skill required to frame outcomes in a field where change is difficult to conceptualize should not be underestimated.[47] Third, the process of formulating objectives is a political as well as a conceptual one. In social welfare, where objectives are implicitly normative and ideological, it is usually desirable to involve the major interest groups who will be party to the program effort. Tradeoffs, compromises, and conflict resolutions may be necessary in order to engender the commitment and support necessary to effectively achieve the desired end result. In this connection, some observers have suggested that the culture of the social agency may lend itself to a planning process that emphasizes building goals and objectives from the bottom up, rather than from the top down.[48]

2. Defining activities necessary to support the objective.   This step in action planning focuses attention on the relationship between activities and objectives; the impact model referred to earlier. It is essentially concerned with the question, "How will *X* activity contribute to the achievement of *Y* objective?" By *activities* we refer not to processes, but to actions to be completed, outputs to be attained in the service of achieving stated objectives. Thus, establishing intake procedures, training the staff in one or more methods of service delivery, finalizing contractual arrangements with other agencies, and informing groups and organizations about the new service may all be necessary to realizing the program objectives. Each of these activities has its own outcome, which should be specified in advance.

The process of identifying activities and their relationship to objectives is commonly beset with obstacles in social welfare agencies. In many areas, knowledge is insufficient to enable staff to predict with any certainty that selected activities will result in desired outcomes.[49] Moreover, it is often the case that staff lack control over the resources necessary for activity accomplishment. Uncertain funding, lack of cooperation from other agencies, restrictions imposed by regulatory and policy-making bodies may all undermine program efforts. These can be vexing problems, but it is nevertheless essential that activities by specified, because without a clear notion regarding what is to be done, little else in the way of rational program planning is possible.

3. Timing and sequencing of major activities.   Once the major activities have been defined, it is necessary to determine the order in which they should occur. There are several reasons for this. Some activities must be accomplished before others can be meaningfully undertaken. For example, the training of staff under most circumstances should be completed before services are offered. The time order of activities will enable the manager to determine how resources are to be deployed, and to identify points at which available resources may not be sufficient to complete the projected activity. For example, if one staff member is to be responsible for two activities but has only time enough to complete one by the target date, it may be necessary to postpone one activity in order to avoid overtaxing that staff person. Finally, sequencing activities permits the manager to anticipate points at which coordination must occur. For example, if the design of the intake procedure is to occur at the same time as efforts are undertaken to inform community groups, the manager is alerted to the necessity of coordinating these efforts in order to insure that information disseminated regarding eligibility criteria is accurate.

The sequencing of activities and target dates for completion permits the construction of a milestone chart (see Figure 4–4), which can serve as a graphic reminder to the manager and staff regarding their progress toward program objectives.

4. Clarifying roles and assigning responsibilities. A critical step in the action-planning process is to identify persons who will have primary responsibility for carrying out major activities and clarifying their relationships to one another. One tool for implementing this step in the planning process is "responsibility charting." The accompanying responsibility matrix (see Figure 4–5) adapted from Raia, illustrates an approach to responsibility charting.[50] As can be seen, the tool requires some agreement on objectives, necessary activities, and definitions of levels and types of responsibility. In the hypothetical case displayed, the program has the objective of placing 100 hospitalized mental patients in community living arrangements. This may involve such activities as developing assessment and selection procedures, training staff, contracting with community residential facilities, and so on. For each of these activities it is necessary to indicate the type of responsibility that will be carried by various actors in the agency. This is done preferably in consultation with relevant participants and after some agreement has been reached over the language used to denote responsibility levels. A somewhat similar approach can be utilized to clarify the authority of persons involved in each of the activities.[51]

5. Identifying the resources needed for each activity. As the action plan suggested above emerges, the manager and staff must concurrently consider the resources that will be required for implementation. The two processes are interactive, since resource constraints and the projected costs of activities fundamentally influence the range of available alternatives. Con-

OBJECTIVE:

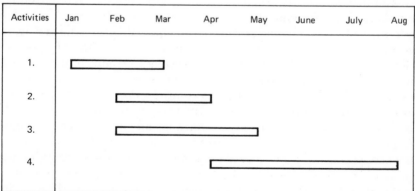

FIGURE 4–4   A milestone chart.

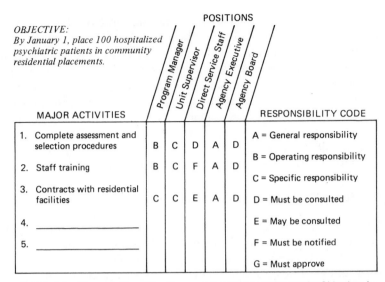

POSITIONS

OBJECTIVE:
By January 1, place 100 hospitalized
psychiatric patients in community
residential placements.

MAJOR ACTIVITIES	Program Manager	Unit Supervisor	Direct Service Staff	Agency Executive	Agency Board	RESPONSIBILITY CODE
1. Complete assessment and selection procedures	B	C	D	A	D	A = General responsibility
2. Staff training	B	C	F	A	D	B = Operating responsibility
						C = Specific responsibility
3. Contracts with residential facilities	C	C	E	A	D	D = Must be consulted
4. _____						E = May be consulted
5. _____						F = Must be notified
						G = Must approve

FIGURE 4-5 Responsibility matrix. *Source:* Adapted from *Managing by Objectives* by Anthony P. Raia. Copyright © 1974 Scott, Foresman and Company. Reprinted by permission.

versely, the task of estimating costs with any precision becomes possible only when activities have been specified in some detail. Where program activities have been "fit" with available funds and resources, the action plan has emerged.

The process outlined above may be repeated for subactivities in each activity area. These more specific levels of action planning are in a sense a way of testing the feasibility of the major activities and, therefore, of the program objectives. The extent to which the manager wishes to carry these refinements will be dictated by costs and the time available. In addition, as with any detailed conceptual process, the staff may be impatient to complete the planning and launch into the activities themselves. Increasingly, it appears that social service program personnel may be limited in the amount of time that can be devoted to action planning. For these reasons, program managers seldom have the luxury of extending the action-planning process beyond the first level of activities.

A second planning tool, which has yet to be extensively utilized in social services, is the *Program Evaluation Review Technique* (PERT). Used with some apparent success in industry, PERT is a somewhat more formal approach to program or project planning than that described above.[52] PERT, like other action planning, is an effort to relate means and ends in a rational, systematic fashion. It starts with program objectives and seeks to model all the activities that must be performed, the sequence in which they will occur, the time necessary for each, and the resources required. The relationship of these activities to one another and to the objectives is graphically depicted in a network. The procedures for constructing this network and using it to plan social services have been developed at some length by Lauffer and others.[53] Suffice it to say here that PERT appears to be a useful tool that program managers can use to develop time and re- source estimates. It can also be later used advantageously by the manager to control and evaluate the progress made toward objectives. At this point it appears that PERT may be most useful in planning relatively small pro- grams and projects, where activities and the time necessary for their ac- complishment are possible to estimate with some confidence.

THE RESOURCE ACQUISITION TASK

The task of planning a program does not occur in a vacuum. Even the best-laid plans are likely to be unsuccessful unless the manager has ac- quired the resoucres and support necessary to implement the plan that has been formulated. Thus a major managerial task during the design stage involves securing the inputs that are needed to transform the plan from concept into operation.

The resource acquisition task takes on particular importance during the design phase because new programs tend to have little slack upon which to draw—i.e., resources that can be diverted from existing oper- ations. Moreover, it is during this initial phase of development that the largest inputs of resources are required. Subsequent growth or changes in the program will necessitate additional inputs to be sure, but their mag- nitude will seldom be as large as that needed for startup. Finally, since the new program has no history of past accomplishment, and the credibility and good will that derives therefrom, there is often little leverage available for negotiating exchanges within the organization or with agencies in the community. Despite these problems—and because of them—the program manager enjoys little margin for failure in the resource acquisition task. "Human service organizations," as Steiner has observed, "exist, survive, and grow or die depending upon their ability to command resources. These agencies are forced to operate in environments where the determi- nants are outside their direct control."[54] If anything, this statement is more true of programs than of agencies; at no point is this reality more pressing than during the initial stage of program development.

Earlier, in the discussion of program planning, we spoke of the need to calculate the amounts of money, personnel, facilities, equipment, and supplies required to carry out the intervention strategy selected to achieve program objectives. These tangible resources are, of course, essential; but others, less tangible, are also vital to a developing program. Among these are the support, cooperation, and good will of significant individuals and groups in the task environment. These resources, which may be broadly referred to as *political capital,* take the form of perceptions of, and attitudes toward, the program held by critical actors in the task environment that at least partially inform their decisions and actions regarding the program. A superior's decision to strenuously advocate for a program in a budget hearing, a consumer group's decision to announce the creation of a new program to its members and encourage them to make use of it, an agency's decision to refer its clients to the new program—these and a myriad of similar decisions are necessary to establish the program's legitimacy and strengthen its ability to attract the tangible resources referred to earlier.

There are two interrelated aspects of the resource acquisition task that will be addressed in this section: acquiring funds and mobilizing the support of superiors. We will take up each of these in turn.

Acquiring Funds

Although a well-conceived plan complete with needs assessment, specific and realistic objectives, intervention strategies of proven or at least potential effectiveness, and a sound, justified budget proposal would seem to be both a necessary and sufficient condition for securing financial resources; in practice this is often not the case. Several types of problems can occur that may result in a program receiving less money than is required to carry out its plan.

First, not uncommonly, the program manager comes on the scene after the parent organization or an external funding body has authorized an expenditure for an initial budget period, only to find upon closer examination that the funds allocated are inadequate to support the program that superiors have envisioned. The manager must, of course, accept this reality and hope that in succeeding budget cycles a case can be made for additional funds to expand or strengthen the program. The problem with early underfunding is that it may so weaken the program that subsequent efforts to advocate for an expanded budget become difficult to sustain. This is particularly likely to occur if the expectations of superiors have not been modified to reflect what can realistically be achieved with the funds that have been made available. It falls to the manager, then, to inform organizational leaders and others who may be involved in making budget decisions whether the performance and outcomes they anticipate can be achieved within the amount allocated. This is not always easy for the program manager to do when attempting to build a reputation with superiors; but the failure to provide such a realistic assessment leaves the program vulnerable to unrealistic expectations. This is important because it is much more difficult to argue in retrospect that the program failed because it was provided insufficient funds in the first place.

Second, even where the program director is able to formulate a budget that bears a reasonable relationship to the plan, superiors often find it necessary to authorize less than the amount requested. This can occur, incidentally, even though the budget requested is amply justified and superiors are supportive of the plan proposed. Perhaps the most common reason for this is that established programs and units of the organization tend to have a prior claim on the agency's budget. Previous budget allocations to these units are often seen as commitments; and though much is made of the need to evaluate each of the organizational components *de nova* in preparing budgets, Wildavsky's view of this process seems to more accurately reflect reality:

> The largest determining factor of the size and content of this year's budget is last year's budget. Most of the budget is a product of previous decisions.[55]

Thus, even when those in authority favor the development of a new program, they often find it difficult to fully fund such requests if doing so requires that existing programs get less. Established programs, after all, are likely to have developed an array of supporters, both within and without the agency, who will exert pressure to see that their services are maintained, if not expanded. New programs tend not to have acquired this power base, so distributing funds from existing to new programs, whatever the substantive justification, can have troublesome political consequences for leaders.

Finally, there are instances in which organizational leaders find it impolitic to ask legislators or other funding bodies to fund new programs. Their own preferences notwithstanding, agency leaders will sometimes choose not to press for a new program or fight cuts in budgetary requests if doing so might result in other political or fiscal costs to the agency. For example, advocating for a program when it is unpopular with the chair of a legislative appropriation committee or runs counter to the political climate, can provoke legislative opposition and perhaps bring the entire agency budget under close scrutiny.[56] In still other instances, an agency administrator will have several program development priorities, not all of which can be realistically funded in a given year. The decision to eliminate or scale down the program's budget request may, in this instance, have less to do with the intrinsic merits of the program than a real politik assessment of what the traffic will bear.

Grantsmanship.   Faced with these and related funding problems, or simply to supplement the budget provided by the parent agency, program directors often cast an eye toward grants and contracts as a way of augmenting their resources. The acquisition of external funding frequently affords managers an opportunity to develop and expand services at a much faster rate than would be possible with their normal budget allocation. Indeed, in some instances, where an agency is hard pressed financially, the prospects for initiating a new program may depend on its ability to obtain external support. Other incentives to seeking grants may grow out of a desire to gain credibility or prestige in the community, to increase one's standing or power in the parent agency, to experiment or demonstrate an innovative service, or to extend services to a heretofore unserved population. Any or all of these factors may be operative in a program manager's decision to seek grant or contract funds.

The technology of grantsmanship has received a good deal of attention from scholars, practitioners, and consultants in recent years. An instructive literature is available on this subject that can provide useful suggestions for how to formulate grant proposals and compete for funds.[57] Our intent here is not to review this literature in detail, but rather to highlight some aspects of the grantsmanship process that appear especially significant for managers in this early stage of program development.

Perhaps the most crucial step in the grantsmanship process is a realistic assessment of the costs and benefits of external support. Let us briefly touch on some of these issues.[58] Program grants from government agencies are intended as incentives to stimulate service delivery organizations to take up programmatic objectives that the funder believes are important. They are generally not intended to provide support for ongoing programs and usually are "one-shot" short-term arrangements. Acquisition of such grants facilitates the development of new programs, but since funding is time limited, the critical issue of the parent agency's (or the community's) continuing fiscal responsibility is simply delayed. In practice, it is common to see new programs start with a flourish under the impetus of a government grant, only to see them severely curtailed or discontinued when the grant is terminated and the agency is unable to assume responsibility. The consequences for clients who have come to rely on the program's services, for the program staff who must seek employment elsewhere, and for agency-community relationships can be easily imagined, if they have not been experienced.

In the near term, reliance on grants to fund new programs frequently produces other issues with which the manager must contend. Program goals and objectives are perhaps more tenuous during the design phase than at any other point in a program's history. At the same time, as Lohman points out, programs that enter the competition for scarce grant funds are in a "buyer's market" where, in order to be successful, they must tailor proposals to the goals and objectives of funding bodies.[59] Where the program objectives coincide with those of the funder, well and good; but the more common case, it appears, is one in which the program manager finds it necessary to modify existing objectives or to add new ones in order to make the proposal attractive. While this often seems a small price to pay for support, the extent to which it may reduce the program's autonomy and undermine its original intent is often obscured.[60] For example, a program originally intended to *advocate* for runaway youth would not seem greatly compromised by a grant that had as its objective *reuniting* runaways with their parents. But pursuing this objective over time would likely affect the client population served, the technologies employed, the qualifications of the staff recruited, and so on. Such changes may be desirable, but this should not obscure the fact that the original purpose of the program has been significantly modified.[61]

The letter contained in Figure 4-6 illustrates the impact that the policies and regulations of a funding organization can have on program operations. In this instance, a youth service agency, which had contracted with a state department of social services to provide crisis intervention for youths and their families, found that its ability to prevent out-of-home placements for youths was being constrained by the policies of the funding body.

Relying on grants as a source of support for new programs can have other concrete implications that are often not anticipated. The most obvious of these are the time and energy involved in administering the grant—collecting and reporting information, often duplicating existing data collection procedures, writing interim and final progress reports, and conferring with site visitors—all of which may detract from ability of the manager and staff to attend to the internal development of the program. Less obvious perhaps is the probability that the external funding body will pose an additional burden on the program manager to reconcile the expectations of the funding agency with those of superiors and heads of other units in the organization. To the extent that the grant requires the program to engage in activities or provide services that are not understood, or run counter to agency policies and procedures, the program manager must often play a mediating role that involves interpreting demands and constraints to each side and negotiating compromises. Managers who do not attend to this mediating role may find that their programs have become politically isolated in the parent organization. Where this happens, of course, long-range support after termination of funding can become problematic.

Our purpose here is not to argue against the acquisition of funds through program grants. Clearly this is often a necessary and desirable course of action. The intent merely is to suggest the importance of weighing the potential costs of this approach and the problems that may confront the manager and staff who choose to pursue this strategy for program funding.

Notwithstanding these problems and dilemmas, a program manager may decide to become involved in grantsmanship. Though, as Lohman suggests, grantsmanship is more an art than science,[62] a number of useful guidelines can help the manager increase the probability of success, avoid common mistakes, and minimize unnecessary expenditures of staff time and effort.

The first and perhaps most obvious step in this process involves systematically collecting information about potential grants and contracts. A number of source documents are available to aid in this search—for example, the *Catalog of Domestic Assistance Programs,* the *Federal Register,* and the *Commerce Business Daily*—all of which are published by the federal government. The *Foundation Directory,* the *Foundation Grants Index,* the *Foundation News,* and the *Grantsmanship Center News* are also useful sources for keeping abreast of trends and activities in grant making in both public and private arenas.[63]

To supplement the information available from regularly published sources, it is also helpful to make personal inquiries. Administrative personnel in federal, state, and local human services agencies can often provide additional information about grant and contract-making activities in their organizations as well as trends and priorities. A program manager should ask to be placed on mailing lists in order to be notified when grants or contracts become available.

When a promising source of grant or contract funding has been identified, a number of steps should be taken in preparation for developing the proposal, time permitting. These include:

1. Analyzing the request for proposal (RFP) or announcement to determine if the program has, or can muster, sufficient technical capability and resources to carry out the project.

2. Contacting the funder to clear up ambiguities that may appear in the RFP, obtaining additional information about the intent of the funded activity and application procedures, and determining the nature and qualifications of likely competitive bidders. Wilkerson suggests that a letter or prospectus that foreshadows the project proposal will sometimes provide the funder an opportunity to give specific feedback, which may then help program personnel in shaping the final proposal to the needs and interests of the grantor.[64]

3. Identifying and obtaining information from other organizations that have a history of successful performance in the program area of concern. Proposals are likely to be better received if the bidder reflects an awareness of past and current relevant developments and results in the field and either incorporates or builds upon them in a proposal. If possible, it is also helpful to obtain copies of past successful proposals.

4. Mobilizing the support and endorsement of other agencies, community groups, and professional associations whose cooperation will be necessary in implementing the proposed project. Early consultation with such groups may not only yield useful ideas for the proposal, but will also initiate or strengthen relationships that may later be necessary in order to effectively carry out the funded activity.[65] In the process of building a local support network, it is wise to determine, as fully as time and resources permit, whether there is a need for the service contained in the proposal and, given the need, whether clients are likely to utilize the services if available. The reader may wish to refer back to the discussion on needs assessment earlier in this chapter for ideas on ways of approaching this problem.

5. Developing the proposal itself. The action-planning format presented earlier

Ms. Terri Jones
Department of Social Services
Regional Office

Dear Ms. Jones:

Youth Services has carefully reviewed the proposed 1980–81 Family Crisis Intervention contract and I regret to inform you that we will not renew our contract with the Department of Social Services at this time. Although Youth Services has, for many years, provided family crisis intervention services as an alternative to out–of–home placement, it is our feeling that the current contract, and the system as a whole, works against the goal of crisis resolution without out–of–home placement. This is most unfortunate because we believe that the legislative intent of RCW 74.13.020, "to maintain the family unit and avoid the necessity of out–of–home placement," is very clear and very appropriate.

Our primary concern with the current contract is the requirement that contract agencies are required to assure responsibility for providing crisis services to youth already placed by Department of Social Services staff in shelter care or receiving homes. Not only would we have the responsibility of delivering services, but services "of sufficient intensity to return the child to his/her own home within the first seventy-two hours, excluding Sundays and holidays, if the child is in shelter care" (IV–A–9).

This requirement concerns us for several reasons. First, it means that one set of workers in the Department of Social Services make the placement decisions and another set (contractors) are required to return the child home. This obviously means the client will be faced with a fragmentary and confusing set of circumstances. This concern is amplified because Department of Social Services' own figures show that since 1978 thirty-seven percent of the clients who have sought family crisis intervention from the Department and who have received one hour or more of service, were referred to shelter care for out–of–home placement. Thus 1,200, out of the 3,277 persons who received one hour of service, were placed. In our experience with family crisis, this is an unusually high rate of placement, and certainly if we were to be responsible for undoing placement within seventy–two hours we would want to review the legitimacy of those placements in the first place. Youth

Services is concerned that the net effect of this new requirement is that more children will be placed, rather than fewer, and that this violates both legislative intent and good family crisis practice.

A related structural problem is having clients come to the Department of Social Services to start services and to move on to another agency to finish them. This requirement has been a concern of Youth Services since the beginning, and we would like to raise the issue again. Frankly, we are sure that this requirement has reduced the ability of your Department and the contractors to insure that families in this state get effective services. The fragmentation, loss of motivation, and confusion that the requirement promotes in clients is immense. I have little doubt that this requirement has done more to sabotage the effectiveness of the system than any others. It seems very clear to me that the Department could develop explicit criteria so that a client would be able to come directly to a local agency and receive services. This is the method that is used to fund mental health centers, drug abuse clients, and a wide variety of other human services supported by state funds. Certainly as heavily audited as the program has been, it would have been no more expensive to allow the agencies to admit their own clients and then to monitor the appropriateness of those admissions. I believe that a comprehensive system that allows a client to deal with one agency and one set of workers is much more likely to be successful for the families of our state; certainly it would reduce the chances that a family would be "lost in the shuffle" of people and paperwork that now exists.

It is our hope that the Family Crisis Intervention program will, with additional experience and legislative review, become more responsive to the needs of our citizens, and that Youth Services shall once again be able to be a formal part of that system as a cost-efficient community-based provider of services. In the meantime, we shall continue to serve those adolescents and their families who seek our services directly.

Sincerely,

Robert Smith
Executive Director, Youth Services

FIGURE 4-6 The impact of a state funding agency policy on program operations.

is one approach to addressing this task. Here are a few more points regarding the preparation of the proposal narrative.

a. Proposal guidelines and instructions may vary considerably in what they ask for and in the specificity of their instructions for proposal development. In each case, however, the applicant will be asked to respond to certain tasks (e.g., goals and objectives, plan of operation, methods of operation, budget), and it is important to respond to each explicitly and completely. Data, writing from the perspective of a federal project officer, suggests the importance of this simple prescription:

> One of the biggest single reasons that people don't get awards is simple nonresponsiveness: not responding to tasks. When the review panel members check against the RFP to see if the proposal is at least nominally responsive . . . , it often is not. If a proposal is not responding to every task that's required, it becomes an easy candidate for being out of the competitive range.[66]

b. Clarity and brevity, though widely counseled, are often not achieved in proposals. It is important to keep in mind that reviewers may have a large stack of proposals to get through, so the easier a document is to follow and understand, the more likely it is to receive a good reading. In this connection several things are helpful: developing the narrative so that it follows closely the sequence set forth in the instructions; placing complex, lengthy material in an appendix for reference, reserving for the narrative only those points that are essential; taking great care to see that the proposal is written in simple, straightforward language and is carefully edited for syntax, grammar, punctuation, and spelling; and utilizing graphs and charts to clarify complex ideas or procedures.

c. Most sophisticated reviewers will anticipate problems that may be encountered in implementing a proposal, no matter how sound a design. It may be useful, therefore, to identify those difficulties in the proposal, the alternatives available for addressing them, and the solutions that have been chosen and why. Reviewers may not agree with the solution chosen, but the fact that the applicant has shown an awareness of potential pitfalls and ways in which they might be handled is likely to be considered a strength.[67]

Finally, in the process of developing a grant, a program manager must see to it that organizational superiors are informed about the proposal and committed to providing the resources necessary for its implementation. Funded projects inevitably entail costs for the parent agency, some of which may not be readily apparent when the proposal is submitted. If superiors are not clear about what they have committed, or if the funded project makes unanticipated demands on the agency, a program may lose internal support even when it has been successful in gaining external support. Much of what is discussed in the next section about mobilizing the support of superiors is applicable in this respect to grantsmanship as well.

Mobilizing the Support of Superiors

In addition to financial resources, a program must have the active support of organizational elites. This would seem to be assured since it was they who originally agreed to the need for the program and authorized its establishment. Yet, between the time a program is mandated and its operating plan is developed, several things may occur that effectively undermine this support base. Indeed, it is increasingly recognized that moving from policy decision to program operation is fraught with numerous obstacles that often prove vexing to decision makers and program managers alike.

Perhaps the most common problem is that the program which ultimately evolves departs in some significant ways from the one originally intended by policy makers. A number of factors, usually in some combination, may contribute to this situation. To begin with, general policies must be specified and elaborated before they can be passed down to the program level. When a policy originates in Congress, for example, it will ordinarily pass through several levels in a federal or executive department (e.g., H.H.S.) before it reaches the agency responsible for delivering the service. Williams comments on this attenuated process and how it may alter the meaning of the original policy:

> The legislation [federal law] then moves to a federal agency charged with responsibility for implementing it. Top agency personnel, often working with persons and groups previously involved in the development of the legislation, will hammer out broad directives, but eventually matters will be turned over to lower-level headquarters staff to develop (and subsequently extend and reinterpret) detailed regulations and guidelines. It is through these documents that the word passes to the field, first going to federal regional office staff that serve as intermediaries between headquarters offices and those who will administer and operate projects. In serving this function, these staff provide additional interpretations. All along the way, many minor and perhaps some major choices are made that in sum can substantially alter a policy's original intent.[68]

But this process of specification and elaboration hardly ceases when the policy is received by the agency responsible for service delivery. The agency executive, perhaps the board, and in larger organizations, the planning staff and division head may lend their own interpretations to the policy before it finally filters down to the program level. This extended process may result in policy directives that are not only at variance with what policy makers originally envisioned but even what was transmitted by organizational leaders. It is not too surprising under these circumstances that program staff frequently find that the design they have fashioned is given less than full support by agency superiors or those further up the line.

The slippage and distortion that can occur as policy is translated through successive levels, though important, is only one factor that erodes support for program design. Other factors may also be significant. For example, in the course of designing a new program, staff must often attend to the needs and interests of potential consumers, other agencies in the community, and professional groups. Frequently, the program manager finds that in order to gain acceptance and legitimacy, the new program must reflect the concerns and priorities of these groups as well as those of organizational superiors. For example, extensive licensing requirements pertaining to health and safety standards of building may not be acceptable to day care providers or foster parents who are unable to afford the capital investments involved. Client groups may insist that a new program be decentralized, or include an outreach component in order to provide potential consumers reasonable access to the program. A police department may refuse to refer delinquents to a court diversion program until it is assured that the juveniles will be required to undergo a mandatory period of counseling. Any of these program modifications may seem reasonable on its face, but the cumulative effect of these accommodations can give rise to a program design that differs substantially from the one originally contemplated by superiors. Thus, a program design, originally thought to be responsive to policy intent, may, when tailored to the needs of local constituents, serve a quite different set of interests. The short-term interests of the program manager would seem to argue for reconciling these differences in favor of superiors, but this choice often has negative residual effects when the program moves into the implementation stage.

Developing a program that has the continued support of superiors can also become problematic if program staff are unable or unwilling to follow policy directives. While staff are likely to have some commitment to and expertise in the program area, they may not have the skills or training required to develop the innovative program. In still other instances, they may have the requisite skills but disagree with certain policy directives on ideological or professional grounds. Weissman's account of the early development of the Lower East Side Union (LESFU) illustrates a case in which the staff failed to follow through on a policy in the design of the program because of a difference with the board over which clients should be eligible for service.

> The disagreement over whether LESFU should serve only those who might be referred to Special Services for Children (SSC) for placement or all problem-ridden families was the first evidence of a difference of opinion between the board and staff. Gold, the . . . only staff member during most of the planning period, had the responsibility for contacting the community and developing a plan for letting individual families know of the LESFU service. She felt a strong commitment to serving the poor of the community. Along with Gold, the first team leader, hired in 1974, would have to bear the burden of explaining to people why they would be denied service even though they had desperate problems unrelated to their children. They resisted this task.[69]

Program staff, as this example illustrates, will often view their involvement in the new program as an opportunity to build a system that reflects their strongly held values and beliefs. This set of dynamics can give rise to a program that in the staff's view optimizes the prospects for quality service, but one that has little correspondence to what organizational leaders consider feasible in light of the realities they face. In this early stage, then, the manager is often confronted with reconciling these divergent views. This is a task of no small importance, because while the support of organizational leaders is critical to program success, so too is the commitment of staff. Fashioning a program that reflects the interests of these two groups may be the most delicate and demanding responsibility of the administrator in the design stage.

The problems discussed above may erode the support originally enjoyed by a program and concomitantly increase its vulnerability to restrictive policy changes, the loss of expected resources, or intrusive monitoring and control by superiors. Among other things, this suggests that the manager cannot afford to take the support of elites for granted. Experience suggests that managers often take the initial mandate of organizational leaders as a self-renewing resource that can be drawn upon at will while they attend to the myriad other tasks and responsibilities that require attention. Adopting such a course can simplify the manager's task in the short run; in the long run, however, inattention to the interests of superiors may render a program politically weak and ineffectual whatever its technical merits.

Managerial strategies for building support among superiors have not received extensive treatment in the literature, largely, one suspects, because the major preoccupation in administrative practice has been with obtaining the compliance of subordinates. However, several guidelines in the literature may be useful to program managers working with elites. The first concerns a determination by the manager of what Delbecq has called *planning complexity*.[70] Defined as the nature of the organizational system with which the advocate (in this instance, the program manager) must engage in order to plan a program, complexity is determined by the following variables:

1. The number of groups involved in the planning effort
2. The extent to which the values of individuals and groups in the system vary and/or are in conflict
3. The extent to which the new program requires structural change (e.g., reorganization or reassignments) in the parent organization
4. The extent to which the new program must be supported by funds diverted from existing organizational programs and functions
5. The extent to which the program employs technologies and/or skills that are unfamiliar in the larger organization

The more these factors are present in the planning situation, the greater its complexity. An assessment of this complexity, according to Delbecq, is essential for the advocate seeking to gain the support of organizational decision makers. This analysis suggests the time, money, staff expertise, and political coalitions the manager must be able to mobilize in order to involve superiors and influentials in the planning process, inform and persuade them, and, where necessary, mediate conflicts that arise. When the manager's resources are insufficient to deal with the complexity anticipated, he or she must acquire additional resources or, failing this, modify the program proposal in a way that increases its acceptability to those whose support is needed (e.g., by reducing its size or eliminating controversial elements). In either case, a central purpose for assessing planning complexity is to insure that the manager and staff stand a reasonable chance of winning the approval and support of organizational leaders and other influentials. This much is essential, because if there is a "mismatch between planning complexity and the resources of the advocate group," the likelihood of gaining acceptance for a program may be significantly reduced.[71]

A second strategic consideration facing the program manager concerns the nature and extent of superiors' participation in the program-planning process. A common tendency is for managers to design the essential elements of a program and *then* present it to superiors for their approval. Delbecq suggests, rather, that the early and continuing involvement of elites in program planning is desirable. This may include early dialogue with leaders regarding their interests and expectations, negotiation and agreement around the processes to be employed in designing the program (e.g., the groups to be involved, frequency and timing of progress reports, time schedule for completion of tasks, and resources necessary for planning), and the appointment of a coordinating committee consisting of selected superiors who will oversee the planning process and provide key input on decisions in program design.[72] While this strategy of involvement entails time and energy costs for the manager and staff, it keeps the program visible as it develops and maintains its priority among the array of competing requests and demands that inevitably come before decision makers. Moreover, to the extent that superiors have been close to the planning process, they are more likely to be identified with the plan ultimately presented for approval and thus prepared to support its adoption.[73] Before a final proposal is presented, there should be a preliminary, informal review of a "draft" concept paper; such a review serves as a vehicle for a dialogue and mutual problem solving and allows for flexible adaptations to ideas and suggestions.

> This dialogue . . . removes the stigma of self-serving advocacy, enlarges the basis of sponsorship and demonstrates that while client and professional concerns have been incorporated into the thinking of the advocate group the concept is still flexible.[74]

In the final analysis, this process of early and continuing engagement with elites may not eliminate resistance to the final program proposal.

Managers must therefore seek to overcome resistance through the exercise of influence with superiors, or settle for modifications that may not be desirable or acceptable to themselves or their staffs.

Binstock and Morris, in their analysis of influence utilized by planners to gain the approval of organizational decision makers (a situation not unlike that of the program manager), suggest that attempts to overcome resistance are likely to be more effective when the planner identifies the types of influence to which decision makers are receptive and focuses his or her resources along these pathways.[75] Agency elites may be variously responsive to influence based on: obligation, friendship, rational persuasion, selling, coercion, and inducement.[76] The manager's task is to determine which of these pathways is open and to mobilize resources which activate that potential. For example, if the manager determines that rational persuasion is a viable pathway, then he or she may concentrate on presenting evidence regarding client or community need for the program, or data regarding the efficacy of the treatment approaches proposed. If obligation is a potential point of influence, the manager may wish to draw upon his or her own credibility derived from past accomplishments in the organization, or favors done for superiors. Elite responsiveness to inducement may suggest the desirability of emphasizing funding possibilities the program will make possible, or the prospect of maintaining a competitive advantage over other agencies in the community. Where elites are interested in maintaining agency prestige, the manager may use the spectre of unfavorable publicity, sanctions by standard-setting bodies, or negative community reaction, in order to elicit a favorable decision on the program proposal.

This is not to suggest that managers can always find ways to influence their superiors' decisions. Elites may not be open to influence, or if they are, the manager may be unable to martial the necessary resources.[77] Still, it is the manager's responsibility to press for a decision outcome which, consistent with professional judgment and community need, maximizes the potential effectiveness of the program. The strategic considerations discussed here are not a substitute for a quality program, but they serve to underscore that the intrinsic value of a plan is often not sufficient to gain the support and approval of superiors.

SUMMARY

In this chapter we have examined selected administrative tasks and technologies that seem particularly relevant to the organizational context and the developmental goals of programs during the design stage. The planning and resource acquisition tasks discussed at some length do not exhaust those that must be addressed by managers engaged in initiating a program, but they do appear to be particularly instrumental in achieving the goals of program capability and credibility. As the program moves from the design stage into full-scale implementation, these attributes provide a necessary foundation. Failure to substantially achieve these developmental goals is likely to undermine the implementation process, since the manager and staff will not have received the support, resources and clarity that are required to effectively launch the delivery of services. In addition, to the extent that the time and energy of program staff are spent addressing design-stage goals, they will be unable to give their undivided attention to the consuming process of implementation. It is to that stage of program development that we now turn.

NOTES

[1] A recent example is PL96-272, the Adoption Assistance and Child Welfare Act of 1980 in which Congress requires that states provide a case plan for each child in foster care and a case review system to determine the continuing necessity for and appropriateness of the placement. At this writing there is some question about whether this law will be fully implemented in light of funding cutbacks.

[2] See, for example, Daniel A. Felicetti, *Mental Health and Retardation Politics: The Mind Lobbies in Congress* (New York: Praeger, 1975).

[3] Henry Mintzberg, *The Nature of Managerial Work* (New York: Harper & Row, 1973), pp. 79–81.

[4] The *organizational environment* includes agency superiors and the heads of other units with whom the program manager will be in interaction. The *external environment* includes legislative, planning, and accrediting bodies, consumer and citizen groups, and other agencies providing parallel or complementary services.

[5] Throughout this book the terms "superiors," "leaders," and "elites" will be used interchangeably to refer to persons in the organization to whom the program manager is ultimately accountable. The governing board, the executive director, and other high-level administrators are primary examples.

[6] Charles Perrow, "Analysis of Goals in Complex Organizations," *American Sociological Review,* 26, No. 6 (December, 1961), 856–66; and Felice Perlmutter, "A Model of Social Agency Development," *Social Casework,* 50, No. 8 (October, 1969), 469–70.

[7] Mayer N. Zald, "The Power and Functions of Boards of Directors: A Theoretical Synthesis," in *Human Service Organizations,* Yeheskel Hasenfeld and Richard English, eds. (Ann Arbor, Mich.: University of Michigan Press, 1974), p. 181.

[8] Anthony Downs, *Inside Bureaucracy* (Boston: Little, Brown, 1967), p. 9.

[9] For a discussion of how citizen participation has become incorporated in recent social legislation, see Jack Rothman, "Macro Social Work in a Tightening Economy," *Social Work,* 24, No. 4 (July, 1979), 276–77.

[10] Downs, *Inside Bureaucracy,* pp. 6–7.

[11] Daniel Katz and Robert L. Kahn, *The Social Psychology of Organizations* (New York: John Wiley & Sons, 1967), p. 78.

[12] Amitai Etzioni, *Modern Organizations* (Englewood Cliffs, N.J.: Prentice-Hall, Inc., 1964), pp. 64-65.

[13] William Rosengren, "The Careers of Clients and Organizations," in *Organizations and Clients,* William Rosengren and Mark Lefton, eds. (Columbus, Ohio: Charles E. Merrill, 1970), p. 27.

[14] Gordon L. Lippitt and Warren H. Schmidt, "Crises in a Developing Organization," *Harvard Business Review,* 45, No. 6 (November-December, 1967). 105.

[15] Fremont Kast and James Rosenweig, *Organization and Management:A Systems Approach* (New York: McGraw-Hill, 1970), p. 437.

[16] *Ibid.,* p. 438.

[17] Stephen P. Robbins, *The Administrative Process,* 2nd ed. (Englewood Cliffs, N.J.: Prentice-Hall, Inc., 1980), p. 132.

[18] There are, of course, instances when certain staff cannot reconcile themselves to the program as it has evolved, or to their role within it. Resignations, transfers, and dismissals often occur at this point.

[19] Robbins, *Administrative Process,* pp. 136-37.

[20] Jonathan Bradshaw, "The Concept of Social Need," in *Planning for Social Welfare,* Neil Gilbert and Harry Specht, eds. (Englewood Cliffs, N.J.: Prentice-Hall, Inc., 1977), pp. 290-96.

[21] Richard Thayer, "Measuring Need in the Social Services," in *Ibid.,* pp. 297-98.

[22] Robert M. Moroney, "Needs Assessment for Human Services," in *Managing Human Services,* Wayne F. Anderson, Bernard J. Frieden, and Michael J. Murphy, eds. (Washington, D.C.: International City Management Association, 1977), p. 131.

[23] André L. Delbecq, "The Social Political Process of Introducing Innovation in Human Services," in *The Management of Human Services,* Rosemary C. Saari and Yeheskel Hasenfeld, eds. (New York: Columbia University Press, 1978), p. 318.

[24] Milbrey McLaughlin, "Implementation as Mutual Adaptation: Change in Classroom Organization," in *Social Program Implementation,* Walter Williams and Richard F. Elmore, eds. (New York: Academic Press, 1976), p. 126.

[25] Moroney, "Needs Assessment," pp. 142-48.

[26] *Ibid.,* pp. 142-43.

[27] Such interviews may also serve the secondary purpose of alerting key actors in the community to the presence of a new program and establishing a basis for subsequent contact.

[28] Moroney, "Needs Assessment," p. 144.

[29] California League of Cities, "Collecting Information: Basic Methods," in *Planning for Social Welfare,* Neil Gilbert and Harry Specht, eds. (Englewood Cliffs, N.J.: Prentice-Hall, Inc., 1977), pp. 311-16.

[30] Moroney, "Needs Assessment," p. 147.

[31] André Delbecq and Andrew Van De Ven, "A Group Process Model for Problem Identification and Program Planning," in *Planning for Social Welfare,* Neil Gilbert and Harry Specht, eds. (Englewood Cliffs, N.J.: Prentice-Hall, Inc., 1977), pp. 333-48.

[32] Anthony P. Raia, *Managing by Objectives* (Glenview, Ill.: Scott Foresman, 1974), pp. 41-45.

[33] Perry Levinson, "Goal-Model and System-Model Criteria of Effectiveness," in

Planning, Programming, Budgeting, Fremont J. Lyden and Ernest G. Miller, eds. (Chicago: Markham Publishing Company, 1972), pp. 288–89.

[34]Edward Schoenberger and John Williamson, "Deciding on Priorities and Specific Programs," in Wayne F. Anderson, Bernard J. Frieden, and Michael J. Murphy, eds. (Washington, D.C.: International City Managers Association, 1977), p. 166.

[35]Walter H. Ehlers, Michael J. Austin, and Jon C. Prothero, *Administration for the Human Services* (New York: Harper & Row, 1975), pp. 83–84.

[36]*Ibid.,* p. 86.

[37]Roger A. Lohman, *Breaking Even: Financial Management in Human Service Organizations* (Philadelphia: Temple University Press, 1980), pp. 152–55. For a basic discussion of budgeting strategies, see also John J. Stretch, "What Human Services Managers Need to Know about Basic Budgeting Strategies," *Administration in Social Work,* 4, No. 1 (Spring, 1980), 87–98.

[38]Roderick K. Macleod, "Program Budgeting Works in Non-Profit Institutions," in *Social Administration,* Simon Slavin, ed. (New York: Haworth Press, 1978), pp. 253–55.

[39]Lohman, *Breaking Even,* pp. 140–42.

[40]*Ibid.,* p. 142.

[41]A good argument for how outcome-oriented budget techniques like PPBS and cost-benefit analysis can help human services programs assess the quality of their services and avoid the pitfall of perpetuating existing operations for their own sake is found in Marc L. Miringoff, *Management in Human Service Organizations* (New York: Macmillan, 1980), pp. 115–27.

[42]Raia, *Managing by Objectives,* pp. 11–12.

[43]Several critics of MBO have suggested that it may have limitations as a management approach in human services agencies. Raider, for example, has observed that unstable funding, a shifting or uncertain clientele, interprogram competition, and staff turnover can often undermine MBO. See Melvin C. Raider, "Installing Management by Objectives in Social Agencies," in *Social Administration,* Simon Slavin, ed. (New York: Haworth Press, 1978), pp. 283–85.

[44]Raia, *Managing by Objectives,* p. 68.

[45]*Ibid.,* pp. 70–75.

[46]Raider, "Installing Management by Objectives," p. 289.

[47]*Ibid.,* p. 286.

[48]*Ibid.,* p. 287. See also Vernon R. Weihe, "Management by Objectives in a Family Service Agency," in *Social Administration,* Simon Slavin, ed. (New York: Haworth Press, 1978), pp. 278–79.

[49]Michael L. Lauderdale, "A Review of Management by Objectives" (unpublished), School of Social Work, University of Texas, n.d., p. 25.

[50]Raia, *Managing by Objectives,* p. 77.

[51]*Ibid.,* pp. 78–81.

[52]See, for example, *Managing Projects and Programs Series.* Reprints from Harvard Business Review, 61–108. For applications of this technique to social welfare agencies, see Armand Lauffer, *Social Planning at the Community Level* (Englewood Cliffs, N.J.: Prentice-Hall, Inc., 1978), pp. 163–75.

[53]*Ibid.,* and James Naughten, *Human Service Project Planning and Management Using PERT/CPM* (University of Washington, 1978), unpublished manuscript.

[54]Richard Steiner, *Managing the Human Service Organization* (Beverly Hills, Calif.: Sage Publications, 1977), p. 152.

[55]Aaron Wildavsky, *The Politics of the Budgetary Process*, 2nd ed. (Boston: Little, Brown, 1974), p. 13.

[56]*Ibid.*, pp. 21-31.

[57]See, for example, Armand Lauffer, *Grantsmanship* (Beverly Hills, Calif.: Sage Publications, 1979); Lohman, *Breaking Even*, pp. 57-79; Albert E. Wilkerson, "A Framework for Project Development," in *Leadership in Social Administration*, Felice D. Perlmutter and Simon Slavin, eds. (Philadelphia: Temple Universtiy Press, 1980), pp. 157-72; Robert Lefferts, *Getting a Grant* (Englewood Cliffs, N.J.: Prentice-Hall, Inc., 1978).

[58]This discussion draws heavily upon Lohman, *Breaking Even*, pp. 61-62.

[59]*Ibid.*, p. 62.

[60]For a discussion of some potential consequences of external funding for new programs, see Jerald Hage and Michael Aiken, *Social Change in Complex Organizations* (New York: Random House, 1969), pp. 98-99.

[61]Lauffer, *Grantsmanship*, pp. 32-34.

[62]Lohman, *Breaking Even*, p. 61.

[63]A good discussion on grant source information is found in Lauffer, *Grantsmanship*, pp. 49-57, 89-90.

[64]Wilkerson, "Framework," p. 166.

[65]Lauffer, *Grantsmanship*, pp. 68-69.

[66]Lois-Ellen Datta, "Preparing the Winning Proposal" (unpublished manuscript), Center for Social Welfare Research, School of Social Work, University of Washington, n.d., p. 12.

[67]*Ibid.*, pp. 13-14.

[68]Walter Williams, "Implementation Problems in Federally Funded Programs," *Social Program Implementation*, Walter Williams and Richard F. Elmore, eds. (New York: Academic Press, 1976), p. 17.

[69]Harold H. Weissman, *Integrating Services for Troubled Families* (San Francisco: Jossey-Bass Publishers, 1978), p. 30.

[70]Delbecq, "Social Political Process," pp. 310-14.

[71]*Ibid.*, p. 314.

[72]*Ibid.*, p. 317.

[73]*Ibid.*

[74]*Ibid.*, p. 322.

[75]Robert Morris and Robert H. Binstock, *Feasible Planning for Social Change* (New York: Columbia University Press, 1966), pp. 113-27. For an excellent discussion of the strategies often used by middle managers to influence their superiors see, Stephen Holloway, "Up the Hierarchy: From Clinician to Administrator," *Administration in Social Work*, 4, No. 4, (Winter, 1980); pp. 1-14.

[76]*Ibid.*, p. 117.

[77]*Ibid.*, p. 121.

CHAPTER FIVE

Program Management in the Implementation Stage

Programs seldom emerge from the design stage with a full-blown capacity for service delivery. Except in rare instances (e.g., where well-developed program models are available and can be easily replicated), there is inevitably an intervening period of capacity building during which the program must be incrementally elaborated and refined and adapted to internal and external realities. This period, which we shall refer to as the *implementation stage,* is a critical one for the manager since it affords an opportunity, perhaps unparalleled in the history of the program, to fashion the fundamental character of the program. This foundation, for better or worse, will do much to determine the program's ultimate effectiveness. In this chapter we turn our attention to the implementation stage and selected management tasks that must be addressed in order to translate program potential into competent performance.

IMPLEMENTATION STAGE: ORGANIZATIONAL CONTEXT

The implementation stage, as the name suggests, commences as the program swings into full operation. Assuming that significant progress has been made toward the developmental goals sought during the design stage (i.e., establishing credibility in the host organization and creating a capability for service delivery), the resources, energy, and attention of the manager and staff are now increasingly devoted to the job of delivering the services the program was created to provide.[1]

During the implementation stage, the array of environmental forces impinging on a program becomes somewhat more complex. Organizational superiors who exercised a dominant role in the formulation of the program during the design stage will often become less intimately involved. Having given their approval to the program plan and allocated funds for its operation, the lack of time and expertise usually requires that they defer to the program manager on matters of implementation. Organizational leaders will, of course, continue to monitor the program as it unfolds, because until it has achieved a relatively predictable level of performance and is fully absorbed into the fabric of the parent agency, problems will arise that require their intervention.[2] For the most part, however, such involvement is likely to be sporadic and problem focused rather than continuous and pervasive.

While relationships with agency superiors become less critical during this stage, those with groups and organizations in the community are likely to take on added importance. Perhaps the central issue bearing on programs at this stage of development is the need to establish a clientele.[3] For some programs whose clientele is assured by virtue of legislative mandate,[4] this may be less of a concern; but in most instances securing a stable, ongoing clientele is by no means a certainty. Problems involving community awareness, geographic access, attitudes toward the services provided, and cultural values, among others, may result in the underutilization of the program, even when the need for it has been amply documented. If this situation persists for long, it can render a program vulnerable to external criticism, funding cutbacks, and competitive initiatives. The inability to attract and serve a clientele not only weakens the program's claim to its service domain, but also deprives it of a population of beneficiaries who can be called upon to support budget requests, expansion proposals, and the like. Achieving what Downs refers to as an "initial survival threshold" is largely contingent upon the program's ability to acquire a stable client population.[5]

Faced with this problem, there is a tendency for programs in this stage to provide a broad and flexible array of services in order both to respond to the clients seeking help and to attract others in the target population.[6] Whereas the original design may have called for a specific kind of service to a well-defined client group, new programs, especially those with few takers, often find it necessary to relax these specifications in order to attract their allotment of clients. Examples might include expanding the geographic boundaries of service; relaxing income eligibility criteria; and providing more of some service such as crisis counseling for which there is an immediate demand, and less of long-term treatment for which there is a decreasing demand. In some cases, program managers find it necessary to provide services in decentralized locations (e.g., store fronts and churches) that are closer to potential consumers as an inducement, or to extend the program's hours of operation to evenings and weekends to accommodate working persons or parents without child care. While all of these steps may attract a clientele, they may also cause role confusion for the staff, internal conflicts over goals and priorities, and difficulties with internal coordination and management control.[7]

Programs at the implementation stage also have the task of breaking into the existing service delivery system. Previous linkages established by the host organization with other agencies may provide initial entry to this system, but each new program must ultimately fashion its own set of relationships with other service providers.

New programs are often substantially dependent upon established agencies in the service delivery network for such things as information, visibility, client referrals, and timely responses to referrals. Though commitments of cooperation and support may have been obtained when the program was being planned, it is during the implementation stage that these arrangements are first subjected to the test of daily operation. The constraints of time, limited resources, communication problems, and procedural conflicts often undermine the most carefully cultivated agreements. These obstacles to interorganizational cooperation can temporarily paralyze a new program and even threaten its very existence. Because these lateral relationships are so important, and yet so fragile, new programs tend to be especially sensitive to feedback from other service providers and somewhat more amenable to making programmatic and procedural changes that will reduce conflict or strengthen relationships with agencies in this network. An example will illustrate the point.

A new court diversion program was established by a law and justice consortium to provide diagnostic assessment, intensive counseling, referral, and temporary residential care for first-time juvenile offenders. The program was based on the assumption that if offenders could be spared the labeling and depersonalization that occurred in the juvenile court, they would be more amenable to treatment and rehabilitation. The original plan, worked out with the chief of the city police, the county sheriff, and the director of the juvenile court, called for police officers who apprehended juvenile offenders to refer the youth directly to the court diversion program. Three months after the program was in operation, the rate of referrals was only one-half of what had been anticipated. Most of the youth apprehended by city and county police continued to be referred to the juvenile court, where they were processed in the usual manner. After some investigation, the program manager found that many police officers preferred not to refer directly to the diversion program; the police believed that unless the juveniles were first placed under the jurisdiction of the court they would not follow through on referrals and thus remain free in the community to commit additional delinquent acts. Though initial referral to the juvenile court undermined the diversionary purpose of the program, the manager felt that cooperation from line officers was unlikely until they were first assured that juveniles were being monitored by the court. Further discussion with the chief of police, sheriff, and juvenile court resulted in a revised plan under which all juveniles would first be taken to the court where probation officers would make a determination about whether to refer the youth to the diversion program. Shortly thereafter, the number of referrals to the court diversion program increased dramatically.

In this instance, we see clearly illustrated the dependence of a new program on existing agencies. Without the active cooperation of the police, the idea of providing an intensive individualized service to juvenile offenders outside the juvenile justice system could not be realized. Though the revised referral procedure violated a central premise on which the program was originally based, it was, nevertheless, a compromise that became necessary in order to insure the continued operation of the program.

Relations with other agencies may have less dramatic effects on program implementation than that illustrated in this example, but the process by which a new program becomes integrated into the community service delivery network usually requires accommodations that result in some modification of the program's original plan. The extent to which this occurs is probably very much related to the program's need for the resources possessed by other agencies, but some process of mutual accommodation is usually necessary.[8]

In addition to potential consumers and other agencies in the community, programs are also likely to affect—and be affected by—other units in the parent agency. New programs of any magnitude will almost invariably have implications for other parts of the organization. Issues of power, influence, and resources are likely to arise at the design stage as we have noted; but such concerns tend to take on special urgency when the program becomes a *fait accompli.* To begin with, a new program is likely to place additional demands on the administrative support systems in the parent agency—e.g., personnel, staff development, evaluation, budgeting, and planning. Recently initiated programs not only require special support and assistance, but they may engage in practices that conflict with prevailing agency goals. For example, a few years ago a new client assistance program mandated by federal legislation was established by a state vocational rehabilitation agency to engage in outreach and advocacy for disabled persons who had not traditionally been served by that organization. The program experienced some early success in identifying and referring poor, minority, and chronically mentally ill clients for service. Unfortunately, many of the vocational counselors in the agency perceived these new clients as poorly motivated and untrainable. Since, in their view, the mission of the agency was to make clients employable, the counselors saw little value in devoting scarce resources to clients who had little chance of achieving this goal. As a result, a high percentage of the clients referred by the client assistance program were denied service or covertly discouraged from continuing. Within a year after it had begun operation, it became clear that the mission of the client assistance program and that of the parent agency were in conflict. Conflict and strain are frequent accompaniments to this process of integrating new programs into the fabric of the parent organization.

New programs can also disrupt the routines or impose additional work on other service units in the agency. For example, a new volunteer program may require that professional personnel in various other departments spend additional time training and supervising volunteers who are recruited; a community outreach program may stimulate a demand for agency services, thereby placing additional pressure on an already burdened intake staff; or the addition of a homemaker or chore services program may increase the case management responsibility of caseworkers. Though these and similar program developments may be perceived as net additions to the capability of an agency, articulating them with existing subsystems frequently poses problems for both new and established work units.

Finally, as new programs are implemented, they sometimes threaten to alter the balance of power in the host agency. Hage and Aiken comment on this process:

> Frequently the addition of a new activity means the creation of new social positions in the organization. The occupants of these new positions will fight for power, for the right to make rules, and for a share of the rewards in the organization.... [They] will want more authority in order to establish their new activity successfully.... They will demand more space and other resources with the plea that these are needed if the activity is to be a success.[9]

To the extent that new programs seek authority and resources at the expense of already established units, the latter may withhold cooperation or actively resist the efforts of the new unit to become established. The resolution of these conflicts can have serious long-term ramifications. If the new program manages, in fact, to increase its influence *vis à vis* other units, it may do so at some cost to interunit communication and coordination. If, on the other hand, the new program is unable to gain the influence necessary to successfully implement its program, its innovative potential may be seriously compromised.[10]

During the implementation stage, the internal dynamics of programs also take on a quite different character. Programs entering this stage must often contend with how to integrate an influx of front-line practitioners. In the design stage, as we noted in the last chapter, the core staff is likely to be small and committed to the mission of the new program. By contrast, the new staff, most of whom will be recruited into lower-level positions, seldom have the same sense of ownership or level of enthusiasm as the founding group. In addition, new staff who have been drawn from other parts of the agency may retain a sense of loyalty to former units, or have an investment in previous behavior patterns; such tendencies may make them somewhat cautious about their involvement in the new venture.

The existence of an enlarged and more heterogeneous (in terms of motivation) work force increases the possibility of disagreement over program objectives, intervention strategies, and work processes. This—combined with a necessity to flexibly adapt services to the needs of the new clientele or the preferences of community agencies—introduces a good deal of unpredictability and inconsistency into program operations. Program managers will have varying degrees of tolerance for this, but at some point they are likely to see a need for increased control and coordination. Thus before a program moves very far into the implementation stage, managers frequently attempt to develop policies and procedures to guide subordinate behavior and bring about greater consistency in performance. The establishment of reporting systems and the creation of a supervisory hierarchy to train, socialize, and oversee new staff are not uncommon at this point.[11]

Efforts to bring greater consistency and uniformity to the behavior of subordinates are, however, likely to meet with some difficulty because of the newness of the program. Premature attempts to specify rules and procedures run the risk of constraining staff who inevitably must address novel and unanticipated problems in their interactions with clients and others. If the staff are too constrained in dealing with these contingencies, both program flexibility and staff morale may suffer. Such efforts by management may also engender resistance in front-line staff, particularly those whose professional training has led them to place high value on practitioner autonomy. Problems with subordinate noncompliance and conflict between line workers and superiors often emerge in this context and frequently engender countervailing efforts by workers to gain a greater voice in administrative decision making.

Program growth during the implementation stage is also frequently associated with the elaboration of administrative structure. As the varied needs of the client population become clear and services and technologies are refined, there is a frequent tendency toward internal specializations and the development of corresponding subprogram units. Thus, an outpatient service in a mental health clinic may divide into two units dealing respectively with children and adults. Services to walk-ins, initially shared on a rotating basis among staff, may now be lodged in a separate crisis unit.

These and similar kinds of internal specialization are likely to be followed by two developments: First, the supervisory cadre that is formed to oversee these subunits increasingly mediates relations between front-line staff and the program manager. The communication chain, in consequence, becomes more attenuated and the manager tends to have less and less face-to-face interaction with workers in the program. Second, as the membership of these subunits stabilizes and their functions become crystallized, workers and supervisors are likely to develop allegiances to these work groups and become identified with their subobjectives. This process is often accompanied by a decrease in communication between subunits and a corresponding need on the part of managers to institute mechanisms—such as staff meetings—that will facilitate communication and coordination.

While the movement toward a more formal, elaborate structure presents potential problems, the failure to develop mechanisms for internal control and accountability can be equally troublesome. Weissman's account of the development of the Lower East Side Family Union (LESFU) reflects some of the difficulties that can occur. In the first two years of its operation, a failure to establish clear lines of authority, reporting requirements, and consistent supervision had given rise to conflict among staff over the goals of the new agency and the ways in which services would be implemented. Weissman observes:

> Initially the mechanism used in LESFU to gain enthusiastic staff participation was the maximal inclusion of the staff in decisions concerning the agency. Emphasis was placed on the group, not the individual. As a group the staff would decide the best method for running the agency. This system fostered adherence to some norms and made it less likely that the [service] model would be developed as planned.[12]

Indeed, fully two years after initial funding, the agency was not operational. Only after hiring a director who instituted regular reporting requirements, clarified roles and responsibilities, and began to take responsibility for making critical decisions, was a full complement of staff finally hired and the program implemented in accordance with the initial plan.

DEVELOPMENTAL GOALS

While the design stage of program development revolves around the question of survival, during the implementation stage the issue of *competence* becomes the central and overriding concern. Having acquired the resources necessary to move from concept to operation, the program now confronts the challenge of actualizing its promise—of establishing itself as a viable instrument for achieving the service goals and objectives its founders envisioned.

In the pursuit of competence, several developmental goals loom particularly important for the program manager. The first involves securing a *domain* for the program and establishing its legitimacy in this area. By domain, we refer to the array of social problems with which the program deals, the clients in these problem populations that are actually served, and the services that are provided to them.[13] This domain defines the real parameters of the program, serves as the focal point for its identity, and provides a basis for its continuing claims on resources. It is also the arena in which the program seeks to develop and consolidate its technical expertise.[14]

A second developmental goal, closely related to the first, is achieving a greater measure of certainty in relationships with groups and organizations in the environment (both internal and external to the parent agency).[15] As long as the program manager must meet diverse and unpredictable external expectations and is unable to count on the support and cooperation of groups and organizations in the environment, the program's internal operation is likely to be rent with ambiguity and discontinuity. Under these circumstances, it becomes difficult, at best, to fashion a coherent program effort.

Domain and environmental certainty goals both contribute to, and are fostered by, the development of the program's internal capability. In the last analysis, the program must be able to deliver services in a reasonably efficient and reliable manner. A structure that will support and facilitate service delivery and the acquisition of personnel with appropriate knowledge and skill are critical elements of this internal capability.

We turn now to the management tasks that must be addressed in the service of realizing these goals.

MANAGEMENT TASKS AND ISSUES
IN THE IMPLEMENTATION STAGE

THE RESOURCE ACQUISITION TASK

In the last chapter we focused on those elements of the resource acquisition task concerned with obtaining the funds and internal organizational support necessary to design and initiate a program. The acquisition and renewal of these resources continues to be an important managerial responsibility in the implementation stage, but at this point the task takes on two added dimensions: (1) attracting and maintaining a stable clientele whose needs can reasonably be addressed by the program's services and technologies; and (2) developing a network of reciprocal relationships with groups and agencies in the community and other units in the host organization whose support and cooperation are essential to the program's operations. Both kinds of resources—i.e., clients and interagency support and cooperation—as we shall see, are instrumental in enabling the program to to define its service domain and achieve greater certainty *vis à vis* the external environment—two of the principal goals sought during the implementation stage.

Contacting, Engaging, and Maintaining a Clientele

All social programs "must somehow solve the problem of bringing their services or technologies to their clients. . . ."[16] This imperative, which unfortunately is often lost in the hectic process of planning a program and acquiring the resources and support necessary to commence operation, becomes a compelling reality as the program enters the implementation stage. Clients, of course, not only provide the "raw material" for treatment technologies, they may also be an important source of revenue,[17] help to publicize and legitimate the program with other potential consumers, and provide confirmation regarding the value of the services to evaluators, funders, and policy makers.[18] The failure to attract and engage a clientele calls into question the very reason for a program's existence and often severely weakens its claim to resources. As Steiner comments, "There is nothing quite so disturbing as a well-funded service operation waiting with open doors for clients that never appear."[19]

Despite the importance of clients as a resource, the task of contacting, engaging, and maintaining relations with them is often neglected by program managers. Too often one sees a seller's mentality in new programs, a mentality that grows out of the belief that if quality programs are provided they will be utilized by those in need. In still other instances, managers and staff are lulled into complacency because theirs is the only program of its kind available in a geographic area, or because the data available from needs assessments indicate the existence of a large pool of potential clients. Whatever the reason for failing to vigorously seek out and establish a clientele, experience suggests that many programs founder during the implementation stage because this task has not received adequate attention.

Three elements of this task are especially important: informing the at-risk population regarding the availability of the program services and the conditions of eligibility; developing mechanisms and processes that will minimize obstacles or facilitate access to the service; and creating conditions and processes that will promote trust between the agency and its clientele. Each of these is addressed below.

Informing the population at risk.   Persons who might potentially benefit from the services provided must know of their existence before they can utilize them. Though this may appear too obvious to mention, ignorance of the existence of social programs is often widespread. Data from a recent national survey indicated that a significant percentage of people with social and health problems did not know of government programs available to help them. For example, among those people with various disability and unemployment problems, approximately one-third were not utilizing a relevant and available public program. Among these nonusers, a significant percentage of them did not know of the existence of a service to which they might turn. Fifty-five percent of nonusers with medical and hospital needs did not know of Medicaid; a similar percentage were unaware of job training and workmen's compensation programs, and so on.[20] The programs in question were national or statewide in scope and had been in existence for a number of years. If we consider newer programs of much smaller scope that are likely to be somewhat less visible, the problem of adequately informing a population at risk of the availability of services becomes apparent.

Three critical publics should be reached if a population at risk is to be adequately informed of the new program. There are first of all those organizations and programs (some of which may be in the parent agency) who have ongoing contact with the clientele of interest. These include not only providers of direct services, but those engaged in information, referral, and access services as well. A second audience is the consumer-based groups whose primary function is advocating for and representing the rights and interests of the at-risk population to which the program is targeted. Some of these groups focus on the needs of specific consumer groups (e.g., tenants' rights associations, welfare rights groups, Parents Anonymous), while others are concerned with more heterogeneous populations, among whom are persons the program seeks to serve (e.g., community councils, neighborhood associations, churches). Finally, there are the potential clients themselves, some of whom may not be known to, or in contact with, the agencies or associations mentioned above. These persons are often the most difficult to reach.

In communicating with these publics it is important that the program manager and staff convey an accurate and complete picture of what services will be provided, where, who will be eligible, and how clients can gain access to the services available. In the early stages of operation, especially, it is critical that all program personnel in contact with the community provide a consistent message. A failure to do so may generate expectations that will later be disappointed, or promote confusion about the purposes and scope of the program. If nothing else, a lack of clarity about the program among potential consumers requires that time and energy be spent in correcting misimpressions, turning away applicants who are inappropriately referred, or worse, attempting to accommodate client needs the program was never intended to address. Before a program goes public the staff should be thoroughly familiar with the plans and procedures that will guide interaction with the clientele. If there are disagreements regarding philosophy, scope, or operation, these should be surfaced and reconciled before the informational effort is undertaken. There is nothing quite so harmful to relations with the community as staff members using the public forum to press for conflicting views regarding the purpose of the program.

Several commonly used means of disseminating program information are: public media, including TV and radio spot announcements and news features; brochures, leaflets, and newsletters; speeches, presentations, and announcements; agency staff meetings and professional conferences; and special events such as open houses and agency tours.[21] These techniques are often supplemented by the manager's participation in local planning and coordinating bodies (e.g., a council of social agencies), professional associations, and contacts with administrators of other agencies.

Though these techniques are necessary for informing other agencies and programs about the availability of the new program, they are often insufficient for reaching persons in the at-risk population who are not in contact with the formal service network. This may be particularly true of potential consumers who are socially isolated, alienated from, or cynical about, social programs, or fearful about the consequences that may follow if they request help. In these instances, the program manager and staff must resort to additional measures. Frequently these take the form of outreach programs including, for example, leaflets in mailboxes, door-to-door contacts, relationships with community caretakers (e.g., bartenders and storekeepers), and outstationed offices.[22] The employment of indigenous paraprofessionals, though by no means a panacea in this regard, has also been found under certain circumstances to be an effective technique for engaging difficult-to-reach clients.[23] In some instances, persons from the community have also been brought onto boards and advisory committees to serve, in part, as a bridge to the larger target population.[24]

In an effort to attract potential clients, new programs are sometimes tempted to "oversell" their capability. The tendency to promise more than can be delivered not only runs the risk of damaging the program's image in the community but also of severely diluting staff efforts.[25] At the same time, new programs, particularly those that are not well funded, must maintain a margin of flexibility so as to be able to respond to community expectations that often emerge clearly only after the program has been implemented. This delicate balance between affirmatively representing the program and accurately reflecting its purpose and capacity (while at the same time adapting to input regarding client needs and expectations) is at the heart of this process of making contact with the population at risk.

Facilitating client access.   Having informed the population at risk regarding the availability of the program's services, the manager and staff must also be attentive to the problems that may impede client access to the program. That access is a problem is reflected in a recent report of the National Conference on Social Welfare:

Social services are often a positive force in improving the lives of those who are reached. However, many people do not have access to the services they need. Even when they make contact with agencies, too frequently they fail to obtain the quality and quantity of needed care and help.[26]

The report goes on to indicate that

... 60 percent of the people who seek social services are tuned away from agencies; only 17 percent of the remaining applicants seen by agencies are actually served; and only one of five people referred from one service to another ever reach the agency to which they were referred....[27]

Potential impediments to client access are numerous and may involve such diverse factors as geographic distance, lack of public transport, physical barriers (as in the case of physically disabled persons who cannot negotiate physical barriers), ethnic or cultural barriers (as with clients who are unable to speak English), restricted hours of program operation (e.g., no evening or weekend hours), and the unavailability of child care.[28] Other factors intrinsic to program operation can also pose obstacles for clients seeking a service. Among these may be a waiting period before the requested service is initiated, complicated time-consuming eligibility requirements, staff insensitivity to cultural differences, and inappropriate or intrusive requests for personal information.

Many of these barriers to service cannot be foreseen when the program is being designed. Some that can be anticipated (e.g., physical distance, lack of child care) can only be corrected with additional resources. In either case, it is important that clients' experiences in accessing the program be systematically monitored. If the program is being underutilized or if clients are failing to return for subsequent visits, the manager and staff should know whether this is due to access difficulties. Access can be monitored in a number of ways, including consumer surveys, follow-up telephone calls, and the auditing of case records. The procedures for doing so may be less important than the manager's commitment to knowing what clients experience in the process of utilizing the service provided.[29]

There is a common tendency for human service professionals to think of service utilization exclusively as a benefit to clients. Increasingly, however, it is being recognized that the act of utilizing a service involves costs to clients as well. Many of these costs—in emotional and physical energy, or time lost—are incurred by clients in overcoming the obstacles noted above. At some point the need for a service may be overshadowed by the opportunity costs (i.e., the options the client foregoes in expending time and energy required to use the service).[30] The need, even the desire for help, will not be acted upon if the client concludes that the utilization is too costly. The task of the program manager is to determine what these costs are for clients and, where possible, to minimize them.

Building trust.   There is, finally, the matter of creating conditions and processes in the program that facilitate the building of trust with clients. The fact that trust is difficult to define makes it no less an important ingredient in relations with consumers. Clients must know about and be able to gain access to a service, but this will be of little value unless they have confidence in the service offered by the program.[31] In this regard, Hasenfeld observes:

> Clearly, without trust the staff cannot hope to gain access to the client's life space and employ intervention techniques that require exposure of the client's private domain, and the client cannot hope to obtain the moral commitment of the staff to respond to his needs.[32]

The development of trust is probably most directly affected by the worker-client interaction, but conditions and processes in the program environment will do much to facilitate this linkage. It has been hypothesized that trust tends to occur most readily when congruence exists between client expectations and the goals of the program.[33] Thus in the first instance it would seem essential that program managers build a strong intake and assessment procedure that permits the identification of client needs and expectations and a thorough exploration of whether the program can be responsive. The manager's responsibility in this involves assigning skilled and knowledgable workers to perform this function; providing intake staff with sufficient time, training, receptionist support, and diagnostic assistance (such as psychological testing or medical examinations) to enable both clients and workers to make an informed choice about whether to proceed with service. Additionally, it is important to emphasize to staff the importance of providing clients with full information about entitlements and privileges as well as responsibilities and obligations.

What the client wants and the agency can provide are seldom cast in concrete at the outset. Typically both parties to this transaction modify expectations and goals in an effort to seek complementarity. In order for this process to occur, however, the worker must have some flexibility and discretion in accommodating client needs. To be sure, such flexibility should occur within well-defined parameters; but within this area of discretion, it is important for the manager to delegate both responsibility and authority to workers at the front line. In some service areas the demands of equity and accountability may severely circumscribe the exercise of discretion by practitioners; nevertheless, the manager should support and reinforce efforts by workers to adapt sensitively to the individual needs and goals of clients, and where possible mediate arbitrary agency rules and procedures.[34]

Hasenfeld has also argued that trust between organization and client is fostered when the latter is perceived and treated as a subject rather than an object, "as a person who can actively participate in decision making about himself, a person who can control his fate."[35] Among other things, this posture is facilitated when clients are encouraged to take an active role in their own treatment planning and are afforded an opportunity to provide feedback regarding the policies, procedures, and services to which they are exposed. To some extent these features can be designed into program services, but the maintenance of this posture with clients is probably very much related to whether similar conditions obtain in relations between the manager and staff in the program. That is to say, if the program manager wants the staff to treat clients as subjects, workers themselves should be so treated. When norms such as openness, respect, reciprocity, and shared decision making are present in staff relations, they are more likely to pervade interactions with clients as well.[36]

Developing Relations with Agencies and Units in the Environment

Since few, if any, programs are self-sufficient, one of the manager's critical tasks is to build a system of reciprocal relations with selected organizations in the community and other units in the host agency that will permit the program to acquire the resources it requires in order to effectively pursue its objectives.

There are several kinds of resources that new programs are likely to need from other organizations and units. We have already commented upon how new programs must sometimes rely on other service providers for *client referrals*. *Personnel* are a second important resource. Though it is the individual who ultimately contracts with the program or agency for services, the nature of the personnel pool can be influenced by such varied entities as the personnel department in the parent agency, or the governmental unit of which it is a part, professional schools and associations, and labor unions. Each of these bodies may act in ways that affect the flow of potential applicants to the new program, as well as the qualifications of the applicant pool. A third resource category is what might be called *technical assistance*. In varying degrees, programs rely on expertise and information to facilitate their work. Within the host organization the program may require support services such as preparing a budget, writing a grant, developing a training program for new employees, evaluating services, accessing data in a computer, and the like. From time to time, program personnel will require information or direction regarding the availability of funding sources, the interpretation of federal and state legislation and administrative regulations, the location of citizens to serve on committees and boards, information concerning emerging social problems and new services, and so on. A fourth type of resource involves the *cooperative service activities* of other organizations and units upon which the program depends to effectively pursue its mission. For example, a protective services program may find it difficult to effectively deal with abusive and neglectful families if it does not receive timely cooperation from the police, the court, a homemaker service, or a mental health clinic. Hospital social service departments frequently are unable to develop adequate discharge plans for patients if physicians wait until the last minute to refer clients for this service. A mental health clinic outpatient program may be severely hampered in treatment planning for patients if hospital records are delayed or provide insufficient information. These, and countless other examples that might be mentioned, reflect the central importance of cooperative service activity to program operations. Such cooperation is, in a real sense, a vital resource.

Even this brief description of the varied resources a program may need to effectively implement its services suggests something of the importance of building relationships with other agencies and units. But how does the manager proceed? How does a person acquire the resources necessary to consolidate the program service domain and simultaneously avoid undesirable intrusions and control from without? This area of management responsibility is not well understood. The process of forging interorganizational and interunit relations is affected by a host of local and individual circumstances that make generalizations hazardous. What follows, then, must be considered tentative. Certainly there is need for further theoretical and empirical work in this area.

There appear to be at least three elements to this task: identifying and analyzing the program's organizational set; establishing contact with other agencies and units in this set; and negotiating exchanges of resources.

Analyzing the organizational set.   Every program is enmeshed in an *organizational set,* which may be defined as those organized entities with which the program is, or is likely to be, in interaction.[37] For the purposes of this task, the manager should be concerned with identifying those entities, within and without the host agency, that are in a position to give or withhold resources the program will need to achieve its objectives and the factors that may influence their decisions in this respect. The literature on inter-organizational relations suggests that a critical variable in such an analysis is the degree of interdependence between two organized entities.[38] Reid defines interdependence as follows:

> Two organizations may be said to be interdependent if one organization perceives that its own goals can be achieved most effectively with the assistance of the resources of the other. Interdependent organizations are then drawn into exchanges of resources to serve one anothers goals.[39]

Two elements of this definition are important. The resources exchanged must have some instrumental value for both parties, and both parties must perceive that an exchange of resources is in their respective best interests. The manager, then, must assess not only what resources he or she may need from others in order to further program operations, but the resources that can be exchanged in return and the value placed on them by the other organization or unit. Let us take the example of a new community education program in a mental health center which is set up to disseminate information about the clinic's services. To carry out this responsibility the program manager is likely to need time and information from other program heads in the agency. These persons, in turn, may feel that community education will serve only to generate additional service demands on their already overtaxed programs. Given this perception, their inclination to exchange resources with the new program is not likely to be very great, because in return for resources they give the new program, they will likely receive a resource—clients—that is already in abundant supply. But imagine for a moment that the community education program is also to be directly involved in lobbying the state legislature for increases in the state budget for mental health services. Here it is likely that cooperation from other department heads will be more readily forthcoming, since the resource being exchanged in return for their cooperation is the potential of additional funds to strengthen or expand their operations.

Exchanges of resources may not be solely determined by self-interest. Within organizations, for example, transfers of clients, technical assistance, and so on may be required by superiors; and established units may well be constrained to cooperate with a new program or run the risk of losing favor or support. In still other instances, interunit cooperation may occur because of friendship or obligation. Interorganizationally, agencies will sometimes lend assistance and support to a new program even if what they receive in return has no immediate implications for their self-interests. For example, such things as community crisis, informal relationships between managers, and moral commitments to the goals of new programs sometimes variously stimulate other agencies to provide resources without any immediate prospect of furthering their own aims.[40] There is, however, little to suggest that these factors are sufficiently powerful in themselves to sustain long-term exchange relationships. In the context of fiscal constraints and budget cuts that increasingly face program heads, this appears to be particularly true. Rather, it appears that perceived interdependence on the part of both parties to an exchange is a necessary, if not a sufficient, condition for sustained cooperation. Assuming this to be the case, the manager who is seeking resources should assess the nature and degree of his or her program's interdependency with other organizations and units in the organizational set. This assessment should provide some direction regarding where to seek interorganizational linkages or, alternately, suggest the kinds of inducements that may be necessary to create a basis for exchange.

Having identified the other agencies and units in the organizational set with whom resource exchanges appear desirable, the manager must also determine whether such arrangements are feasible. An awareness of interdependence is one thing, but initiating and maintaining these relationships is quite another. To obtain some estimate of feasibility it is important, first of all, to know something of the environmental context in which each potential cooperating agency or unit operates, including the inducements and constraints for interorganizational cooperation that may exist in laws, regulations, funding arrangements, and administrative policies under which they operate.[41] Examples here might include the availability of grants that require interagency collaboration, the enactment of legislation that mandates coordination between previously independent organizations, or pressure from planning bodies aimed at eliminating overlap or competition between agencies. A less tangible, but equally salient, aspect of the organizational environment is the ideology that prevails in that service sector. Such phrases as "deinstitutionalization," "mainstreaming," and "diversion" are often more than just buzz words, but rather reflect deep philosophical commitments that can have a strong impact on decision-making processes in organizations.

A second variable affecting interorganizational relations is the size of the organization or unit with which the program intends to establish an exchange. Relationships with larger organizations are generally more difficult to sustain because of the number of people who must be consulted or who will be party to implementing the agreement.[42]

A third consideration is the nature of the other organizations' or units' decision-making processes. Decision making may be simply conceptualized on a continuum ranging from centralized at one end—where very few people make decisions on behalf of the organization—to decentralized on the other—where many people are involved in making decisions. In dealing with centralized organizations, the manager may, given otherwise favorable conditions, find it easier to initiate exchange agreements. However, to the extent that subordinates have not been involved in, or do not subscribe to, those decisions, implementation and maintenance of these agreements may prove difficult. The experience of some workers at LESFU in trying to develop coordinated services for troubled families is a case in point:

> LESFU referred neglect cases to Special Services for Children (SSC), the public agency for protecting the rights of abused children. An arrangement was worked out with a special unit in SSC to accept LESFU referrals and to coordinate their efforts.... Unfortunately, arrangements with SSC were worked out at higher levels of the organization. Some workers in the special unit were not willing to cooperate, or to accept LEFSU judgments about neglect. *This conflict occurred because the top leaders of SSC did not understand the pressures and constraints under which workers in the special unit operated.* [Emphasis added.][43]

Conversely, while it may be more difficult to initiate agreements with organizations that use a decentralized decision style, implementation and maintenance are likely to be somewhat less problematic because the actors involved in making the decisions will also tend to be involved in carrying them out.

A fourth area bearing on the feasibility of interorganizational arrangements concerns the costs and benefits of such relationships. Agencies and units in the horizontal network are likely to calculate not only what is to be gained in an exchange, but what is likely to be sacrificed as well—e.g., loss of control, additional time and energy spent on communication and reporting, manpower necessary to maintain the liaison and monitor arrangements, and so on. What may at first appear an inviting opportunity to work cooperatively sometimes loses its appeal as the effort, money, and delay involved become apparent.[44]

In summary, then, the program manager should approach the task of acquiring resources for the program by: (1) identifying organizations and units with which the program is, or is likely to be, in interaction; (2) assessing the degree of actual or potential interdependency that exists between the program and each of these entities; and (3) determining the feasibility of initiating and maintaining exchange relationships. It is important to add here that this is an ongoing analytic process for the program manager. The assessment of opportunities for resource exchange must be constantly updated to reflect changes in the program and in the other agencies and units with whom transactions are being conducted. Moreover, the fact that there may be little basis on which to build an exchange relationship at any given point in time should not necessarily be seen as a prescription for inaction. Indeed, under certain circumstances, the manager may give priority attention to cultivating conditions that will be conducive to future exchange relationships, even though there is little to be gained in the short run. Interorganizational relationships, in other words, are not solely the product of immutable, external forces, but are conditioned by the discretion and aspirations of the administrative actors involved.

Establishing contact.   A second major dimension of the resource acquisition task involves the manager in establishing personal contact with the network of agencies and units that control or influence the flow of vital resources to the program. In what Mintzberg calls the *liaison role,* the manager initiates a number of relationships with other administrators to variously exchange information and favors, learn about their preferences, goals, and problems, and explore mutual interests.[45] These contacts not only provide much of the information necessary to making the analysis discussed above, but also create channels that can later be used to communicate about problems in, or possibilities for, interorganizational exchange. To effect these contacts, the manager joins associations, attends conferences and community forums, holds luncheon meetings, and engages in similar activities whose purpose, in part, is to become visible and seek out opportunities for interaction. Many of these activities appear to be symbolic when viewed in isolation, but they serve the purpose of placing the manager "in touch" with the organizational set.

Negotiating exchanges.   Assessing and making contact with the organizational set provides the foundation for the third aspect of the resource acquisition task: *negotiating agreements.* Here the manager is concerned with establishing the terms of exchange with other agencies or units. The resources to be exchanged, as we suggested earlier, may be of several kinds (e.g., clients and technical assistance) but the responsibility of the program manager is to negotiate an arrangement that will maximize the interests of the unit, or alternately minimize threats to its service domain and internal capability.

Since the program manager's negotiations are with agencies and units over which he or she has no formal authority, and since the parties are normally concerned with advancing their own interests, such relationships have varying degrees of tension and conflict. Sometimes the needs of both parties can be easily accommodated in an agreement, but it is more common to find "a mixture of conflict and mutual dependence that binds parties to one another, yet compels each to contend for a division of resources in accordance with their differing interests."[46] Under these circumstances, the primary medium through which differences are resolved is trading, wherein the two parties agree to exchange resources in a way that protects the integrity and survival of their respective programs and yet facilitates cooperation.[47] Such agreements almost invariably require compromise and concessions; and though both parties may not benefit equally, it is important that each feel that there has been some net gain to them. Lacking this, the prospects for maintaining the agreement are not particularly good.[48]

What is the nature of these exchanges? One common type, a contractual agreement, involves the provision of a particular type of service to a designated clientele in return for money. In the case of a new program, the manager may make a contract more attractive to the funding agency by agreeing to provide services at a lower unit cost than other agencies. Exchanges may also revolve around a division of labor, such that the manager agrees to send all cases requiring a particular type of service (e.g., parent-child conflict) to another agency, in return for assurances that his or her program will receive in return all cases in which foster care may be needed. Yet another type of exchange may revolve around new opportunities that will benefit both parties. Inviting another agency to be a collaborator in a newly funded project that promises to expand its staff or extend its jurisdiction, in return for training or access to research expertise, would be an example.

Issues and dilemmas in interorganizational relationships. While resource exchanges with agencies and units in the organizational set are often vital to successful program implementation, such relationships can also pose issues and dilemmas for managers. One issue arises from the fact that new programs are likely to be more dependent on these arrangements than their counterparts. Established agencies have functioned, and can probably continue to do so, without the assistance of the new program. Add to this that developing new relationships takes time and effort and often involves some alteration in modes of operation, and it is not difficult to understand why existing agencies or units are often slow to enter into new cooperative arrangements. The dilemma facing the manager under these circumstances is how at once to induce the other party into an exchange, offering resources that are attractive enough to offset the forces of inertia, without at the same time overextending or unduly encumbering the program's capacity. In their eagerness to launch the program, managers often fall prey to a "borrow now—pay later" stance where, in order to enlist the assistance of other parties they make commitments without clearly determining how they will meet them later on. Some manifestations of this are overbidding on contracts, promising services that cannot realistically be provided by the program staff, agreeing to performance criteria or accountability requirements that cannot feasibly be met, and so on. Needless to say, if such commitments are not honored, the program's credibility (especially the manager's) with other agencies and units is likely to suffer. On the other hand, the effort required to deliver on unrealistic promises may overextend the staff, lower its morale, or prompt some staff to quit.

Either outcome, of course, is likely to severely weaken a new program. Clearly it behooves the manager to assess the short-term advantages of such exchanges against their long-term costs. In some instances, it may be wiser to forego resources that will permit rapid program development in the interests of long-term program viability.

There are occasions, however, when program managers will have little choice but to participate in interorganizational agreements, knowing that the terms of the exchange are unfavorable to their program. Perhaps the best that can be done under these circumstances is to confront the likely consequences as soon as possible and plan for ways to minimize them. Curtailing certain program functions, reassigning staff, or transferring funds are among those steps that managers often take to deal with such contingencies.

Actual or potential competition with other agencies or units is also frequently an issue during the implementation stage.[49] When the program is competing for a finite client pool or for limited funds, competition can have serious consequences. Several options are available to managers. They can proceed independently of the other agency or unit and seek to gain a share of the resources available in that service arena. Choosing this course is likely to engender conflict and perhaps make an eventual reproachment more difficult. A second alternative is to seek some agreement that divides labor and resources between the parties; however, unless the new program has some leverage, the established agency or unit is not likely to look too favorably on an arrangement that reduces its domain. A third option is for managers to seek out a joint venture which might range from a formalized cooperative arrangement to some kind of merger. This course may entail a loss of identity or operating autonomy for the program, as well as a loss of control for the parent organization. Any of these options (and the variants thereon) are likely to have profound implications for the character of the program and, indeed, even for its survival.

A final issue for managers concerns reconciling agreements made between the program and its organizational set with the preferences and expectations of their superiors. As various agreements, large and small, formal and informal, are made, their cumulative impact on program operation is likely to be quite significant. In order to effectively engage in building these horizontal relationships, program managers will need to have a clear understanding with their superiors regarding the parameters of discretion that can be exercised. In turn, it is important that managers obtain the informed approval and support of superiors, especially for the more important interorganizational arrangements that are developed. If neither of these conditions are present, the managers' ability to follow through on these arrangements is likely to be severely compromised.

DEVELOPING AN ORGANIZATIONAL STRUCTURE

Even as managers are engaged in establishing a clientele and forming lateral relationships with other agencies and units, they must also address the task of building an organizational structure that will promote reliable and efficient program performance and insure a modicum of internal accountability.

Although a rudimentary organizational structure will have been created during the design phase, the increased size and heterogeneity of the staff, and the process of elaborating and refining services in response to unforeseen problems and changing circumstances, are now likely to create the necessity for a substantially more complex and formalized set of structural arrangements. Before proceeding, we should point out that the extent of a manager's responsibility for structuring his or her unit is likely to vary with the nature of the parent organization. Programs located in larger, mature bureaucratic agencies will often have imposed upon them the structural characteristics of the host agency. This needn't be a problem for the manager (indeed, it may simplify the task), except insofar as such inherited arrangements prevent the program from dealing with contingencies in a flexible way. Where this occurs, a manager may find it necessary to press for discretionary authority to diverge from established organizational procedures and policies.

What is *organizational structure?* In the simplest terms it can be defined as the "established pattern of relationships among components or parts of the organization."[50] More specifically, structure consists of those formal, relatively stable arrangements that prescribe how the functions and duties of an organization are to be divided and then coordinated, how authority is to be distributed, and how work responsibilities are to be carried out. Structure, as we define it, does not encompass relationships, sentiments, and norms that emerge spontaneously in the course of interaction between organizational members, though these informal processes can do much to influence the nature of formal relationships. Organizational structure is less a description of what is, than a blueprint for how activities should be orchestrated to achieve desired objectives.

Because organizations seldom, if ever, function in precisely the manner formally prescribed, there is a tendency to minimize the influence of structure on behavior, to think of it as window dressing that obscures what really happens in organizations. And while it is true that structure alone does not determine behavior in organizations, there is considerable evidence to suggest that it exerts a significant influence on a wide variety of processes and outcomes in human services organizations including, for example, morale and job satisfaction,[51] attitudes and behaviors toward, and expectations of, clients,[52] efficiency,[53] and turnover and absenteeism.[54] A review of this evidence would take us far afield, but suffice it to say that designing the formal structure of an organization or program is likely to be one of the manager's most consequential tasks.

Perhaps the most common way of depicting structure is the *organizational chart,* or what is sometimes referred to as the *table of organization.* This instrument is a graphic representation (usually a very rough and simplistic representation) of the major functional subunits and administrative positions in an organization, and their hierarchical relationship to one another. Most organization charts focus on lines of authority and communication between superiors and subordinates, and less, if at all, on horizontal and diagonal relationships between actors in parallel subsystems. Figure 5-1 provides an example of a table of organization for a community mental health agency. Typically, this kind of chart is supplemented with more detailed narrative descriptions about the functions of various subunits; position descriptions for each class of employee; an operations manual containing rules, regulations, and operating procedures; and an assortment of memos and directives explaining all of the above.

There are a number of dimensions of formal structure, but for purposes of this discussion we shall concentrate on four that bear directly on program reliability, efficiency, and internal accountability. The first two of these variables, *job specialization* and *departmentalization,* refer to the degree

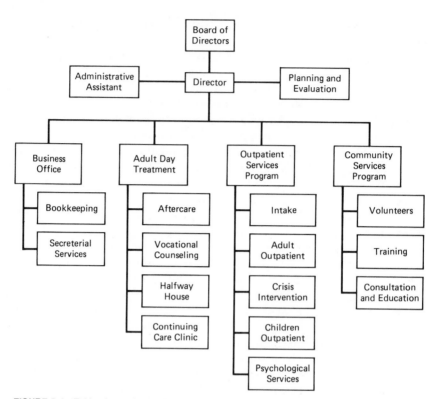

FIGURE 5-1 Table of organization for a community mental health clinic.

of complexity or horizontal differentiation in an organizational unit—i.e., the extent to which labor is divided among participants in the program. *Centralization* and *formalization,* the other two variables of structure, are measures of vertical differentiation, or the extent to which authority is distributed among positions in the administrative hierarchy.

Each of these dimensions or variables can be visualized on a continuum (little to much, low to high), and the manager must determine how much or little of each is to be designed into the structure of the program. After defining each of these concepts, we shall then identify some of the factors that should be considered in making these choices.

Horizontal Complexity

Job specialization refers to the extent to which roles and activities are differentiated in an organizational unit.[55] Put more simply, specialization is reflected in the number of positions or job classes that have distinct responsibilities. The greater the number of functionally distinct positions, the greater the specialization. Thus, for example, a residential treatment program for disturbed children may divide its front-line staff into two job classes—e.g., social workers and child care workers—with employees in each class performing essentially the same responsibilities. A second program of similar size and purpose may adopt a more complex division of labor. Social workers, for example, might be assigned to several job classes, including intake and assessment workers, individual and family therapists, and community placement and supervision specialists. Child care functions might likewise be disaggregated into specialties like recreation, group life coordination, and custody. The more job responsibilities are divided into these specializations, the more complex the organization's division of labor.

Several arguments are advanced for job specialization in organizations, most of which grow out of the experience of industry.[56] The more narrowly defined the responsibilities of workers, the easier (theoretically) it is for the worker to master the skills and activities required of the job. As the worker spends more time with fewer activities, the repetition should increase the efficiency with which the activities are performed. Second, the narrower the range of job responsibilities, the easier, it is argued, it is for the manager to define performance standards and therefore control and evaluate the work of employees. Third, since jobs that are broadly defined are likely to require varying levels of knowledge and skill, there are reputed advantages to be gained by ordering positions in accordance with levels of technical expertise required. In this way more highly trained and experienced workers can concentrate on those activities that require their expertise, while less trained and experienced employees can be assigned less demanding duties. Finally, dividing labor into more narrowly defined specialization potentially enables the organization to flexibly deploy employees to make the best use of their interests and aptitudes. Some workers may be more skilled at, or interested in, diagnostic assessment or short-term crisis treatment, while others may prefer long-term treatment arrangements. Specialization permits the manager to take advantage of these differences in motivation and capacity.

The principle of dividing labor so as to increase productivity, efficiency, and expertise is by no means new or foreign in social welfare organizations. In larger agencies especially, one is likely to find heavy emphasis placed on job specialization and, if anything, there appears to be an increasing trend in this direction for many of the reasons just mentioned.[57] At the same time, the manager who is contemplating how best to divide labor in his or her program must weigh the potential benefits of job specialization against its potential problems and dysfunctions. Among these may be: the boredom, monotony and fatigue experienced by workers in narrowly defined, repetitive jobs; the development of parochial perspectives on client need and a consequent tendency to atomize client problems; the diminished use of worker discretion and judgment in responding to client need; the diverse and inconsistent demands placed on clients as a result of having to relate to diverse specialists; and difficulties in coordinating the work of numerous specialists.[58] In recent years approaches such as case management, case advocacy, and treatment teams have developed, in part, to offset some of the negative consequences of extensive specialization; but the costs of these solutions (in terms of increased time and coordination and energy devoted to group processes) must also be assessed against the benefits of complexity.[59] On the individual worker level, some organizations, most notably in the business sector, have adopted job enlargement and job rotation strategies as an antidote to employee dissatisfaction with highly specialized routine work.[60] The benefits and limitations of these approaches to excessive specialization have yet to be systematically investigated in social welfare organizations, though some research evidence shows a correlation between job content in human services and worker burnout.[61]

Departmentalization, the second dimension of complexity, concerns the degree to which the activities of a program are grouped into distinct administrative subunits (departments, bureaus, offices), each with its own leadership and areas of responsibility.[62] Though departmentalization is closely associated with job specialization, it is a conceptually distinct phenomenon and should be addressed separately.

As programs increase in size they tend to become more departmentalized, if for no other reason than that a single manager finds it increasingly difficult to oversee and effectively relate to the activities of a large number of subordinates. One purpose of departmentalization, then, is to reduce the manager's span of control—i.e., the number of subordinates for whom he or she carries direct supervisory responsibility. Clearly a program manager with thirty employees will find it much more manageable to relate to four supervisors, each of whom is responsible in turn for seven subordinates, than to deal directly with all thirty employees.

But the size of an organizational unit is only one of several reasons for departmentalization. A second rationale lies in the desirability of clustering cognate activities into a subunit so as to facilitate the interaction and coordination of actors whose jobs are highly interdependent. The formation of project teams to design and implement an experimental service would be one such example. Subunits may also be formed in order to concentrate technical expertise and create a critical mass of specialists who perform support functions for an entire program. Budget and planning offices, research departments, and training and staff development units are examples. The types of clients served by a program may also provide a basis for departmentalization. Such factors as age, ethnicity, or type and severity of problem may result in client groups with sufficiently distinct service needs as to justify the formation of units on this basis. Processes or technologies utilized may also serve as a criterion for internal differentiation, such that intake is organizationally separated from ongoing treatment, licensing from placement, information and referral from crisis intervention, and so on. Finally, some programs are separated into geographic units in order to ease client access or foster responsiveness to the unique cultural or social characteristics of various communities or regions.

Despite the potential advantages of departmentalization, however, tradeoffs are frequently involved. The increased number of subprogram managerial and supervisory personnel necessary to oversee subunits often results in added administrative overhead. The more subunits, the more time and energy managers and others must devote to maintaining inter-departmental communication and coordination, resolving conflicts, and attending to work flow. Employees frequently develop loyalties to their unit that cause them to give higher priority to departmental interests than to the achievement of overall program objectives. When this occurs, the account-ability and control that should follow from departmentalization may suffer. In extreme cases such as that reported by Maypole, a unit or department may become so identified with its own objectives, that it attempts to with-draw from the parent program and become functionally autonomous.[63]

Among the most important negative consequences of departmentali-zation may be the discontinuity and fragmentation experienced by clients. Although these difficulties are more often attributed to a lack of inter-agency coordination, it is not uncommon to see two or more subunits in a single program providing overlapping services, failing to coordinate their interventions, or disseminating inconsistent messages about service eligibil-ity. These and other problems are likely to occur with more frequency as the organization is divided into subunits that share responsibility for deal-ing with the client group.

These problems with departmentalization, and some of those as-sociated with job specialization as well, have prompted a search for organi-zational forms that will at once allow for a rational division of labor and at the same time prevent or mitigate some of the difficulties they frequently generate. One such structural alternative is the *matrix organization,* where parallel subunits of an organization or program operate in the traditional hierarchical manner, but specialists from each of these departments are assigned to functional teams to work on some common task or problem.[64] Each specialist continues to be administratively responsible to his or her departmental superior, but also works under a team leader and with repre-sentatives of other departments in order to develop a coordinated ap-proach to the problem or clientele at hand. Team members must carry out the policies and procedures of their respective departments, but they are also responsible for articulating these departmental requirements at the team level so as to produce an organic, internally consistent approach to their common task.

The structure that emerges resembles the grid displayed in Figure 5-2. Here we have staff from four units in a foster home program assigned

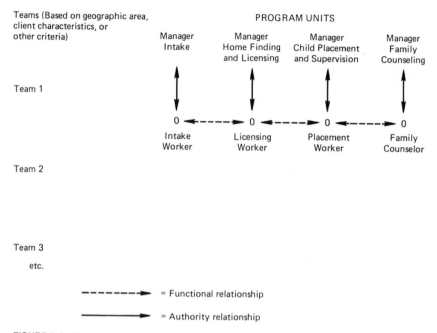

Teams (Based on geographic area, client characteristics, or other criteria)

PROGRAM UNITS

	Manager Intake	Manager Home Finding and Licensing	Manager Child Placement and Supervision	Manager Family Counseling

Team 1

	Intake Worker	Licensing Worker	Placement Worker	Family Counselor

Team 2

Team 3

etc.

‐ ‐ ‐ ‐ ‐ ‐ ‐ ► = Functional relationship

———————► = Authority relationship

FIGURE 5-2 Matrix structure for foster home program.

to teams. Each team is responsible for a number of families with children in need of foster care services. The team assumes the entire responsibility for each case, including initial assessment, home finding and licensing, placement and supervision of children who require foster homes, and counseling with natural parents in order to facilitate the return of children to their homes.

While the matrix structure is useful for addressing some of the dysfunctions of organizational complexity, it is no panacea. The worker is placed at the intersection of the vertical and horizontal systems in a program and must be skilled at mediating their respective demands and expectations. This is almost certain to produce ambiguity for the single worker and at least occasional conflict among workers from several departments.[65] Immersion in the team's group processes and a commitment to the team's effectiveness must be balanced with the need to be responsive to the directives and norms of the home department. Dissonance and role strain are frequent byproducts of this arrangement. From the departmental manager's point of view, such arrangements may weaken his or her control over subordinates and reduce the flow of upward information needed for accountability. Evaluation of subordinates can also prove problematic, since much of the primary data about a worker's performance will be provided by the team leader, who may have quite different criteria for judging the quality of work than the administrative superior. The team leader, of course, will perceive the lack of line authority as a constraint. If the worker is unable or unwilling to cooperate with other team members and has the support of his or her superior, the team leader may have few formal options available to correct this situation (e.g., reassignment or dismissal).

To say that matrix organization is no cure-all is not to dismiss its potential as a structural alternative. Indeed, given what appears to be an increasing trend toward job specialization and departmentalization, the matrix approach shows promise as a way of retaining the essential benefits of complexity, without undue sacrifice to quality, integrated services.

Vertical Differentiation

As the chief official of an organizational unit, the manager has been delegated the responsibility, and presumably the authority, necessary to carry out the program's objectives. Viewed broadly as the legitimate right to make decisions, direct the actions of subordinates, allocate resources, and invoke rewards and sanctions, *authority* is a central instrument through which the manager obtains compliance from subordinates and coordinates their efforts toward the attainment of program objectives.[66]

Questions of authority and compliance assume considerable importance for the manager during the implementation stage. The increased size of the program staff and its growing heterogeneity, as we mentioned earlier, heighten the prospects for disagreement over program priorities, methods to be employed, and the interpretation of policy. In addition, since even the most detailed program plan will not anticipate all the contingencies that might arise during the implementation stage, subordinates in a program will have to modify or elaborate policy in order to deal with unanticipated realities. These ad hoc, individual adaptations can, over time, significantly alter the original intent and nature of the program.

These and related processes will provoke a number of questions for the manager: What kinds of decisions will be made by subordinates? Under what circumstances? What means can be employed to insure that decisions, once made, are carried out in a reliable and consistent manner? In what areas should rules and regulations be formulated to guide subordinate behavior? How will such rules be enforced? How can the manager insure his or her ability to monitor the performance of staff? The manner in which these and similar questions are answered by the manager does much to determine the nature of the authority structure that is to be employed in a program.

Discussions of authority and compliance evoke images of the classic pyramid hierarchy that starts at the top with the program administrator and fans out symmetrically to link all employees in a superior-subordinate relationship. These pyramidal representations reflect the span of control of administrative personnel at each level in the organizational unit. The greater the span of control, the fewer the administrative levels and the flatter the hierarchy. Conversely, the smaller the span of control, the more the administrative levels and the steeper the hierarchy. For example, in Figure 5–3 we see two programs of equivalent size that have different hierarchical configurations because of variations in the span of control.

But while the configuration of the authority hierarchy tells one something of how authority is distributed, it reveals little about how it is actually exercised. To approach this question, the concepts of *centralization* and *formalization* are useful. *Centralization* may be defined as the degree to which the authority to make decisions is concentrated with a few or diffused among many in an organizational unit. The greater the number of decisions made at upper levels in the program, the greater the centralization.[67] Conversely, the more authority for decisions is delegated downward, the more decentralized the organization. The extent to which a program is centralized or decentralized may vary with the decisions under consideration. For example, budget and personnel decisions may be reserved for the program director, decisions regarding which service delivery methods to employ may be delegated to department heads or unit supervisors, while treatment decisions may be made at the front line. In short, programs are likely to be characterized by varying degrees of centralization and decentralization in different decision areas.

Formalization refers to the degree to which the program relies on rules and procedures to govern employee behavior.[68] Administrative regulations, procedure manuals, forms, job descriptions, and memos are among the most frequently used instruments for conveying rules, but less formal means such as custom, tradition, and verbalized agreements also serve this purpose. The more detailed these prescriptions and the more they are consistently enforced, the more formalized the program. Again, as with the variable of centralization, formalization may vary considerably in different

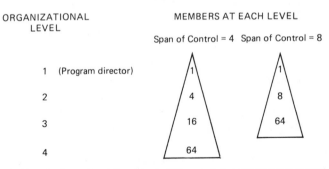

FIGURE 5-3   Span of control and depth of hierarchy in two organizations of equal size. *Source:* Adapted from Stephen P. Robbins, *The Administrative Process,* 2nd ed. (Englewood Cliffs, N.J.: Prentice-Hall, Inc., 1980), p. 199.

activity areas. In matters such as determining client eligibility, conducting employee evaluations, or processing grievances, procedures to be followed may be quite explicit and uniformly enforced. In other areas—say, the frequency of supervisory conferences, coordination between workers, or the conduct of treatment interviews—rules and procedures may be less specific or, indeed, lacking.

Formalization is essentially a mechanism for reducing discretionary behavior or routinizing decision-making processes so as to increase reliability and consistency in performance. Though rules and procedures are often criticized for promoting inflexibility and undermining initiative and creativity, they can also reduce role ambiguity, clarify interrole expectations, and constrain the arbitrary use of authority.

Though centralization and formalization tend to be positively associated in the structure of organizations, they may vary independently. In Table 5–1 we see four possible structural combinations. Cell 1 would contain programs in which broad decision-making authority is concentrated in a few top-level administrators, and rules and regulations exist to guide most important areas of transaction between the staff and with clients and organizations in the community. In cell 2 would be found those programs in which the program manager has delegated a great deal of decision-making authority to subordinates (and they, in turn, to their subordinates), but the latitude that subordinates can exercise is likely to be circumscribed by the presence of quite detailed rules and regulations. Cell 3 represents those programs that contain few detailed prescriptions; most decisions of any significance are made by the program manager and his or her immediate subordinates. This combination is often found in small programs where it is possible for the director to command and process the necessary information to make decisions in a range of areas. Programs in cell 4 include those in which the manager's subordinates are given the authority to make a number of different kinds of decisions and are relatively unencumbered by procedures and regulations.

Unfortunately there is no litmus test to help the manager determine how much or how little centralization or formalization should exist in a program's structure.[69] Rather, as was the case with structural decisions on

TABLE 5–1   Combinations of Centralization and Formalization in Program Structure

	Centralization	
Formalization	High	Low
High	1	2
Low	3	4

job specialization and departmentalization, the optimum degrees of centralization and formalization are likely to vary with the circumstances. For example, contingency theorists have advanced the notion that the structural characteristics of an organization should vary to accommodate the nature of the technology employed and the environment in which the organization operates.[70]

With regard to technology, there is some agreement that where technology (i.e., the techniques employed to accomplish the work of the organization) is repetitive, standardized, routine, and easily programmed, decision making is better centralized in the upper reaches of the hierarchy. Under these circumstances, it is argued, managers should decide what is to be done, when, and how, and prescribe the actions of subordinates through direction, rules, and procedures. Conversely, where technology is nonroutine, variable, complex, and indeterminate, contingency theory suggests that authority should be delegated downward and rules minimized so as to permit subordinates the flexibility and discretion that is necessary to performing their jobs.[71]

The *environment* in which an organization (or program) operates is also thought to be a critical determinant of organizational structure. In general, both theory and research point to the conclusion that organizations with less formalized and centralized structures are likely to be more effective in the face of an unstable and changing environment. For example, in such an environment rapidly changing demands and expectations require the staff to alter patterns of operation, adopt innovations, and proactively problem solve in order to deal with the threats and opportunities that arise. When, on the other hand, the environment of the organization is relatively constant and predictable, contingency theory suggests that a top-down authority structure, characterized by centralized decision making and formalization, is more appropriate.[72]

Given the complex and indeterminate technologies employed in most social welfare programs and the uncertain environments in which they typically operate, contingency theory suggests that highly formalized and centralized structures are not appropriate. Moreover, when applied to programs at the implementation stage where, as we have previously indicated, service delivery techniques are evolving and where relations with external groups are still unstable, this line of analysis would indicate the need for caution in prematurely centralizing authority or developing elaborate sets of rules and procedures.

When one adds to this that high centralization and formalization tend to produce undesirable secondary consequences such as lowered morale and job satisfaction[73] and strain in relations with professionals who desire autonomy,[74] the need to proceed carefully in building the authority structure becomes all the more apparent.

Still one might argue that in the last analysis the need for coordination and accountability dictates the necessity for a degree of centralization and formalization. While this may be true, a body of administrative thought argues that delegation and discretion, rather than eroding the manager's authority, actually enhance it. Caplow's comment nicely summarizes this point of view:

> When subordinates are given more autonomy their emotional commitment to the organizational program often increases in a dramatic way. On the technical side, their familiarity with operational details often enables them to run a given operation more effectively within broad guidelines than under tight instructions. One paradoxical result is that the manager who gives the fullest possible autonomy to his subordinates may find his power over them enhanced rather than diminished. . . . On each level the transfer of a substantial part of the superior's decision-making prerogative . . . tends to increase the subordinate's commitment and contribution to the organization and thereby reinforce, rather than diminish, the authority of each superior.[75]

At the very least, Caplow's comments suggest that designing a structure to maximize authority may not be the most judicious approach for eliciting compliance and coordination from subordinates. We will return to this topic again in the next chapter.

DEVELOPING AND MAINTAINING STAFF CAPABILITY

One hardly need argue that the quality of a program's front-line personnel—their knowledge, skill, and commitment—is a critical ingredient in successful program implementation. The managerial tasks discussed earlier create the potential for the implementation of services; but in the last analysis, those who deliver the services and interact with clients to effect changes in their life circumstances, are responsible for bringing this potential to fruition.

Front-line personnel are important to the performance of all organizations, but in social welfare they play an especially important role because of the nature of the technologies employed. As previously indicated, services provided by most social agencies rely heavily on the application of technologies that are nonroutine, complex, and indeterminate. The variability of clients' needs and requests and the difficulties involved in understanding the problems they present, when combined with the relatively unspecific nature of the techniques employed and the still considerable uncertainty about their efficacy, makes it unfeasible for the organization to prescribe uniform technical processes. This creates a situation in which social agencies must rely heavily on the discretion, judgment, and skill of individual workers.[76] The differences between this state of affairs and that which is found in many industrial organizations are illustrated in the following comment:

In a manufacturing plant, technology is typically tangible in that the process of assembling the elements results in a concrete product be it clothing, automobiles, or toothpaste. This kind of technology is generally characterized by a high degree of routinization. Once the operational system is in place, the tasks are clear, the causative relationships apparent, the process highly repetitive, the product standardized. Some technologies are so perfected that human input becomes marginal.[77]

Given the heavy reliance on front-line staff in social service programs, it follows that managers should invest a good deal of time and energy in developing and sustaining this capability. Moreover, at no time in a program's history is this task likely to be so important. Not only will the initial cohort of staff do much to shape the character of the service delivery system, they will also build an informal system of norms, sentiments, and relationships that will exert, for better or worse, a powerful socializing influence on later generations of employees. Finally, this initial group of workers will become a repository of institutional experience, skill, and wisdom that can be drawn upon, formally and informally, to train new employees and thus promote program continuity.

Staff capability can mean many things, but we shall here be concerned with the extent to which front-line workers utilize their time productively in the provision of services to clients and the degree to which they skillfully employ methods and techniques that, according to professional knowledge and the requirements of the program plan, are thought to be the most effective with the population being served.

Developing and maintaining staff capability is a multifaceted task that, in one sense, touches every area of managerial responsibility. More specifically, however, two elements of this task bear quite specifically on the capability issue. These are: recruiting and selecting workers, and training and staff development.

Recruitment and Selection

Building an effective staff capability must start with selecting employees who have the potential for competently performing the tasks and activities that will be required in the program. Indeed, some would argue that there are no managerial decisions that so vitally influence the ultimate success of a program than the choice of its personnel. Staff development, as we shall see later, is vital to fully developing the capability of front-line staff, but such efforts are likely to be fully successful only when the staff have the basic qualifications necessary to perform the necessary work.

From the managerial perspective, recruitment and selection is basically a process of maximizing the fit between the jobs that must be done and the people who will do them. Let us first describe this process in general terms and then discuss some of the substantive issues that managers frequently contend with in carrying out this task.

The recruitment and selection process consists of several interrelated steps.[78] Any systematic process of selection must begin with a specification of the positions (jobs) to be filled, since these serve as criteria against which applicants will be evaluated. Usually referred to as job descriptions, these statements typically include the duties and responsibilities entailed in a job: the major tasks, activities, and processes involved; key working relationships with superiors, colleagues, and other agencies; the skills needed; and the personal qualifications required. But how are these job descriptions developed? Observation suggests that this is frequently an armchair exercise where the manager simply draws from past experience the advice of colleagues or from a mental image of what he or she anticipates will be necessary to accomplish the work of the program. In some cases this informal process may suffice, but the frequency with which employees can be heard to complain that the job description under which they operate has only the vaguest resemblance to their actual work suggests that job descriptions should be developed with greater care.

Fortunately, there are aides available to assist the manager in developing more refined job descriptions. One such aide is the *Dictionary of Occupational Titles,* published by the U.S. Training and Employment Service, which lists and briefly defines thousands of current job titles in the United States. Though standard classifications like this one are unlikely to provide an exact description of the positions in a given organization, they can be used as a point of departure.[79] Second, in recent years several task banks have been developed, which describe the tasks involved in a large array of social welfare jobs. Perhaps the best known of these is the National Health, Education, and Welfare Task Bank, developed by the Upjohn Institute. This bank describes the tasks associated with a number of jobs in social welfare, the functions and behaviors involved in various tasks, the level of complexity of these functions, and the objects toward which they are addressed (i.e., people, data, or things).[80] The Florida Human Services Task Bank, developed by Austin and his colleagues, also provides a detailed description and analysis of the functions and tasks that are performed in a variety of human services jobs.[81] (See Table 5–2). Third, the *Standards for Social Service Manpower,* published by the National Association of Social Workers, can serve as a guide for determining the functions that should be performed by social workers at several job levels and the qualifications necessary for each.[82]

These and similar classificatory schemes can be quite useful to the manager in conceptualizing the nature of the work to be performed in a program, as well as the qualifications of personnel. However, since programs and services are quite varied, it is likely that the manager will find it necessary to supplement this information. This can be done, variously, by

TABLE 5–2   Components of the Florida Human Services Task Bank

Function	Role	Substantive Areas
Linkage	Broker	Arranging consumer services
	Consumer advocating	Pleading/advocating for individual consumer's interests
Mobilization	Activating	Developing resources and support for consumers and social services
	System advocating	Generating support for service system change, adjustment, modification
Counseling	Counseling	Guiding and advising consumers
	Consulting	Training staff and lay people
Treatment	Rehabilitating	Providing behavior treatment (therapy) to dysfunctioning consumers
	Care giving	Regulating consumer activities; providing medical assistance and physical/medical treatment for consumers; providing daily living care for consumers
Administration	Client programming	Collecting and recording consumer information; planning and authorizing consumer services; evaluating and processing consumer information
	System researching	Collecting, organizing
	Administering	Coordinating administrative matters; planning administrative activities; managing the personnel process; managing and monitoring operational procedures; carrying out support activities

Source: Michael J. Austin, "Defining the Nature of Human Service Work for Personnel System Management," *Administration in Social Work,* 1, No. 1 (Spring, 1977), 38.

visiting other already established programs in the same service area, viewing their job descriptions, observing the work of employees, or interviewing front-line supervisors. The manager might also seek out expert informants who know about the subtleties of service delivery in a particular area and the qualities required of workers dealing with the program's clientele. Systematic job analysis techniques can also be useful in this process: for example, *Functional Job Analysis* and the Position Analysis Questionnaire.[83] In Functional Job Analysis, for example, the jobs of employees are conceptualized in terms of the functions performed in working with data, people, and things. Functions vary in level of complexity, ranging from relatively simple to complex. Thus the purpose of the analysis is to identify the component functions of a job and determine the extent to which each function within a job is oriented to data, people, or things. The graphic Figure 5–4 summarizes functions and the objects to which they are directed. Take the case of a social worker in the emergency room of a hospital. Analysis might reveal that 50 percent of this persons' job involved the functions of *treating* patients and their families, 20 percent *instructing* or *consulting* with interns or medical students regarding the history or social circumstances of patients recently admitted, 10 percent *taking instruction* from other members of the medical team or the social service supervisor, and 20 percent *compiling* information about patients and *analyzing* it for purposes of social assessment. This analysis would lead us to conclude that the emergency room social worker performs functions of moderate com-

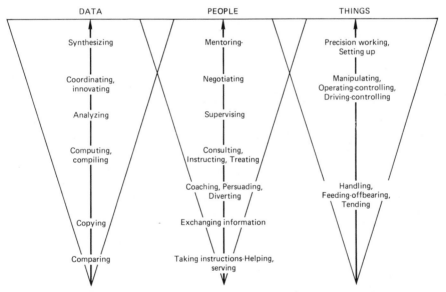

FIGURE 5–4   Summary of worker function scales. Each successive function reading down usually or typically involves all those that follow it. The functions separated by a comma are separate functions on the same level separately defined. They are on the same level because empirical evidence does not make a hierarchical distinction clear. The hyphenated functions: *Taking Instructions-Helping, Operating-Controlling, Driving-Controlling,* and *Feeding-Offbearing* are single functions. *Setting-Up, Operating-Controlling, Driving-Controlling, Feeding-Offbearing,* and *Tending* are special cases involving machines and equipment of *Precision Working, Manipulating,* and *Handling,* respectively, and hence are indented under them. *Source:* Sidney A. Fine and Wretha W. Wiley, *An Introduction to Functional Job Analysis: A Scaling of Selected Tasks from the Social Welfare Field* (Kalamazoo, Mich.: Upjohn Institute for Employment Research, 1971), p. 31.

plexity, 80 percent of which are directly concerned with people and 20 percent of which involve dealing with information. Techniques like Functional Job Analysis might be applied to analyzing the work of program staff in early stages of implementation in order to build more complete and accurate job descriptions for subsequent employees.

Once job descriptions have been formulated, the manager (or the personnel department if it is responsible for recruitment) is in a position to recruit a pool of applicants. Advertising and disseminating information about the available positions may be accomplished in a number of ways including placing notices in newspapers, professional journals and newsletters; notifying employment services; informing professional colleagues who may be in contact with potential applicants; and making visits to universities and professional schools. In order to insure the adequate representation of minorities, women, and other groups in the applicant pool, it is sometimes necessary to target information to specific groups, associations, and publications, at both local and national levels. In many large cities, for example, associations of minority human services workers can assist in this task.

Having recruited a pool of applicants, it is then necessary to obtain information about the candidates. The kind of information to be obtained is a matter of some importance, since it will provide the basis for predictive inferences about the likely success of applicants for the job in question. Generally, three major categories of information are sought: biographical, test, and interview.[84] Biographical information may include educational background, previous employment, and various personal items such as age, sex, and marital status. It may also include letters of reference, which speak to the applicant's aptitude, skill, and past performance. In some cases, particularly in public social agencies operating under civil service or merit systems, applicants may also take paper-and-pencil tests to measure their knowledge or aptitude in areas pertaining to the job. Biographical and test information usually provide the basis for screening the applicant pool and deciding which among them seems best suited for the position. These persons are normally interviewed by either the manager or some independent group such as a civil service commission, and a final determination or recommendation is made regarding the most qualified candidates. Interviews, though considered a useful and even indispensable basis for making personnel decisions, can be subject to a number of biasing influences that have raised some to doubt about their value as predictive indicators.[85] Structuring employment interviews in advance, training interviewers, administering questions uniformly to various applicants, and separating the responsibility for conducting the interview and evaluating the results are some of the measures that have been proposed for improving the utility of this means for assessing job applicants.

Finally, an applicant being offered a position should be given full information regarding the job, salary, fringe benefits, and pertinent personnel policies and procedures so that an informed decision regarding employment with the agency can be made.

Cross-cutting this process of personnel recruitment and selection are several issues that often take on special implications for managers. New programs in established agencies are likely to inherit a well-developed, agencywide personnel system that is a product of public law or a complex of administrative regulations and executive policy. While such personnel systems can provide the new managers with much needed information and direction in their staffing function, they often impose constraints and inflexibility on the recruitment and selection process. One such constraint occurs when the manager attempts to develop a new job classification that has previously not existed in the agency, only to find that the process of acquiring approval involves endless red tape, elaborate justifications, hearings, and the concurrence of personnel boards or civil service commissions. The time required to secure this approval sometimes delays recruitment efforts and may result in the manager's adapting an existing job classification, even though it does not accurately reflect the job that is to be done or the qualifications desired of candidates. The difficulties this can entail in recruitment and selection are obvious.

In those cases where responsibility for the recruitment and screening of personnel is born by a separate personnel department or an independent agency, as is the case in many state and local public jurisdictions, program managers must often deal with delays in the appointment process or, worse yet, with being sent applicants that are not qualified to perform the job.[86]

A recent phenomenon in public social agencies has been the widespread declassification of social service positions, whereby the educational and experiential requirements for entry to a job class have been lowered. For example, positions previously requiring a master's degree in social work and two years' direct practice experience may be redefined so that a bachelor's degree and one year of experience serve as the minimum requirements. Managers can, of course, choose the most qualified persons from the applicant pool, but the lowering of entry qualifications and the concomitant reductions in salary levels will discourage potential applicants who have more than the minimal credentials. To the extent that this trend continues, program managers in public social services may find themselves recruiting from a pool of persons who have only the barest qualifications.

Another issue in recruitment and selection can arise if a new program is launched at a time when the parent agency has placed a freeze on new hires. This can, of course, have serious implications for the manager. If the program represents a significant departure, philosophically or technically, from what has previously existed in the agency, the manager may wish to recruit externally in order to bring in persons whose past experience and current skills are especially attuned to the needs of the innovative venture. In this connection, Hage and Aiken point out the limitations of recruiting among existing agency employees.

> ... if decision makers recruit internally, they are likely to select individuals who may be unaware of the full potentialities of the new program. The longer job occupants remain in an organization, the more they tend to develop a particular, and sometimes limited, point of view that can seriously mitigate the extent of the proposed change....[87]

This should not suggest that internal recruitment is necessarily a bad strategy for new programs. There may be persons in the agency who are well suited to the needs of the program. However, where this is not the case, limitations on external recruitment can pose a severe constraint.

These and related personnel issues can pose especially difficult administrative problems for the program manager. At best they require that the manager spend a good deal of time and energy to effect changes in personnel policies and practices, seek exceptions to policy, or work out informal arrangements. At worst, an inflexible personnel system may require that he or she settle for staff who have insufficient skill, experience, or commitment to the program idea. In either case, the manager is well advised to become intimately familiar with and skilled in dealing with the agency's personnel system so as to mitigate these possibilities.

Staff Development

Staff development is an essential complement to employee selection. However exacting and rigorous the procedures for selecting personnel, however capable the persons finally chosen to fill front-line positions in the program, there will inevitably be some discrepancy between their knowledge and skill and the demands of their jobs. This gap between performance and job requirements does not necessarily reflect on the quality of personnel (though, of course, the less successful the agency in recruiting qualified and capable workers, the wider the gap is likely to be), but rather grows out of the fact that programs and the environments in which they operate are in a relatively constant state of change. These changes, varying in scope and intensity, impose new expectations and require adaptation, learning, and the acquisition of new skills. Fine, for example, has identified several kinds of changes occurring in and around social agencies that are likely to generate the need for new knowledge and skills among staff. These include: changes in policies, procedures, and work routines; the introduction of new technologies; changes in the status of employees; and changes in the expectations of external groups and organizations.[88] One might add to this list other change-inducing factors such as new theories about the etiology of social problems and changes in community values and attitudes. The point is that these events and processes, usually in some interdependent combination, require staff to think and act in different ways. In many instances these transitions are negotiated by workers themselves with little formal assistance. In others, however, the acquisition of new knowledge, skills, or the development of attitudes must be facilitated by the organization. This is the point at which staff development becomes critical.

Though staff development is (or should be) a continuous process throughout a program's history, it is likely to take on special significance during the implementation stage. At no point in a program's history is the ratio of new hires to the total number of employees likely to be higher. At the very least, each new employee must become familiar with the program's objectives, policies, and procedures and attuned to the nuances of group life in the organization. In many instances, particularly where the program is an innovative departure, they will also need to be trained in the use of new techniques. All of this would be difficult enough if the program was well defined and relatively stable; but as we have already indicated, this will seldom be the case. The uncertainty that surrounds engaging a new clientele, developing relations with other agencies and units, and implementing a new service delivery system requires a posture of experimentation, and this is likely to result in rapidly changing demands upon the staff.

There appears to be general agreement that staff development includes those formal activities in agencies that are intended to enhance the role performance of employees in the interest of increasing their contributions to the achievement of organizational or program objectives.[89] The more traditional approach to staff development places primary emphasis on the acquisition of job-relevant knowledge and skills by individual employees; but there is an increasing recognition that staff development may also serve the purpose of improving the quality of the work environment— i.e., by promoting conditions that are conducive to improved performance. Weiner notes this dual purpose:

> Traditionally staff development has been concerned with enhancing staff knowledge and skills. While this remains the primary mission, a secondary purpose involves the use of these activities to foster improved communication and work group cohesion in regard to clinical, case management, and administrative issues.[90]

This expanded concept of staff development recognizes that though it is necessary for employees to have a command of the technical skills required in their work, such skills are often not effectively utilized in a context of poor communication, mistrust, and destructive competition. In short, effective role performance by employees is more than the sum of their individual technical competencies.

Accordingly, we may suggest that staff development can be appropriately addressed to an array of concerns and issues that impact the role performance of employees. These may include, but are not limited to, knowledge and skills specific to a particular job, attitudes toward work and the employing organization, interpersonal relationships between employees, and modifications in administrative policies and practices.

Staff development normally implies (indeed, the name suggests) that the organization intends to change employees in order to improve *their* performance. These efforts may be informed by employee perceptions of performance deficiencies. Still, staff development activities are usually conceived as one-way transfers of information, techniques, or problem-solving skills. Less often are these activities explicitly conceived as an opportunity for the program manager and other administrative personnel to obtain feedback from the front line about policies and practices that may need to be altered. Here the focus is not solely on changing the individual to better perform his or her job, but one of effecting a process of *mutual adjustment* in which both subordinate and superior learn from one another and jointly problem solve.[91] Clearly, if this approach is to be effective, the program manager must make staff development an integral component of the administrative process. Among other things, this may involve assigning definite responsibility for staff development to one or more persons in the program, insuring that such persons have access to the program manager and are involved in program planning, and arranging for the manager's participation in selected training activities.[92] Without effecting these linkages between staff development and administrative decision making, staff development as a mechanism for mutual adjustment is likely to be perceived as game playing by subordinates.

The program administrator's role in staff development is likely to vary with the size and complexity of the parent organization. In large agencies, this function is frequently lodged in a separate department or division that may service a number of programs, including the manager's. In smaller agencies, the program manager often carries overall responsibility for this function, though he or she will usually delegate specific operating responsibility to a subordinate. In either case, the manager should take an active role in the planning and oversight of these activities in order to insure that they are instrumentally related to program purposes and objectives.

There are three principal components to the building of a staff development program: assessment, strategy selection and delivery, and evaluation.[93] *Assessment* involves determining if there is a discrepancy between current and desired future levels of staff performance. There are several aspects to this determination. First, it is necessary to know the extent to which front-line staff are meeting the requirements of their jobs as currently defined. Some ways in which this is done are periodic supervisory evaluations, ongoing management information reports (e.g., caseload trends, number of service units delivered, types of dispositions made, number and types of client complaints, fair hearings requested), and program audits and self-reports from staff. These sources of information provide indicators regarding areas of work that need improvement and may suggest the desirability of staff development efforts.

Another facet of assessment concerns an estimation of the skills that staff are likely to require, given anticipated future changes in the program. Earlier, we commented on several types of change events which, singly or in combination, require the acquisition of new knowledge and skills by employees. The task of the administrator is to anticipate these developments where possible, and determine the nature and extent of the new skills that will be required in order to face them. This "future orientation" to staff needs assessment is cogently expressed by Fine:

> Training needs must grow out of knowing how the system works and what are the basic requirements of present and potential work processes, as well as a sensitive understanding of what workers can and will do under future working conditions. Training needs are generated by an equation which includes on the one hand the predicted future characteristics of the work and the work organization and, on the other hand, the anticipated characteristics of the worker.[94]

More concretely, if the manager foresees the introduction of new services or technologies, a critical part of preparing for these changes is determining whether the staff have the capability necessary to implement them.

Assuming a gap exists between staff performance levels and current or future likely job requirements, it is then necessary to understand the reasons for this discrepancy. It is common to attribute these performance gaps to insufficient skill, knowledge, or motivation of workers. Too seldom are organizational conditions or management processes inspected to determine if the shortfall in performance is due to these factors as well. Are performance standards or job requirements realistic? Are workers given adequate support and direction by their superiors? Are there procedures and policies that impede effective work performance? Do organizational conditions elicit the workers' commitment to program objectives? These and related questions must be asked if performance deficiencies are to be fairly assessed and appropriate staff development strategies chosen. Such an analysis may, indeed, suggest that the problems are better dealt with through means other than staff development.

The second step in formulating an approach to staff development concerns the *selection* and *implementation* of strategy. In order to make an informed choice of strategy it is first necessary to specify the behavioral objectives sought—i.e., what employees should be able to do that they are currently not doing or cannot do. These may range from objectives such as proficiency in operating equipment, or compliance with work routines or regulations, to more complex and difficult-to-define objectives such as the ability to employ certain diagnostic or treatment techniques.

Having specified objectives, one may then examine the alternative staff development strategies available to determine those most likely to be effective and feasible. There are a variety of potential staff development strategies including, for example, formal orientation, staff meetings, case conferences, supervisory guidance and instruction, in-service training, continuing education, and organizational development.[95] Determining which of these is likely to be most effective in achieving the desired behavioral objectives is a complex matter that involves, at the very least, the content to be imparted, the preferences of the workers themselves, their educational backgrounds and learning styles, their personal needs and interests, stages of career development, and so on.[96]

A concomitant concern in selecting a staff development strategy is administrative feasibility. Are there personnel in the organization with the knowledge and skills necessary to implement the strategy selected? If not, are competent consultants available in the community? What are the direct costs (e.g., consultant fees, salary costs, travel, material and equipment costs, and rentals) and indirect costs (e.g., salaries paid workers in attendance, lost time from work) of mounting the staff development effort selected?[97] The most potential effective strategy may not always be feasible, yet experience suggests that staff development activities that are chosen primarily on the basis of low cost and administrative convenience are often not worth doing.

Like any intervention in a complex human process, staff development does not lend itself to easy evaluation. Yet in time of fiscal constraint, when such activities are likely to come under close scrutiny, the evaluation of staff development becomes especially urgent. It is not our purpose here to discuss the various evaluative methodologies that can be employed to assess training.[98] Suffice it to say training should be evaluated at several levels. The first and most common approach to evaluation deals with the knowledge and skills learned, and the attitudes or perceptions that are modified as a result of involvement in the staff development activity. This kind of evaluation seeks to determine whether, and to what extent, the learning or change objectives of the activity (e.g., in-service training) were accomplished. A second level of training evaluation addresses the more difficult question: Was what was learned through staff development subsequently translated into on-the-job behavior? A third level concerns the extent to which changes in work behavior are maintained over time: Do they become, in other words, a stable part of the worker's behavioral repertoire? Or are they transient and diminishing over time? A fourth level focuses on whether changes in work behavior are reflected in improved performance for workers individually and for the program as a whole. This, it will be recalled, brings us full circle to the issue that generates the need for staff development in the first place—i.e., the perceived gap between current and desired work performance.

Because evaluation at each successive level requires more time, resources, and methodological sophistication, it is not too surprising that few assessment efforts ever look beyond the first level. Yet until this kind of research evidence is obtained, administrators will have little basis for systematically determining whether staff development, in fact, impacts performance, how such efforts should be modified, and the administrative conditions needed to sustain behavioral changes. Increasingly, it appears that if staff development is to escape the status of a desirable but dispensable amenity, administrators will have to insist on evaluation as a necessary component of this activity.

SUMMARY

Organizational dynamics at the implementation stage are heavily conditioned by the program's need to establish a clientele and form a system of reciprocal relations with groups and organizations in the environment. At the same time, the addition of staff to carry out service functions often introduces an element of unpredictability into the program's performance and is likely to engender a search for ways to effect greater consistency, coordination, and control. The developmental goals sought during this period revolve around building program competence; defining and securing a service domain; reducing uncertainty in relations with units and organizations whose cooperation and resources are required to effectively implement the program plan; and developing an internal capability for service delivery. Three managerial tasks were thought to be particularly important in moving a program toward these goals: (1) resource acquisition, which involves attracting a clientele and negotiating exchanges with other units and organizations; (2) structuring the organization so as to promote efficiency, coordination, and accountability; and (3) developing and maintaining staff, which at this stage concerns personnel selection and employee development. Each of these tasks was discussed at some length, together with strategies and techniques that might be employed and issues that can arise as they are being carried out.

NOTES

[1]To the extent this has not occurred, program staff are likely to remain embroiled in the design-stage tasks of planning and resource acquisition. A continued preoccupation with these tasks can result in less than adequate attention to the tasks of implementation.

[2]Jerald Hage and Michael Aiken, *Social Change in Complex Organizations* (New York: Random House, 1969), pp. 100–4.

[3]Tony Tripodi, Phillip Fellin, and Irwin Epstein, *Social Program Evaluation* (Itasca, Ill.: F. E. Peacock Publishers, 1971), pp. 31–33.

[4]An example would be a public child-protection services program established under a law which requires that all cases of suspected neglect and abuse be referred to the program.

[5]Anthony Downs, *Inside Bureaucracy* (Boston: Little, Brown, 1967), p. 9.

[6]William Rosengren, "Careers of Clients and Organizations," in *Organizations and Clients,* William Rosengren and Mark Lefton, eds. (Columbus, Ohio: Charles E. Merrill, 1970), pp. 121–22.

[7]*Ibid.,* p. 127.

[8]See William J. Reid, "Interorganizational Coordination in Social Welfare: A Theoretical Approach to Analysis and Intervention," in *Readings in Community Organization Practice,* 2nd ed. Ralph Kramer and Harry Specht, eds. (Englewood Cliffs, N.J.: Prentice-Hall, Inc., 1975), pp. 120–22.

[9]Hage and Aiken, *Social Change,* pp. 100–1.

[10]*Ibid.,* p. 101.

[11]Daniel Katz and Robert L. Kahn, *The Social Psychology of Organizations* (New York: John Wiley & Sons, 1966), pp. 79–80.

[12]Harold H. Weissman, *Integrating Services for Troubled Families* (San Francisco: Jossey-Bass Publishers, 1978), p. 57.

[13]James R. Greenley and Stuart A. Kirk, "Organizational Characteristics of Agencies and the Distribution of Services to Clients," *Journal of Health and Social Behavior,* 14, No. 1 (March, 1973), pp. 70–79. These authors differentiate between *claimed domain,* what an agency says it will do, and *de facto domain,* what it actually does. The claimed domain is likely to have been defined during the design stage. During the implementation stage, programs seek to solidify these claims, though as Greenley and Kirk point out, the services provided are often at some variance with what was originally intended.

[14]Gordon L. Lippitt and Warren H. Schmidt, "Crises in a Developing Organization," *Harvard Business Review,* 45, No. 6 (November-December, 1967), 106.

[15]Yeheskel Hasenfeld, "Organizational Dilemmas in Innovating Social Services: The Case of Community Action Centers," in *Human Service Organizations,* Yeheskel Hasenfeld and Richard A. English, eds. (Ann Arbor, Mich.: University of Michigan Press, 1974), pp. 687–92.

[16]Tripodi, Fellin, and Epstein, *Social Program Evaluation,* p. 32.

[17]This is particularly the case in programs operating under fee-for-service, contract, and vendor arrangements.

[18]Yeheskel Hasenfeld, "Client-Organization Relations: A Systems Perspective," in *The Management of Human Services,* Rosemary C. Saari and Yeheskel Hasenfeld, eds. (New York: Columbia University Press, 1978), p. 195.

[19]Richard Steiner, *Managing the Human Service Organization* (Beverly Hills, Calif.: Sage Publications, 1977), p. 160.

[20]Daniel Katz, Barbara Gutek, Robert L. Kahn, and Eugenia Barton, *Bureaucratic Encounters* (Ann Arbor, Mich.: Institute for Social Research, 1975), pp. 46–47.

[21]See Walter H. Ehlers, Michael J. Austin, and Jon C. Prothero, *Administration for the Human Services* (New York: Harper & Row, 1976), pp. 270–82.

[22]Tripodi, Fellin, and Epstein, *Social Program Evaluation*, pp. 33-35.

[23]Jack Rothman, *Planning and Organizing for Social Change* (New York: Columbia University Press, 1974), pp. 175-78 and 186-87.

[24]*Ibid.*, pp. 372-74.

[25]Marc L. Miringoff, *Management in Human Service Organizations* (New York: Macmillan, 1980), pp. 162-63.

[26]National Conference on Social Welfare, *The Future for Social Services in the United States* (Columbus, Ohio: National Conference on Social Welfare, 1977), p. 16.

[27]*Ibid.*, p. 16.

[28]David F. Gillespie and Susanne E. Marten, "Assessing Service Accessibility," *Administration in Social Work*, 2, No. 2 (Summer, 1978), 183-97.

[29]See Steiner, *Managing the Human Service Organization*, pp. 174-76, for a discussion of techniques for assessing clients' perceptions of service.

[30]Gillespie and Marten, "Assessing Service Accessibility," p. 187.

[31]Harold Lewis, "Management in the Non-Profit Social Service Agency," in *Social Administration*, Simon Slavin, ed. (New York: Haworth Press, 1978), pp. 9-10.

[32]Hasenfeld, "Client-Organization Relations," p. 197.

[33]*Ibid.*, p. 198.

[34]Robert D. Vinter, "The Social Structure of Service," in *Issues in American Social Work*, Alfred J. Kahn, ed. (New York: Columbia University Press, 1959), p. 267.

[35]Hasenfeld, "Client-Organization Relations," p. 199.

[36]For a discussion of how agency characteristics impact service transactions, see Robert D. Vinter, "An Analysis of Treatment Organizations," in *Human Service Organizations*, Yeheskel Hasenfeld and Richard A. English, eds. (Ann Arbor, Mich.: University of Michigan Press, 1974), pp. 40-46.

[37]"Introduction," in *Human Service Organizations*, Hasenfeld and English, eds., p. 540.

[38]See Reid, "Interorganizational Coordination in Social Welfare," pp. 118-28; John E. Tropman, "Conceptual Approaches in Interorganizational Analysis," in *Strategies of Community Organization*, 2nd ed., Fred M. Cox, John L. Erlich, Jack Rothman, and John E. Tropman, eds. (Itasca, Ill.: F. E. Peacock Publishers, 1974), pp. 144-57; and Stephen M. Davidson, "Planning and Coordination of Social Services in Multiorganizational Contexts," *Social Service Review*, 50, No. 1 (March, 1976), 117-37.

[39]Reid, "Interorganizational Coordination in Social Welfare," p. 120.

[40]*Ibid.*, pp. 121-22.

[41]Davidson, "Planning and Coordination, pp. 123-26.

[42]Tropman, "Conceptual Approaches," p. 152.

[43]Weissman, *Integrating Services*, p. 107.

[44]Reid, "Interorganizational Coordination in Social Welfare," p. 122.

[45]Henry Mintzberg, *The Nature of Managerial Work* (New York: Harper & Row, 1973), pp. 63-65.

[46]Simon Slavin, "Concepts of Social Conflict: Use in Social Work Curriculum," in *Social Administration*, Simon Slavin, ed. (New York: Haworth Press, 1978), p. 535.

[47]Tropman, "Conceptual Approaches," pp. 148-50.

[48]Davidson, "Planning and Coordination," p. 129.

[49]Robert W. Wilson and Paul Akana, "Coordination with Intergovernmental and Private Agencies," in *Managing Human Services,* Wayne F. Anderson, Bernard J. Frieden, and Michael J. Murphy, eds. (Washington, D.C.: International City Management Association, 1977), pp. 232-33.

[50]Fremont Kast and James Rosenweig, *Organization and Management: A Systems Approach* (New York: McGraw-Hill, 1970), p. 207.

[51]Michael Aiken and Jerald Hage, "Organizational Alienation: A Comparative Analysis," in *The Sociology of Organizations,* Oscar Grusky and George Miller, eds. (New York: Free Press, 1970), pp. 517-26; Paul Weinberger, "Job Satisfaction and Job Retention in Social Work," in *Perspectives on Social Welfare,* Paul Weinberger, ed. (New York: Macmillan, 1974), pp. 478-79; Joseph Olmstead and Harold Christensen, *Effects of Agency Work Contexts: An Intensive Field Study,* (Washington, D.C.: U.S. Department of Health, Education, and Welfare, 1973), I: 107-25.

[52]Thomas P. Holland, "Organizational Structure and Institutional Care," *Journal of Health and Social Behavior,* 14, No. 3 (September, 1973), 241-51; and Patricia Y. Martin and Brian Segal, "Bureaucracy, Size, and Staff Expectations for Client Independence in Halfway Houses," *Journal of Health and Social Behavior,* 18, No. 4 (December, 1977), 376-90.

[53]Charles S. Glisson and Patricia Y. Martin, "Productivity and Efficiency in Human Service Organizations as Related to Structure, Size, and Age," *Academy of Management Journal,* 23, No. 1 (March, 1980), 21-37.

[54]Christensen and Olmstead, *Effects of Agency Work Contexts,* pp. 117-22.

[55]Hage and Aiken, *Social Change,* pp. 33-38. These authors use the concept "complexity" to designate the degree of occupational specialization and the extent of professionalization that exists.

[56]Stephen P. Robbins, *The Administrative Process,* 2nd ed. (Englewood Cliffs, N.J.: Prentice-Hall, Inc., 1980), pp. 196-98.

[57]Wilbur Finch, "Social Workers Versus Bureaucracy," *Social Work,* 21 No. 5 (September, 1976), 370-75.

[58]See *Ibid.* for a fuller discussion of the problems of specialization.

[59]See Robert Morris, "The Human Services Function and Local Government," in *Managing Human Services,* Wayne F. Anderson, Bernard J. Frieden, and Michael J. Murphy, eds. (Washington, D.C.: International City Management Association, 1977), pp. 29-30.

[60]See, for example, Robert L. Kahn, "The Work Module: A Proposal for the Humanization of Work," in *Work and the Quality of Life,* James O'Toole, ed. (Cambridge, Mass.: MIT Press, 1974), pp. 199-226.

[61]Ayala Pines and Ditsa Kafry, "Occupational Tedium in the Social Services," *Social Work,* 23, No. 6 (November, 1978), 499-507.

[62]Robbins, *Administrative Process,* pp. 204-7.

[63]Donald Maypole, "The Drive for Organizational Differentiation and In-house Politics: An Executive Director's Dilemma," *Administration in Social Work,* 4, No. 4, (Winter, 1980), 83-94.

[64]Steiner, *Managing the Human Service Organization,* pp. 120-23.

[65]*Ibid.,* p. 123.

[66]See Robbins, *Administrative Process,* pp. 223-29, for a discussion of authority.

[67]Hage and Aiken, *Social Change,* pp. 18-21.

[68] *Ibid.*, pp. 21-23.

[69] Even with regard to span of control, the once fashionable tendency to enunciate formulae—e.g., no less than four subordinates, no more than nine—has given way to the recognition that such factors as the nature of the functions performed by subordinates and the complexity of the interactions between them will greatly influence the number of people an administrator can effectively supervise. See Robbins, *Administrative Process*, pp. 200-3.

[70] See Kast and Rosenweig, *Management and Organization*, pp. 507-19.

[71] Charles Perrow, *Organizational Analysis: A Sociological View* (Belmont, Calif.: Brooks-Cole, 1970), pp. 75-91; and Jay R. Galbraith, "Organization Design: An Information Processing View," in *Perspectives on Behavior in Organizations*, J. Richard Hackman, Edward E. Lawler, and Lyman W. Porter, eds. (New York: McGraw-Hill, 1977), pp. 207-14.

[72] Kast and Rosenweig, *Management and Organization*, pp. 507-18; and Wendell L. French and Cecil H. Bell, *Organization Development*, 2nd ed., (Englewood Cliffs, N.J.: Prentice-Hall, Inc., 1978), pp. 185-91.

[73] Hage and Aiken, "Organizational Alienation," pp. 517-26.

[74] Finch, "Social Workers Versus Bureaucracy," pp. 370-75.

[75] Theodore Caplow, *How to Run Any Organization* (Hinsdale, Ill.: Dryden Press, 1976), pp. 26-27.

[76] "Introduction," in Hasenfeld and English, eds., *Human Service Organizations*, pp. 12-14.

[77] Miringoff, *Management*, p. 20.

[78] This discussion draws heavily upon Ehlers, Austin, and Prothero, *Administration*, pp. 162-66. For a more detailed discussion of selection practices, see William C. Howell, *Essentials of Industrial and Organizational Psychology* (Homewood, Ill.: Dorsey Press, 1976), pp. 106-80.

[79] Howell, *Essentials*, pp. 107-8.

[80] Sidney A. Fine and Wretha W. Wiley, *An Introduction to Functional Job Analysis: A Scaling of Selected Tasks from the Social Welfare Field* (Kalamazoo, Mich.: Upjohn Institute for Employment Research, 1971).

[81] Michael J. Austin, "Defining the Nature of Human Service Work for System Management Personnel," *Administration in Social Work*, 1, No. 1 (Spring, 1977), 31-41.

[82] National Association of Social Workers, "Standards for Social Service Manpower," in *Social Administration*, Simon Slavin, ed. (New York: Haworth Press, 1977), pp. 383-95.

[83] See Howell, *Essentials*, pp. 108-17, for a discussion of these instruments.

[84] *Ibid.*, pp. 164-76.

[85] *Ibid.*, p. 165.

[86] Richard P. Shick, Rose W. Boyd, and Barry Bader, "Civil Service Systems: A Short History," in *Managing State and Local Government: Cases and Readings*, Frederick S. Lane, ed. (New York: St. Martin's Press, 1980), pp. 77-78.

[87] Hage and Aiken, *Social Change*, p. 97.

[88] Jean Fine, *Planning and Assessing Agency Training* (Washington, D.C.: U.S. Department of Health, Education, and Welfare, 1979), pp. 41-44.

[89] For example, see *Ibid.*, p. 6; Gertrude Cohen, "Staff Development in Social Work," in *Encyclopedia of Social Work*, John B. Turner, ed. (New York: Na-

tional Association of Social Workers, 1977), II: 1541; Harvey Weiner, "Administrative Responsibility for Staff Development," in *Leadership in Social Administration,* Felice D. Perlmutter and Simon Slavin, eds. (Philadelphia: Temple University Press, 1980), pp. 230–48.

[90]Weiner, "Administrative Responsibility," p. 231.

[91]Howell, *Essentials,* p. 181.

[92]Weiner, "Administrative Responsibility," pp. 232–35.

[93]Howell, *Essentials,* pp. 192–97.

[94]Fine, *Planning and Assessing,* pp. 41–44.

[95]Weiner, "Administrative Responsibility," pp. 236–37; and Ehlers, Austin, and Prothero, *Administration,* pp. 183–89.

[96]Fine, *Planning and Assessing,* p. 45.

[97]*Ibid.,* pp. 102–10.

[98]See Howell, *Essentials,* pp. 192–97.

CHAPTER SIX

Program Management in the Stabilization Stage

The stabilization stage is both an end and a beginning. An end in the sense that it represents the potential realization of what the founders of the program had hoped for, and the staff have sought to achieve; a beginning, because even as the program realizes its potential, both internal and external forces inevitably pose new challenges that require change and renewal.

As in the previous two chapters, we shall first highlight some of the organizational dynamics that are common to programs in the stabilization stage, and the developmental goals the manager seeks to achieve in this context. We will then turn to a consideration of three management tasks which, though not unique to this stage, take on special importance in achieving the developmental goals sought during this period.

STABILIZATION STAGE:
ORGANIZATIONAL CONTEXT

As a program enters the stabilization stage, the matter of its survival is no longer a fundamental issue. By this point, it is likely to have established a steady clientele and a group of past beneficiaries who will serve witness to the need for, and the assistance provided by, the program. The program is also likely to have developed mutually beneficial exchange relationships with selected agencies in the community who will view its continuance as a matter of self-interest. Within the host organization, the initial disequilibrium created by the addition of the new program will usually have subsided as cooperative agreements and other adjustments are made to mesh the program with other units. Funding at or near current levels, while by no means a certainty, is reasonably assured, since the program has by now become a part of the agency's budget base and established a recognized claim to its share of future resources. By the stabilization stage, in short, the program will usually have become institutionalized; it will have become a relatively permanent fixture on the organizational scene.[1]

All this is not to suggest that programs in the stabilization stage have an inviolate sinecure free from demands, pressures, and changes in the environment. Like all organizational entities, programs are open systems inexorably influenced by external forces and conditions. The point is, simply, that the question of survival no longer hangs in the balance. Relations with the environment now increasingly revolve around maintaining the integrity and continuity of the program, adapting to changes, and justifying the need for continued support. We will address each of these matters briefly.

As a program becomes stabilized, it is likely to be near the peak of its performance capability. There are several reasons for this. As a result of trial and error and successive refinements in previous stages, personnel will tend to have developed a fund of experience about the types of clients that can most benefit from the program, the services best suited to meeting their needs, and methods of service delivery. As a result, programs will often focus increasingly on a selected group of clients and engage them in more intense and long-term service relationships.[2] As the program settles, personnel often become more skilled in the performance of their jobs. Roles and responsibilities become more sharply defined so that less time need be devoted to clarifying expectations, coordinating efforts, and attending to routine matters.

Unfortunately, even while a program is becoming more directed and coherent, external events that may have little to do with its intrinsic value sometimes arise and threaten to disrupt this internal equilibrium. These forces are myriad, but some of the more common ones are: changes in organizational leadership, which may result in a deemphasis or withdrawal of support from the program; the enactment of legislation that expands or restricts the program's jurisdiction; funding cutbacks; the emergence of a community crisis (e.g., natural disasters, civil disorder, an influx of immigrants); and attacks by community groups or the media that reflect ideological opposition to the thrust of the program.

These and similar events are neither inherently good nor bad, but they can disrupt program operations and, in the near term at least, result in diminished performance. In some instances programs are improved and ultimately strengthened as they accommodate to these environmental pressures. In many cases, however, major discontinuities can divert energy and resources at precisely the point when the program could otherwise be performing optimally. The following example illustrates one such case.

A county agency administering a program of chore services to the low-income elderly had, after two years of experience, developed procedures that were seemingly effective in recruiting and training chore services workers, linking workers and consumers, and monitoring performance. A survey of recipients indicated an overwhelmingly positive reception of the program and a widespread belief that the services provided were instrumental in helping the frail elderly to remain in their homes rather than become institutionalized.

"Unfortunately," the program proved very popular, and the number of recipients eventually served far exceeded that which had been projected by the state welfare department (the funding agency). Cost overruns in the program, together with an anticipated state budgetary deficit for the biennium, required that the state agency reduce the authorization for chore services from the 2,100 persons served in the county to 1,500. Hereinafter, it was decided by the state department, the chore services would be available only to those income-eligible clients who would require immediate institutionalization if chore services were not available. Among other things, this policy resulted in the county agency serving a more fragile and disabled population than had previously been the case. A number of trained and experienced chore services workers were eventually let go and those that remained had to be given additional training in order to deal with new client problems they were encountering. The reduction of services also produced a sharp negative reaction from the elderly community and over several months required that the program administrator spend considerable time meeting with groups and interpreting the policy changes. The long-term effects of these changes on the program were difficult to calculate, but informed observers felt that they served to undermine much of the capability that had been built in the program's first two years.

External events such as those illustrated in this case example can seldom be controlled by the program manager. Where they occur with regularity over a sustained period, their cumulative impact on staff morale and client service can be devastating. To protect against these effects, program staff often develop mechanisms for buffering and neutralizing outside demands. Delays in implementing changes, superficial compliance with new demands, and selective adoption of new procedures are ways frequently utilized to reduce the disruptive impact of external forces. In some cases, these tactics may help maintain program integrity and continuity. However, when they become generalized responses to any force for change, the program can lose touch with its environment.

Another significant aspect of program-environment interaction during the stabilization phase revolves around the issue of accountability. At the design, and to a greater extent the implementation stage, agency superiors and policy-making and monitoring bodies are concerned with whether the program is being put in place as intended: whether, for example, the anticipated services are being delivered, at what cost, how resources are being deployed, the characteristics of consumers, and so on. At the stabilization stage, however, after the program plan has been implemented, organizational leaders and external evaluators often become increasingly interested in the extent to which program objectives have been achieved. Accordingly, they are likely to press the program for information concerning the extent to which clients served have been benefitted, whether changes in the behavior or social circumstances of consumers have occurred, and whether the costs of effecting these outcomes have been reasonable when compared to other program alternatives.

External demands for evidence of program effectiveness and the evaluations that usually follow may set in motion internal processes that have significant implications for program operations. First, program evaluations (both intramural and extramural) normally require more information than the program has readily available. The new and usually more elaborate forms and statistical reports instituted often have the effect of increasing formalization in the program (see the discussion of this concept in Chapter 5) and the time and energy that must be devoted to complying with and overseeing these new demands. Front-line and supervisory staff, who may already be fully extended, find these burdens a distracting annoyance from their principle duties. Second, evaluations often require that services be administered in a consistent and uniform fashion in order to ascertain the relationship between what is done and the outcomes achieved. Among other things, this may circumscribe the flexibility and discretion of front-line workers and cause resentment over what is perceived as intrusion on professional autonomy.[3] Third, in some situations program staff may disagree with the way in which an evaluation is designed and conducted (e.g., the formulation of objectives, data collection procedures, the ethics of randomization and control), thus placing them in conflict with management or external evaluators. Noncompliance with evaluation procedures, or more active forms of subversion, are not uncommon under these circumstances.[4] Fourth, when program staff perceive that their performance is being evaluated against unrealistically high standards, they may selectively focus on those clients who are most likely to benefit from the services provided in order to insure success: a phenomenon that some have referred to as "creaming."[5]

These and related processes are not only likely to confound evaluative efforts, they may even have troublesome effects on the program itself. Such problems are not inevitable, but the frequency with which they occur suggests the need to be sensitive to the potential tradeoffs between accountability and program performance.

The stabilization stage is usually marked by an increasingly elaborate organizational structure.[6] Roles and procedures are developed to codify past experience, routinize decision making, and assure greater consistency in service delivery. As program staff become more knowledgable about the clientele, additional needs are frequently recognized, and specializations requiring their own kind of expertise arise within the program. Increased specialization, in turn, requires greater attention to monitoring and coordination and a concomitant increase in the number of administrative and supervisory staff devoted to this function.[7] The administrative hierarchy becomes more sharply defined, and the formal authority and prerogatives of actors at each level tend to crystallize.

Unless a program is burdened with a legacy of unresolved problems and issues from previous stages, it should, as we have mentioned earlier, be at the height of its capability. Ideally, the energies of the staff can be more fully directed to the attainment of program objectives, since the issues of survival and development, which required so much attention in previous stages, are no longer of paramount concern. Ironically, however, the very attributes and processes that create this potential for effectiveness also contain the seeds of several disabling organizational conditions.

A stabilized program usually has a cadre of experienced staff who have a substantial investment in current modes of operation. Such persons, who often occupy senior practice or supervisory jobs, have probably been instrumental in promoting and gaining the acceptance of certain innovations, developing operating procedures, and institutionalizing practice technologies. Their "sunk costs" in existing program arrangements are likely to be substantial; and their power, security, and convenience contingent upon maintaining things much as they are.[8] Senior staff often play an important role in defending the program against hasty and ill-conceived changes and thereby help to maintain continuity.[9] At the same time, such persons may resist needed change or effectively undermine it once it is initiated. For programs that operate in a rapidly changing policy environment, this can become a serious problem. Thus the program manager, who may be in no position to avoid the imposition of externally imposed change, is confronted with the delicate task of complying with directives while at the same time dealing with staff resistance in a way that does not undermine the morale and commitment of those who may be among the program's most valued personnel resources. A situation encountered by the author illustrates this dilemma:

Ms. A was hired as the coordinator of the social work program by the director of pupil personnel services in a large, urban public school system. Because of recent budgetary cutbacks, the director was seeking ways in which social workers might be used more effectively. One of her ideas was that social workers might be deployed as consultants to teachers and principals in local schools to help them better understand troubled children and develop both organizational and individual teacher interventions aimed at helping these children. Ms. A had experience with this kind of social work program in a previous job and felt that social workers could have more impact working in this way than in counseling one-to-one with children and their families. Ms. A was hired as the social work program coordinator largely because of her previous experience and commitment to this kind of social work intervention.

Members of the social work staff, most of whom had been in their jobs for some years, seemed initially receptive to Ms. A's proposal for shifting the focus of their efforts in the schools. Staff training was provided on consultation practice and organizational change and development interventions, and a memo sent to the school principals outlining the changes contemplated in social work priorities.

Unfortunately, several months after the change in policy, it became clear to Ms. A that social workers, with few exceptions, continued to devote most of their time to providing individual diagnosis and treatment on cases referred by teachers. As the coordinator discussed this problem with her staff, a variety of reasons were given for why the change in service priorities was not occurring as anticipated. A number of workers attributed the difficulty to the fact that principals and teachers did not understand or recognize the value of this new role for social workers. In order to maintain good working relationships with educational personnel it was necessary, in their view, to "move slowly" in implementing the new policy. It also became clear to the coordinator that some of the staff were not comfortable acting as consultants and organizational change agents. Some complained that a loss of direct involvement with children in the schools would compromise their credibility with teachers. As this pattern of resistance emerged, Ms. A became aware that effecting a change in service priorities in the social work program would be more difficult than she had originally anticipated.

Rules, regulations, job specifications, and performance standards are the hallmark of a stabilized program. Frequently, they constitute the distillation of previous successful experience and represent means for ensuring consistent and predictable program responses to recurrent situations. Among other things, they can help to establish and maintain stable patterns of interaction between staff, staff and clients, superiors and subordinates; they can make expectations explicit and facilitate work flow and coordination. To be sure, these aspects of formal structure are often seen as limiting and cumbersome; but without them ambiguity, frustration, and conflict often occur. Over time, however, several problems can result from these arrangements.

One common tendency is for those in positions of administrative authority to become increasingly preoccupied with maintaining the existing

order.[10] Reliability and consistency, once sought as means to program performance, often become desirable ends in their own right. Administrative
control under these circumstances tends to be equated with effective management, and rewards and sanctions are increasingly applied to promote
compliance with directives and procedures. Though lip service may be
given to the value of employee initiatives and innovative practices, departures from standard operations by subordinates are often seen as disruptive to organizational functioning. It becomes increasingly difficult for
front-line staff to experiment with new methods or to modify established,
but ineffective, practices. The policing and enforcement functions of
superiors necessarily create distance and fear in their relations with subordinates and heighten the awareness of power disparities among program
personnel. Spontaneity and free exchange in these relationships becomes
difficult to maintain, since self-disclosure may bring censure. Accordingly,
the communication flow increasingly proceeds from the top down in the
form of formal directives, rules, and guidelines. Information communicated from the bottom up tends to be restricted to that which is specifically
requested by superiors. Ideas, experiences, and perspectives about how the
program might be improved, especially when such information implies
negative feedback, are likely to be withheld. The quality of the information
made available to administrative personnel under these circumstances suffers.

The net effect of these conditions is to introduce rigidity into the
program. The energy of both direct service and administrative personnel is
directed at conserving what is. The capacity of the program to respond
flexibly to changes in the environment can be severely compromised.

DEVELOPMENTAL GOALS

Having secured a place in the host organization and in the community
service delivery system, a program now enters a period in which the focal
concern is fully utilizing the resources and experience acquired in the
interest of maximizing service objectives. The challenge to the manager is
essentially one that Lippit and Schmidt have called "organizational self-
actualization."[11] Lest one think that achieving developmental goals in the
two previous stages is sufficient for program actualization, we need only
observe the frequency with which programs, seemingly on the threshold of
making a significant social contribution, lose their sense of direction and
commitment to purpose and become consumed with internal maintenance
and self-aggrandizement. The stabilization stage, then, is a time of great
potential; but it is also a time of peril in which much that has been accomplished can be undone. The manager plays a central role in determining
which it will be.

Three developmental goals are critical at this stage. The first is building and maintaining an organizational climate that supports and facilitates the performance of program personnel, particularly those who are directly involved in service delivery. Among other things, this requires working conditions and interpersonal processes that will encourage professional growth and self-renewal, elicit commitment to program policies and objectives, and support creative problem solving. The second developmental goal is the creation of a capacity for program evaluation that will allow for systematic feedback regarding what is being done and with what effects. This capacity is necessary not only to comply with the expectations of external constituents, but to generate information that can inform efforts to improve and refine program capability. The third goal, inextricably related to the first two, is to build a capacity in the program that permits it to deal creatively with internal problems and emerging environmental contingencies and to change accordingly. Programs that are unable to respond to threats and opportunities, or to correct internal deficiencies, ultimately run a serious risk of losing touch with the needs of clients and the expectations of supporters and constituents.

MANAGEMENT TASKS AND ISSUES
IN THE STABILIZATION STAGE

STAFF DEVELOPMENT
AND MAINTENANCE

In Chapter 5 we focused on the recruitment, selection, and training of staff as a critical aspect of the manager's staff development and maintenance task during the implementation stage. This continues to be an important ongoing administrative responsibility (especially in times of high turnover or program expansion); but during the stabilization stage, the staff development and maintenance task takes on additional dimensions and complexity. While previously concerned with the acquisition and training of staff for competent performance, the manager now confronts the challenge of sustaining and renewing that competence over time: of creating a program climate that fosters professional growth and a continuing commitment to service objectives.

The importance of this aspect of staff development, and the unfortunate consequences of failing to address it, are amply demonstrated in a significant number of mature programs whose service potential is never realized because the energies and talents of staff are diverted to unproductive conflict, alienation, and the protection of self-interest. Front-line practitioners are the instruments of service delivery; and their attitudes, feelings, and perceptions of work and the work place are likely, for better or worse, to influence how they carry out their tasks and activities. No work environment is trouble free. The manager cannot realistically expect to maintain a climate that is void of interpersonal strain, tension, and conflict. Still, when these conditions become dominant and persistent features in the work place, they are likely to undermine staff performance. Ultimately, of course, the quality of services to clients tends to decline and program effectiveness suffers.

The managerial task, then, is to create and sustain within the program a work environment that supports and facilitates the service delivery efforts of staff and encourages them to actualize their knowledge and skill in relations with clients. It is necessary to observe at the outset that the manager's actions in this regard will not be the sole determinant of the quality of the work environment. Policies and practices in the host organization, over which the manager will have little control, also constitute an important part of the organizational environment. Inadequate salaries, unclear and inconsistent directives from organizational leaders, funding cutbacks, and strikes are some of the many things that may influence the attitudes and behaviors of staff. The program manager can sometimes mediate the worst effects of these environmental influences, but in the last analysis they will be part of the reality that impinges upon staff.

Having entered this caveat, there are important aspects of the work environment that fall more directly within the program director's purview. It is to these conditions and processes and to the ways that the manager can influence their development that we turn in this section. Before doing so, however, let us be more specific about the criteria for judging whether the capabilities of staff are being fully utilized. Until these criteria are clear there is no way of knowing whether the organizational environment is contributing to the intended effects. Two criteria commonly considered important indicators of staff capability are: performance and satisfaction. We shall discuss each of these concepts in turn.

Performance and Satisfaction

Performance refers to the work behaviors manifested by employees, individually and collectively. Though commonly employed as a global concept describing employee behavior, it is in fact a composite of several distinct and not necessarily related components. Performance may be gauged in terms of *productivity or output,* which in social services is usually expressed as the quantity of services delivered. This may be the number of clients seen, interviews conducted, applications processed, or discharge plans finalized. A second component of performance is *efficiency*. Efficiency, as a measure of performance, can be employed in two ways. The first is the relationship between input (e.g., time and money) and output. The lower the level of input for each unit of output in the program, the more efficient the program. A commonly used index of efficiency is the per unit cost of providing a service. Thus, if two programs are producing comparable service outputs, but one manages to do it for $30 an hour and the other for $45 an hour, the former is more efficient. A second, and more complex measure of efficiency is the relationship between input and service outcome, or *service objectives*.[12] Here, for example, one would be interested in ascertaining the costs entailed in achieving program outcomes, such as the placement or maintenance of the frail elderly in community living arrangements. To the extent that the two programs achieve similar objectives, but one does so using less costly methods, it is more efficient. This measure of efficiency requires, of course, that program objectives be measurable and that their achievement be determined.

A third dimension of performance is the *quality of the services* provided. Programs or individual workers may be productive and cost efficient, but may not be performing the work competently. Quality of work has to do with the extent to which practitioners are competently employing methods, techniques, and procedures that are thought to be most desirable for achieving service objectives. Standards of quality may be derived from previous program experience ("we have found that X works best with our clients"), professional norms ("good professional service requires that . . ."), or formal, empirically based prescriptive models of practice which provide guidelines for interventive activities (e.g., task-centered treatment and behavioral therapy). Thus, if a program's services are based on some explicit model, workers' performance can be assessed against this standard of practice.[13] The quality of work standards are both difficult to operationalize and to apply in assessing performance. In consequence, most programs rely on more global, subjective judgments about the quality of the services provided. Supervisory evaluations are most commonly employed for this purpose, but assessments by peers, and in some instances by clients, are also utilized.[14]

A final measure of performance is *service effectiveness*. Here performance is reflected in the extent to which what the worker does for and with clients is causally related to the achievement of service objectives. With the exception of those few programs that engage in formal program evaluations of an experimental or quasi-experimental nature, this kind of performance evaluation is usually based on impression and self-report, where cause and effect is impossible to ascertain in any rigorous sense. There are, however, some promising innovations in the use of single subject design methodology, which can be employed at relatively low cost to systematically assess the relationship between worker behavior and client outcome.[15] We will address the subject of service effectiveness more fully in the section on assessment later in this chapter.

Quality of service and service effectiveness are clearly the most important measures of performance in social service agencies. Unfortunately, they are also the most difficult, expensive, and time-consuming performance variables to evaluate. As a result, there is a tendency to use productivity and efficiency as surrogates of quality and effectiveness. These dimensions of performance need not be mutually exclusive, but it is clear that they address quite distinct phenomena and should not be used as interchangeable measures of performance.

Job satisfaction, or the attitudes and perceptions employees hold regarding work and the work place, is a second major area of managerial concern. Unlike performance, which refers to behavior and its consequences, measures of satisfaction are based on workers' self-reports of subjective feelings toward various aspects of their jobs and the organizational conditions under which they labor. A number of different instruments are available for tapping employee satisfaction,[16] and a few have been developed or adapted for use in social welfare organizations.[17] Such instruments address varied aspects of the work situation including, for example, employees' feelings regarding job, pay, opportunities for promotion, relations with fellow workers, supervisory practices, participation in decision making, and identification with the organization.

It has been commonly observed in the human services that job satisfaction is a necessary precondition to effective performance ("high morale leads to good performance"). However, increasing evidence suggests that these variables may be independent.[18] That is to say, the fact that a worker is satisfied with the work situation may have little to do with how he or she performs on the job. At the very least, it is now apparent that the relationship between satisfaction and performance is far more complicated than had been supposed. Indeed, some have suggested that if there is a causal connection between these variables, it is performance that affects satisfaction and not the reverse.[19]

If this is so, then why should the manager be concerned with job satisfaction? There are several reasons. First, managers have an ethical responsibility for the emotional health and well-being of subordinates, whether or not this has a demonstrable relationship to performance. However, there are practical reasons as well. Job satisfaction among employees appears to be an important correlate of low absenteeism and may be related to turnover, problems that are disruptive and costly to program operations.[20] Experience would also suggest that pervasive low morale among employees is likely to impair communication, problem solving, and cooperation and give rise to conflict, grievances, and work slowdowns. Ultimately, job dissatisfaction may lead to such undesirable side effects as emotional depletion, alienation, and loss of interest in work and in clients—the so-called "burnout syndrome."[21] The human costs of this for the program and its clientele are incalculable.

Let us return to the central question: what managerial processes and organizational conditions are most conducive to good staff performance and high job satisfaction? There are no simple answers to this question. A number of theoretical perspectives, more or less supported by empirical evidence, have been advanced to explain how performance and satisfaction can be improved; but as yet, no single body of prescriptions is applicable across all types of social welfare organizations under varying circumstances.[22] Nevertheless, some themes emerge from theory and practice that suggest that outlines of an approach to developing and maintaining staff performance and satisfaction. Three areas that seem particularly important in this regard are: the nature of supervisory practices, leadership styles, and working conditions.

Supervisory Practices

Supervisors in social welfare agencies, perhaps to a degree unparalleled in other types of organizations, play a vital role in the development and maintenance of front-line staff. In addition to classic administrative responsibilities such as organizing, monitoring, and evaluating the work of subordinates, supervisors in the social services are also expected to foster professional development through educational supervision and to provide their charges with social and emotional support.[23] The supervisor is at once an administrative superior whose task is to see that subordinates comply with policies, procedures, and management directives; a teacher who is responsible for imparting knowledge and cultivating the professional skills of direct services workers; and a consultant who provides social support to subordinates as they confront an array of vexing and emotionally draining client situations. Given this broad array of responsibilities, it is not surprising that supervisors—in their attitudes, behaviors, and practices— do much to influence the working environment of direct service workers.

One of the most critical aspects of supervisory practice appears to be the amount of flexibility and autonomy allowed supervisees in the conduct of their work. Several studies have shown that subordinates who perceive their supervisors as directive, controlling, and restrictive of initiative and autonomy, tend to be dissatisfied not only with the supervision they receive,[24] but with their jobs and other aspects of the organization as well.[25] For example, one study in sixteen health and welfare agencies found that practitioners who felt they had little decision-making discretion and little ability to administer agency rules and regulations were likely to be dissatisfied with their work and with relations with colleagues and superiors.[26] A similar relationship between supervisory practice, job satisfaction, and performance is reported in a study by Christiansen and Olmstead, in which it was found that workers who perceived their supervisors as supportive, nonpaternalistic, and encouraging of autonomy were likely to be performing more ably and to have more favorable attitudes toward their job situation.[27]

At first glance, this might suggest that workers prefer a style of supervision that is detached and uninvolved, but this is clearly not the case. Rather, it appears that practitioners respond favorably to the opportunity to make practice-related decisions and to initiate ideas and activities that seem responsive to client needs and circumstances, but prefer to do so in the context of a supervisory relationship marked by expert guidance, support, and corrective feedback. Kadushin, in his national survey of social workers concerning their attitudes toward supervision, found that among the principle sources of satisfaction were the opportunity to "share responsibility and obtain support for difficult case decisions from somebody with administrative authority," and to receive help from the supervisor in dealing with "problems in my work with clients."[28] Conversely, practitioners cited lack of critical feedback and insufficient assistance in how to deal with clients as a major source of dissatisfaction with their supervisors.[29] Similarly, Kafry and Pines have found that workers who consistently receive support and feedback from superiors regarding their performance are more likely to have positive attitudes about their jobs than those who do not.[30]

In sum, then, it appears that supervisory practices conducive to worker performance and satisfaction are: the ability to foster independence and initiative among subordinates; to provide technical assistance to workers in order to enhance their knowledge and skills; to provide social support to practitioners to buffer the enervating effects of dealing with emotionally demanding clients; and the ability to give both positive and negative critical feedback in order for the workers to know how well they are performing their jobs.

The delicate balance between elements of supervision is often difficult to maintain, especially during the stabilization stage. In more mature programs there are likely to be a number of rules, procedures, and policies to follow. In their role as administrators, supervisors are responsible for seeing that these directives are complied with. Indeed, sometimes supervisors are evaluated in terms of how well their subordinates carry out agency procedures. It is not uncommon under these circumstances for supervisors to place primary emphasis on monitoring and enforcing the observance of rules, while at the same time discouraging the exercise of discretion and the pursuit of innovative departures by subordinates for fear of the censure this may bring from agency leadership. In the short run, this is a safer, more convenient posture; but over time, it may produce deleterious effects on staff morale and undermine independence and creativity in service delivery. The supervisory strategy outlined above, on the other hand, while requiring more intensive and individualized relationships with subordinates, and introducing a degree of unpredictability in staff performance, seems, nonetheless, more likely to produce satisfaction and professional growth in subordinates. Such a posture clearly places heavy interpersonal demands on supervisors and supervisees alike, inasmuch as it requires frequent two-way communication, mutual problem solving, and the development of trust; but the payoff is likely to make the investment a worthwhile one.

In larger programs the manager is seldom involved in the day-to-day supervision of direct practitioners and must, therefore, rely heavily on front-line supervisors to create and sustain a climate of work that is conducive to good staff performance. Under these circumstances, it is important that the program manager attend to his or her relationship with the supervisory staff, because what occurs in this context is likely to be reflected, for better or worse, in the kind of supervisory practices they utilize. Relatively little attention has been given to the supervision of supervisors,[31] but it appears that many of the characteristics of effective supervision with front-line staff apply to relations between the program manager and supervisor as well. In particular, if the program manager encourages autonomy and initiative, provides expert guidance, support, and feedback, and establishes an expectation that problems will be mutually addressed, supervisors may employ similar behaviors in their relations with subordinates.

Leadership and Decision-Making Styles

Participatory management and democratic processes have long been an article of faith in social welfare administration. Stein,[32] Schatz,[33] and Trecker,[34] among others, have emphasized the importance of involving staff in decisions that affect their work, especially where staff have expertise and information relevant to the decision at hand. Drawing largely from the ideology and research of the human relations school, writers on administration and social welfare have broad claims for the efficacy of participative management.

> Participatory management implies that staff will have a voice and a vote in those management decisions that affect their work. Employees who participate in this management style feel more highly motivated and tend to incorporate the organization's goals more readily than employees working in . . . organizations that are autocratic or consultative in nature. Participatory management encourages people to stay in the organization and to improve their performance.[35]

Although the effects of leadership may not be so uniform nor so direct as suggested in this quote, it does, nevertheless, appear to have a significant influence on worker performance and job satisfaction. Before examining the relationship between leadership style and indices of staff performance and job satisfaction, we should first define this aspect of management practice more explicitly.

Managerial behavior with regard to subordinate participation in decision making can be viewed on a continuum ranging from unilateral action (with little or no input from or consultation with subordinates) to the delegation of decision-making authority within broadly prescribed boundaries.[36] This continuum is graphically portrayed in Figure 6-1.

For the purposes of discussion, we shall refer to leadership that falls on the left-hand side of the continuum as *directive* and that on the right hand side as *delegative*. That which corresponds to the middle part of the continuum we shall refer to as *participative*. The program manager who: (1) elicits the ideas, information, and preferences of subordinates in making major administrative decisions; (2) delegates decision-making authority to workers and supervisors in areas where they carry responsibility; and (3) allows practitioners to exercise some discretion in choosing the means for carrying out decisions made at higher levels, is by this definition using a participative form of leadership. A participatory leadership style does not imply abrogation of managerial authority. The program manager retains ultimate authority to reverse or modify decisions made by subordinates and may, in some instances, exercise that prerogative if the interests of clients or those of the program are at stake. Participatory management does not require that all decisions be delegated or that staff be consulted on all matters. In some cases, the decisions to be made are relatively routine. In others, the options are severely constrained so that it does little good to engage in a participatory process. In yet other instances, the manager may be the only one with sufficient information to make an informed choice. Given these contingencies, a manager's leadership style on the continuum is likely to vary with the kind of decision involved, staff capability, and external political constraints. All this is to suggest that style of leadership is

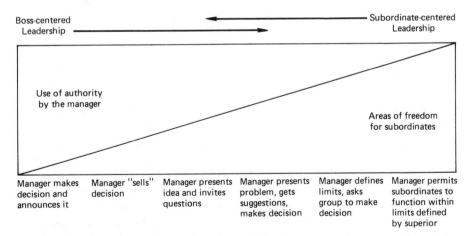

FIGURE 6-1   Continuum of Leadership Behavior. *Source:* R. Tannenbaum and W. H. Schmidt, "How to Choose a Leadership Pattern," *Harvard Business Review*, 1958, pp. 95–101.

likely to be reflected in the modal tendencies of the manager rather than in his or her unerring use of one approach in all decision making situations.

A good deal of evidence suggests that subordinate participation in agency decision making is associated with high job satisfaction. Hage and Aiken's study in sixteen health and welfare organizations, previously cited, examines the relationship between workers' perceptions of how frequently they participate in such decisions as hiring new staff, promotions, and the adoption of new policies and programs, and their satisfaction with work and relations with colleagues and supervisors. Limited opportunities for participation in such agency decisions were found to be significantly related to the dissatisfaction with work and to a lesser extent with negative attitudes toward superiors and colleagues.[37] Other research has shown that workers who have little opportunity to be meaningfully involved in agency decision making are likely to be less satisfied with their jobs.[38]

The relationship between participatory management and worker performance is somewhat less clear. When staff performance is judged in terms of various indices of quality of care or service, evidence suggests that a leader's participatory style and staff performance are positively related. That is, when lower-level staff are given more opportunity to make or participate in administrative decisions regarding such things as program design and personnel assignments, there appear to be concomitant improvements in their work with clients. Holland found, for example, that staff in an institution for the mentally retarded were significantly more individually (as opposed to institutionally) oriented in their resident management practices after the institution was administratively reorganized into decentralized, semiautonomous units, where the staff had greater opportunities to participate in a range of administrative and treatment decisions. Moreover, within each of the decentralized units, the more highly involved the staff were in the planning of resident training programs, the more likely they were to exhibit an individualized orientation in their work with clients.[39]

Research by Martin and Segal, which focused on staff expectations for client independence and self-reliance (a measure of service quality) in twenty-three halfway houses for alcoholics, also lends support to the relationship between leadership style and performance.[40] When the effects of agency size were held constant in this study, workers in halfway houses characterized as more administratively decentralized were found to have higher expectations for client independence and self-reliance. A similar relationship between worker performance and worker participation in administrative decision making has also been observed by Vandervelde in a study of community mental health centers.[41] Here, too, the findings show a strong relationship between worker participation in management decisions and worker effectiveness (as determined by peer and supervisory assessments).

While participatory management appears to be associated with various measures of work quality, there is some evidence that this style may not be particularly conducive to practitioners' productivity.[42] One major study of productivity and efficiency in thirty social welfare organizations in various service fields found that centralization, or the concentration of authority and decision-making power among leaders, had a strong positive correlation with productivity and to a lesser degree with efficiency.[43] In other words, where authority to make decisions was exercised by administrative superiors, productivity increased. Where decisions were broadly shared in an agency, productivity decreased.

It would be premature to conclude from these findings that centralization is the "cause" of productivity and efficiency, but logic and observation suggest that these variables are probably closely linked. Howell's argument is instructive in this regard.

> The participative style is more conducive to creative or innovative solutions and leaves participants more satisfied with the decision that is ultimately reached. However, it does so at the expense of efficiency and, occasionally, the internal harmony of the group. This is because participation is prone to generate more diverse opinions hence more conflict and confusion in the decision-making process—all of which takes more time—than does centralization.[44]

Should one conclude from this that a directive leadership style is preferable in social welfare agencies? Not necessarily. Productivity and efficiency are, of course, desirable performance outcomes; but as we argued earlier, they are neither the only, nor the most important, indicators of performance. Moreover, to the extent that the manager pursues a leadership style calculated to generate productivity, he or she does so at some cost to other areas of staff effectiveness. Glisson and Martin note some of the tradeoffs that may be involved.

> To the extent that high productivity and efficiency require high centralization of authority, however, an important dilemma prevails. As noted by many researchers, a high degree of centralization leads to staff dissatisfaction, a lower quality of client service, and a diminished level of individual worker and organization-level development. . . . Certainly to the extent that a centralized power structure stifles worker experimentation, innovation and openness to change, the chances for discovery of new and better methods appear minimal. The exclusion of professional staff from the decision-making process, . . . is known to result in staff members' adoption of an apathetic orientation toward clients. One is hard pressed, therefore, to make the case that a centralized authority structure contributes to a higher quality of service for clients.[45]

The search for a leadership style that contributes to an optimal mix of satisfaction and quality work, on the one hand, and productivity and efficiency on the other is one of the major challenges to the field of social welfare administration. In the meantime one would hope, existing trends notwithstanding, that productivity and efficiency do not become the sole criteria against which to assess the efficacy of leadership.

Working Conditions

While the interpersonal processes used by managers and supervisors in relating to subordinates are important elements of the organizational climate, so too are the more concrete circumstances under which workers function. For the most part, these aspects of the agency environment have been given little systematic attention in the social welfare administration literature, except insofar as managers are encouraged to provide the resources and amenities that enable practitioners to carry out their duties.

In fact, it appears that these concrete conditions of work may have a significant impact on staff performance and satisfaction. Among the most important of these conditions is the ratio of staff to clients. Some evidence suggests that when workers are responsible for fewer clients the quality of services they provide (as reflected in attitudes toward, and expectations for clients) is better,[46] and the impact of their services on clients greater.[47] Lower caseloads also seem to have a favorable bearing on worker job satisfaction,[48] although one study has indicated that where lower caseloads are accompanied by increased expectations for worker effectiveness, and practitioners lack the skills necessary to meet these standards, satisfaction may decrease.[49] In general, however, it appears that when practitioners are responsible for caseloads that permit them to effectively apply their knowledge and skills, overall quality of service and job satisfaction are likely to increase.

Seemingly mundane aspects of the work situation such as physical space, clerical support, and telephone access also have some impact on front-line practitioners. One study of social workers in public and private child welfare agencies, for example, revealed that practitioners with private office telephones were more satisfied with their jobs than those who did not enjoy these amenities.[50] Since private offices and individual telephones were generally more available in smaller voluntary agencies, it is difficult to know from this study whether these results can be attributed solely to the availability of these resources, but similar findings in at least one other study support the notion that satisfaction may be affected by the adequacy of such physical facilities.[51]

Research by Schwartz and Sample, concerning the comparative effects of experimental work teams and conventional supervisory units in a public assistance setting, also suggests the importance of work conditions for worker satisfaction.[52] Though the primary experimental variable in this study was a team arrangement wherein supervisors and workers shared responsibility for all cases assigned to the unit, an integral component of the experiment was the provision of a unit clerk to relieve workers of repetitive paperwork and telephone interruptions. Moreover, each of the experimental teams was placed in a partitioned office, in contrast to the large, open rooms in which the conventional units operated. One of the findings of this research was that workers in the experimental teams had generally more positive job attitudes than did those in the conventional units. To what extent these differences can be attributed to physical arrangements and clerical support, or to the team form of organization, is not possible to determine, but it seems plausible that the former were at least partly responsible for the outcome observed.

All this would suggest that managers should be attentive to the impact of working conditions on practitioner satisfaction and performance. While the work environment seems most directly affected by the quality of relationships between superiors and subordinates, these tangible conditions are not inconsequential.

In summary, the task of developing a competent, creative, and satisfied staff is accomplished, at least in part, through supportive and technically competent supervision; leadership that allows subordinates a meaningful opportunity to participate in administrative decisions; and working conditions that facilitate the efforts of workers. At the same time, some evidence suggests that if maximizing staff productivity and efficiency are the principle aims of the manager, the administrative approach outlined above may not be the most efficient. This may pose something of a dilemma for the social welfare program manager, but as we have suggested, it is the quality of service to clients and service effectiveness that must ultimately be the manager's principle concern.

THE PROGRAM ASSESSMENT TASK

Assessment may be broadly defined as that managerial task concerned with systematically determining whether program performance meets, exceeds, or falls short of desired standards and objectives. Its primary purpose is to collect and analyze information about program operations and outcomes that may be used by the manager and others for ascertaining whether steps should be taken to alter modes of operation, standards of performance, or both. Assessment, in other words, is a means employed by managers to generate ongoing feedback about program activities and accomplishments so as to determine whether corrective action is necessary.

Information derived from systematic assessment is only one of several factors that may influence managerial decisions and actions. Weirich is quite correct in observing that:

> Decisions are often made on political grounds, for ideological reasons, out of tradition or habit, because of economic feasibility, from personal intuition and bias, or sometimes from simple expediency. Some decisions are never

consciously made: things just seem to happen. Skilled administrators use an informal "intelligence" network as a source of much information . . .[53]

Systematic assessment is neither a sufficient, nor even in some instances a necessary basis for administrative decision making. Still, anyone familiar with the recent history of human services in this country will know that there are strong pressures and inducements for managers to draw upon formal, systematic assessment in making decisions about programs.

Although assessment is primarily a decision-making tool, it serves a variety of other purposes as well. Central among these is enabling the program manager to maintain relationships with superiors and others in the host organization and with groups and agencies in the task environment. Lacking an internal assessment capability makes it difficult, at best, for the manager to demonstrate that the program is in compliance with policies and regulations, to defend budget requests, to respond to critics, and to represent the program's accomplishments. Moreover, assessment plays a vital role in helping to establish and sustain credibility with groups that may affect the flow of resources.

Although assessment is a continuing managerial responsibility throughout the program development cycle, this task takes on special significance during the stabilization phase for several reasons. First, it is only when a program has been refined and elaborated in light of the experience of implementation that the manager is likely to have a clear sense of what can reasonably be expected of his or her unit. The initial program plan should contain criteria against which to assess the early performance of a program; but as we have previously indicated, such plans are likely to be significantly modified throughout the implementation stage. Thus in the early going, the manager is likely to use the feedback obtained to adjust program operations and expectations in light of emerging realities. At some point, however, standards begin to crystallize and the manager must establish baselines (e.g., caseload levels, service units delivered, expenditures) against which to measure program performance. At this juncture, systematic assessment becomes essential.[54]

Second, as programs reach the stabilization stage, their rate of growth in resources and personnel is likely to slacken, even as the demand for services continues to increase. It often happens, therefore, that managers are confronted for the first time with a condition of scarcity in which it is impossible to satisfy the resource needs of all the program's components. Priorities must be established and guidelines developed for deciding among competing demands. Should staff be reassigned from the intake to the treatment unit? Should the size of one program element be reduced so that another can be maintained or expanded? These and related allocative decisions can be made without the benefit of information, but the pressure that surrounds these issues usually requires that the manager be able to justify his or her actions with data. Not uncommonly then, as resources are no longer adequate to satisfy the need for program expansion, managers often intensify their assessment efforts in order to rationalize their choices.

Third, the growing importance of monitoring and evaluation in the stabilization phase is often associated with the temporal nature of accountability systems. For example, some states require that programs or departments be periodically reviewed under the zero-based budget in order to determine whether they should be continued.[55] In yet other instances, programs are funded as demonstrations or special projects under laws that carry a proviso for legislative review after some designated period. Frequently, parent organizations undertake their own reviews of programs in order to provide the board or top-level administrators with an independent determination of whether the program is operating in accordance with agency policy or achieving the objectives set forth in the original authorization. These externally imposed requirements for accountability invariably engender increased, if sometimes reluctant, attention on the part of the manager to assessing program performance.

All this is not to suggest that the assessment task comes into play only during the stabilization phase. Clearly, as Tripodi, Fellin, and Epstein demonstrate, this task is essential in earlier stages as well.[56] Indeed, assessment proves much more difficult in the stabilization stage if the manager has not established such a capability previously. We treat the assessment task in the context of stabilization only because internal dynamics and external constraints are likely to force it upon the manager, personal inclination notwithstanding.

But what of the task itself? How does the manager proceed to assess program performance? There is an extensive literature on program assessment and evaluation, much of which is addressed to the researcher who is attempting to study agency processes or outcomes in order to provide information for administrative or policy decision purposes. Though much of this literature is useful to the manager, it is not our purpose here to focus on the technical aspects of conducting program evaluation research. Our concern, rather, is with assisting the manager to determine the kinds of information that may be needed to support and inform decisions and actions and to choose among the array of tools that are available for generating this intelligence. In this context, we shall focus on how the administrator creates an assessment capability in the program and uses its output, and deal only in passing with the methods and techniques employed to collect and analyze information.[57]

Defined in this way, the program assessment task consists of the following interrelated components.

1. Identifying (anticipating) the kinds of issues, problems, and decisions that are likely to require or create the need for systematic information about program performance.
2. Identifying the nature of the information that will be useful for these purposes.

3. Selecting and implementing the methods to be employed for generating the appropriate information.

We shall take up each of these task components in turn and then conclude with a comment on the manager's role in promoting the utilization of assessment.

Problems, Issues, and Decisions

There is a virtually limitless array of information about program activities, processes, and outcomes that managers might find potentially useful. Clearly, however, in management as in any field of human endeavor, it is unfeasible to obtain all the information one might need, or find useful, to deal with every possible contingency. Doing so would not only impose intolerable costs on the program and divert resources away from its service mission, but also result in an information overload for the manager. Moreover, experience in applied fields like human services, where people are principally concerned with shaping rather than explaining events, shows that information that has no apparent utility for action tends to be information unused. Rothman, for example, in a study of research utilization by agency personnel, found that assessment was considered useful largely to the extent that it was relevant to the work that staff performed. One of his informants captured this perspective in the following comment:

> Information is often presented to us in a way that is too broad, not sufficiently precise or relevant to deal with specific agency problems. It is not practical or related to actions we can take.[58]

Given the need for selectivity and relevance in deciding upon what to assess in a program, it would appear that the manager's first responsibility is to develop a map of future problems, issues, and decisions that are likely to confront the program.[59] Though the map will change with time and circumstance, it can nonetheless serve as a framework for guiding choices about aspects of program performance that should be assessed. Without these guidelines, managers often find themselves in a dependent, reflexive posture regarding what to assess and when.

While issues, problems, and decisions confronting the manager and staff tend to be quite situation specific, there are several predictable types or classes of concern for which systematic information is likely to be needed. In what follows we highlight some of the more important of these, especially as they arise in the stabilization stage of development.

Management control.   *Management control* is a process in which a manager monitors program performance in order to determine whether it is being implemented in accordance with plans and standards, detects significant deviations, and where necessary, takes remedial action.[60]

Like all complex human endeavors, programs are subject to the problems of implementation slippage, error, and distortion; and the manager is inevitably confronted with the responsibility for making adjustments to bring performance into line with expectations, or alternately, for modifying expectations to reflect emerging realities. Remedial action by the manager need not depend on the availability of systematic data, but such information is often critical to good decisions. Indeed, the absence of such information may deprive the manager of cues which suggest that some aspect of the program is not functioning properly.

Management control addresses a wide range of concerns, ranging from relatively minor, short-term operational problems, to those that may require fundamental alteration in the design or purpose of the program. The former might include overexpenditures in one or more budget categories, temporary decreases in staff productivity, indications that two or more program subunits are not adequately coordinating their efforts, and worker noncompliance with agency rules and regulations. Problems of a more significant nature might be reflected in evidence that the program is not serving the intended target population, that client demand for service is decreasing, that available resources are insufficient to sustain the use of a kind of technology, that the quality of service delivered by the program has declined, or that service objectives are not being achieved.

In these and many other performance areas, assessment is vital to the management control process, either to determine that the program is not being implemented in accordance with expectations or for detecting where discrepancies are occurring.

Feedback. Assessment is too often conceived of solely as an instrument for management control. Though this is one of its main purposes, assessment can also be used to provide feedback to subordinates for their development and improvement. Information provided to workers about their practice can be an aid in self-evaluation, educational planning, and personnel deployment. Such feedback can also help to focus supervisor-worker relations by identifying specific areas in which new knowledge or skills might be developed. This, as we saw earlier, is an important aspect of supervisory practice. For example, information regarding the number of court petitions filed by protective services workers may reveal that some workers are having difficulty in dealing with resistive, hostile parents. Data indicating a lack of turnover in case loads, may suggest that workers need some assistance in setting realistic objectives with clients and with terminating relationships when these objectives have been achieved. This kind of feedback can be most useful to workers and their supervisors in dealing with professional development.

Innovation. Assessment can also be useful for stimulating innovations or improvements in services. Information regarding the changing characteristics of clients seeking service, evidence regarding the effectiveness of one technology as compared to another, data concerning unmet needs—these and other products of assessment may stimulate a search for alternative modes of service delivery. For example, data indicating that relatively few foster children are returned to their natural parents, or the average length of placement is steadily increasing, may suggest the need for a case review or permanency-planning mechanism. One youth service agency which had followed the practice of seeing families in conflict for weekly hour-long sessions over several months changed to a crisis-oriented mode of service involving as much as five to seven hours of intervention per week, when it found that this intensive interventive approach significantly reduced the number of children who required placement outside the home.

Accountability/compliance.   From time to time, superiors in the host organization, as well as external funding and regulatory bodies, will require information to determine if the program is complying with laws, administrative regulations, and procedures, or achieving desired results.[61] Legislative committees, federal, state, and local funding agencies, and accrediting and planning bodies are each likely to have their own routine protocols for collecting information from programs under their jurisdiction. The manager, of course, must be in a position to respond to these requests for information. Data required by the parent organization or external agencies will vary, but at base the manager must usually be in a position to provide information concerning the demographic characteristics of clients, the services provided, and outputs generated by the agency, and program expenditures.

Public relations.   Assessment also enables the manager to represent the accomplishments of the program to the larger community—a process that is crucial for building support, correcting misinformation, and defending against unwarranted criticism. Assessment information is also necessary for annual reports, brochures, press releases, speeches, and similar activities that are intended to convey to various publics what the program has done and is planning to do.

Types of Program Information

The foregoing suggests the kinds of information that should be available to program managers as they deal with a variety of problems and decisions. Let us be more explicit, however. Following Tripodi and others, we suggest that there are three major categories of information about programs.[62]

Program effort. Program effort refers to the extent of consumer participation in a program, the quality and quantity of the activities performed, and the resources utilized by personnel in the interest of achieving program objectives.[63] Stated differently, program effort is reflected in information about what is being done, for whom, when, and at what cost. It is a multifaceted concept that includes, but is not limited to, the following dimensions:

1. The number and characteristics of clients who participate in the program (e.g., age, sex, income level, ethnicity, and family composition).
2. The extent to which the potential target population is actually served by the program. Rossi, Freman, and Wright suggest that target population participation can be viewed in terms of coverage and bias.[64] *Coverage* refers to the percent of the target population that is actually served by the program. *Bias* is the extent to which subgroups in a target population (e.g., black, poor, or elderly) are unequally represented among participants in the program. Estimates of both coverage and bias obviously require information about the parameters of the target population—e.g., how many, where located, and what needs.
3. The service experience of clients or consumers, including, for example, the number and frequency of service contacts, time elapsed between request for service and initial contact, and number of clients who prematurely discontinue service.
4. The activities of program staff in service delivery, including caseload levels, units of service provided (e.g., hours of counseling), types of services provided (e.g., diagnosis, treatment, outreach, referral), methods employed (e.g., group, individual, or family treatment), and time expended.
5. Quality of staff performance, as reflected, for example, in evidence that practitioners are utilizing treatment techniques and processes considered desirable, the extent to which program services are being implemented in accordance with specifications, the extent to which staff are complying with administrative regulations, and reporting requirements.
6. Expenditure and resource utilization, including the amount and rate of expenditures in various budget categories (e.g., personnel, travel, training), the utilization of materials and supplies, and the adequacy of space and equipment.
7. The actual costs incurred by the program in delivering units of service, or costs entailed in subunits or elements of a program.

Program effectiveness. Unlike program effort, which is concerned with the inputs and processes employed to achieve objectives, *program effectiveness* focuses on the extent to which objectives themselves are achieved, and whether such outcomes can reasonably be attributed to the interventions applied.[65] Effectiveness, in other words, considers the relationships between the services provided and the outcomes, or results, achieved.

Indicators of program effectiveness might be derived from the following kinds of information:

1. The extent to which program objectives have been achieved, including, for example, whether changes in client behavior, skill, attitude, or status that were expected to occur as a result of program interventions have, in fact, occurred. Client satisfaction with services received are also sometimes used as indicators of program effectiveness.

2. The extent to which treatment or service objectives established for individual clients have been attained. These are outcomes particularized to each case and are generally more specific than program-wide objectives. For example, the latter may focus on the reduction of recidivism among all delinquents served in a program, while individual treatment objectives might be targeted at the acquisition of certain social skills or a reduction in parent-child conflict for specific cases.

3. The variable effects of different kinds or levels of service on subgroups of clients. Such comparisons might involve the relative success of two methods of treatment—e.g., behavioral vs. milieu—or the same method applied for varying periods of time to two comparable groups in an institution for delinquents.

4. The differential impact of services on clients with different characteristics. A uniformly administered service, such as job counseling, may prove to be more effective with some clients (e.g., those with prior employment history) than others.

5. The comparison of outcomes for clients exposed to a program, with those for similar persons in the target population who have received no services.

Earlier in this chapter we noted two different uses of the term *efficiency*. The first and most common measure is the relationship between inputs and outputs. The second is "concerned with the costs and resources of obtaining program objectives; specifically, with the ratio of services extended to results produced."[66] In both cases, resources refer to such things as personnel, time, money, materials, and equipment. Information regarding efficiency may include, but is not limited to, the following:

1. The costs associated with units of program output (e.g., placing a child in a foster home, or delivering a treatment interview).

2. The costs entailed in achieving program objectives, with specific information regarding the component costs attributable to personnel, material, or equipment.

3. The relative costs of different services or approaches used in achieving the same outcomes (e.g., the comparative costs of chore and homemaker services in preventing institutionalization of the elderly).

4. The expenditures entailed in delivering a program compared to the monetary nature of the benefits realized (e.g., the costs of a training program for welfare clients in relation to the savings achieved as a result of reduced welfare benefits).

An assessment of input-output efficiency requires information about program effort. Input-outcome efficiency assessment requires, in addition, information about program effectiveness. If outcome data for clients are not available, input-outcome efficiency evaluation is not possible.

Methods of Program Assessment

A variety of methods are utilized to collect and analyze information about program effort, effectiveness, and efficiency. Detailed discussions of these methods are available in the literature and need not be repeated here. Rather, we shall briefly summarize the salient characteristics of several of the most common approaches and then focus attention on selected problems and issues confronted by managers in designing and implementing each.

Management Information Systems. Probably the most important and versatile tool for program assessment is the *management information system* (MIS). Unlike other approaches to assessment, which tend to be episodic and focused on quite specific questions or concerns, the MIS can provide an ongoing, relatively broad-based, timely source of information about program resources, activities, and performance. A good MIS will provide, or permit the acquisition of, information that addresses many of the managerial problems and issues discussed earlier. Perhaps as important, a well-designed and implemented MIS can provide much of the basic information necessary for other methods of assessment that will be discussed below, thereby reducing the cost and effort necessary to produce original data.

Though the management information system is most often employed to assess program effort, it can be used as a vehicle for assessing effectiveness and efficiency as well. In the case of effectiveness, for example, there has been an increasing interest of late in building into MISs measures of client success and satisfaction in order to systematically examine the relationships between levels, types, frequency, and intensity of service and client outcome. The use of technologies like problem-oriented records, goal attainment scaling, and single subject designs, routinely incorporated into the agency record system, should increase the utility of the MIS for effectiveness assessments.[67]

Virtually all agencies generate information about their internal operations. Records are kept of income and expenditures; case recordings are maintained to reflect something of treatment processes and client progress; periodic reports are submitted to determine caseloads, the types and frequency of services provided and time expended, demographic characteristics of clients, and so on. These and other data sources comprise the management information system. This much will be familiar to all those who have worked in social agencies. In recent years, however, owing largely to the simultaneous escalation of accountability demands placed on agencies and the expansion of information technology, human services organizations have sought to develop more refined and elaborate management information systems.

More advanced management information systems differ from traditional ones in several respects. First, they are characterized by clear and operationalized statements of program objectives, as well as the procedures and activities deemed necessary for the achievement of these objectives. Means-ends relationships in agency operations provide an essential framework for the design and operation of such systems.[68] Second, they tend to be built around decision-making or problem-solving activities of actors at various points in the organization; as key decisions are taken, relevant and timely information is available. This requires an understanding of the decisions that are actually made and the information needs attendant to them.[69] Third, the design and operation of such systems necessitate the use of a standardized language to describe objectives, needs, and activities. Participants in the system must possess a common understanding of the lexicon and adhere to it.[70] Fourth, more advanced systems are computer based—i.e., data generated by the MIS are entered in a computer, which in turn is programmed to perform the desired types of analyses. The use of the computer permits the processing of far more data than is possible in a manual operation, and generally allows for quicker and more sophisticated analyses. See the Appendix for an example of a reporting form that generates service data for computerized information systems.

A well-designed, well-implemented management information system can be an enormously useful—some would say indispensable—aid to the manager in conducting the program assessment task. Among the potential advantages it affords are: access to reasonably comprehensive and systematic data about various aspects of program operations, an improved capability to objectively assess program performance, somewhat greater flexibility in retrieving and analyzing information requested by external organizations, and an enhanced opportunity for rationalizing program decisions. For subordinates, the MIS potentially increases the availability of timely feedback about performance. Under the best of circumstances, such a system can also help to reduce ambiguity about work requirements and procedures.

Despite the potential advantages and the successful application of this technology in a number of social agencies,[71] there remain a number of impediments to its widespread adoption in social welfare.[72] Perhaps the most vexing of these obstacles is the conflict between the assumptions and requirements implicit in MISs and the norms and values that permeate most social agencies. Weirich, for example, has observed that many efforts to introduce information systems come a cropper of the fact that they tend to increase and consolidate the power and control of managers at the expense of subordinates. To the extent that practitioners perceive the introduction of an MIS as an infringement on professional autonomy and discretion, managers often find it difficult to obtain the cooperation needed.[73] Other problems with MISs entail the resistance of front-line workers to the imposition of forms, procedures, and rules that accompany the introduction of MISs, the accountability requirements,[74] and the potential misuses of client information stored in a central facility over which the practitioner has no control.

An equally difficult issue for program managers is cost. "Most social service administrators will realize," notes Weirich, "that an information system requires new resources, but some may not realize just how extensive."[75] Among the costs may be the hiring of external consultants to assist in the design of the system, the lease or purchase of a computer or computer time, personnel to operate and update the system, and the orientation and training of staff in the use of new procedures. Some of this work can be contracted out, but unless the manager has an understanding of what is required, there is a risk of losing control over the nature of the system developed.[76] The benefits of an MIS may justify these costs, but managers should be sensitive to the degree to which the additional investment in management information, in fact, produces a direct or indirect benefit to service delivery. Observation suggests this equation is sometimes not kept in mind; that the quest for more information becomes an end in itself, quite divorced from the program's substantive purposes. All this is to suggest that the manager who is attempting to augment the information capability of a program should be concerned as much with the impact of this technology on the organization as with the technical design and implementation of the system itself.

Outcome evaluations.   *Outcome evaluation* is a process aimed at determining if a program is achieving its objectives and whether such results can be reasonably attributed to the services or interventions provided. It is an approach to assessment basically concerned with ascertaining ". . . whether or not a program has produced more of an effect than would have occurred naturally; that is, either without the intervention or compared with alternative interventions."[77]

Outcome evaluation is specifically well suited for addressing the kinds of questions noted earlier in our discussion of program effectiveness. The results of such studies can be useful for a variety of management purposes, but especially as a basis for deciding upon changes in the program—e.g., whether objectives should be modified, services eliminated or continued, innovations adopted. Increasingly, in a time of economic scarcity, outcome evaluations are also necessary in order to satisfy the expectations of parent organizations or external policy and funding groups that are in the process of making allocative decisions.

Outcome evaluations can take many forms, ranging from those based largely on subjective judgments of program success tendered by clients and staff, to those that are derived from rigorous experimental or quasi-experimental investigations. Examples of the former might include:

follow-up studies of clients after they have completed a course of treatment to determine the extent to which the anticipated benefits of participation in the program were in fact achieved; client surveys, where respondents themselves indicate whether or not they benefitted from the program; and audits conducted by external experts who, based on interviews, analyses of documents and observations, render some judgment on the effectiveness of the program.[78] An example of the latter might be an experimental study, where a probability sample of the target population is selected and randomly assigned to experimental (the group that receives the program's services) and control (the group that receives no service) conditions. Both experimental and control subjects are compared in terms of the outcome variable before services are initiated and after they have been completed. Because of the difficulty of conducting truly experimental studies in human service agencies, an approximation referred to as a *quasi-experimental design* is often employed. One common form of this type of evaluation is the random assignment of new clients in the program to different treatment conditions, such that one group receives those services which are thought to maximize the likelihood of the intended outcomes, while the other receives a less intense, modified, or delayed version of the intervention. Quasi-experimental designs using *constructed controls* (i.e., persons who have had no contact with the program but who are otherwise quite similar in critical respects to those who have) are also sometimes employed so as to compare treated and untreated groups in terms of the desired outcomes. Finally, a quasi-experimental study sometimes uses the clientele of a program as their own controls. Referred to as *reflexive controls,* such clients are measured on the outcome variable before they begin the program and at periodic intervals thereafter to detect changes that are concomitant with the provision of service.[79]

The manager who wishes to undertake an outcome evaluation must determine which of these approaches to utilize. Several factors are likely to play an important part in this determination: time, cost, available expertise, and need for precision. Time is often a critical determinant of choice. Frequently the program manager has little time to plan and implement an outcome evaluation. Decisions made in the parent organization, or by an external funding body, may prompt the need for such an evaluation and yet constrain the dimensions of that undertaking. Under these conditions, the manager may find it necessary to initiate somewhat less rigorous forms of outcome evaluation, realizing that the results may be vulnerable to criticism as a result, or that he or she may find them less useful as a basis for decision making.

The costs of undertaking more rigorous forms of evaluation may also influence choice in this matter. The more rigorous the evaluation, the more the manager is likely to rely on external experts for an analysis of a program's effectiveness. Especially in the case of programs with small budgets, the expense associated with more rigorous evaluations may not be justified, or may so detract from resources for basic program maintenance as to be contraindicated.

As is the case with management information systems, the availability of expertise within the program, or in the parent organization, may determine the magnitude and complexity of the evaluation undertaken. The conduct of experimental or quasi-experimental evaluations ordinarily requires the expertise of a qualified social researcher. Lacking access to such persons, the program manager may find it prudent to utilize less rigorous techniques of evaluation.

The superiority of experimental and quasi-experimental approaches is largely a function of their power to discern whether outcomes experienced by clients can reasonably be attributed to the services provided by the program. Moreover, the more rigorous the techniques, the greater the likelihood that the program's contribution to any changes achieved can be separated from other extraneous influences that may also be contributing to these outcomes.[80] Where it is necessary for the manager to make such precise statements about program effectiveness—where, in short, the stakes for clients, or for program continuation or credibility, are sufficiently high—rigorous forms of evaluation may be indicated.

Efficiency evaluation. The evaluation of efficiency is broadly concerned with determining the costs entailed in generating program outputs or achieving program outcomes.[81] The relationship between costs and results rests at the center of efficiency evaluation. While information about program efforts and program effectiveness is essential to a variety of managerial decisions, it is often not sufficient. The manager must, as well, be concerned with the resources consumed in the delivery of services, the comparative costs of treatment approaches aimed at effecting similar outcomes, and whether the outcomes of a program are justified by the costs incurred. In a day of relatively fixed budgets, it is not necessarily enough that services be well implemented or even that they be effective. Legislative bodies, the larger public, and host organizations are increasingly concerned with how to maintain or increase effort and effectiveness at constant or lower expenditure levels. The manager, of course, is concerned with how to make the most of the resources available. Various forms of efficiency evaluation are essential to decisions of these kinds.

There are three common approaches to efficiency evaluation.[82] *Cost accounting* is concerned with determining the resources required to perform services and supportive activities that ultimately result in program outputs. For example, a cost accounting system would enable a program to ascertain how much it costs to place a child in a foster home, or to complete diagnostic workups for patients in a mental health center. It should be able, moreover, to assess the elements of cost in producing a unit of output, so that those associated with different activities contributing to output can be determined.

Benefit-cost analysis focuses on the relationship between the costs of a program and the outcomes it produces, usually expressed in monetary terms. As in cost accounting, the costs of a program are determined. Outcomes are measured and, where possible, converted to monetary equivalence. For example, a reduced rate of recidivism among delinquents served by a program could be converted to dollar savings that might otherwise have gone toward apprehension, court processing, institutional care, and damage to property or persons. Once derived, these economic benefits are compared to program costs to produce a benefit-cost ratio. The higher the ratio of benefits to costs, the more efficient the program. Figure 6-2 illustrates how costs and benefits associated with a social service program might be conceptualized.

While the logic of benefit-cost analysis is relatively straightforward there are a number of problems encountered when applying it to most social service programs. The one most commonly observed is that the out-

---

Upward Bound was a program of remedial education at the high school level developed in the 1960s. The purpose was to identify high-potential disadvantaged youths who would not be likely to go to college and to provide them with special college preparatory education. Data from a large evaluation of students who had entered the program over a number of years were available which also included information on older siblings of the respondents who had not participated. From the point of view of the participants, the benefits and costs were defined as follows:

Benefits
1. Increased after-tax filetime incomes, measured on the basis of expected ultimate educational attainment of participants and the control group.
2. Stipends paid to participants during the program.
3. Increase in scholarships and college attendance grants to Upward Bound students.

Costs
1. Additional tuition costs required of Upward Bound students because of higher rates of college attendance.
2. Additional expenses of Upward Bound students while in college.
3. Earnings foregone by Upward Bound students while in college.
4. Transfer income over the lifetime foregone by Upward Bound students (e.g., unemployment and welfare).

FIGURE 6-2   List of costs and benefits for the Upward Bound evaluation. *Source:* Peter H. Rossi, Howard E. Freeman, and Sonia R. Wright. *Evaluation: A Systematic Approach* (Beverly Hills, Calif.: Sage Publications, 1979), p. 252. Adapted from W. I. Garms, "A Benefit Costs Analysis of the Upward Bound Program," Journal of Human Resources, 5 (Spring 1971).

comes of social agencies are often difficult to convert to monetary values. For example, what is the monetary value of improved parenting skills, the resolution of marital conflict, or the reduction of inappropriate behavior in the school room? Though each of these outcomes might ultimately be reflected in economic indicators, the assumptions that must be made in order to make this conversion are likely to be tenuous at best.[83] Given these problems, it is not surprising that the most extensive use of benefit-cost analysis has been with programs that produce quite tangible outcomes with fairly obvious economic implications such as vocational rehabilitation and family planning.

Another conceptual problem encountered in benefit-cost analysis is the matter of deciding whose perspective to utilize in calculating costs and benefits. There are at least three points of view that can be taken: costs and benefits to the individual who participates in the program; to the government or agency which conducts the program; and to the community or society. Analyses done from each of these perspectives, as Rossi points out, are likely to yield somewhat different benefit-cost ratios.[84] Lumping costs incurred or benefits achieved from each of these perspectives into a single benefit-cost ratio can be confusing and misleading. For example, in a particular program, one of the benefits derived for individual participants might be an increased utilization of services like subsidized housing or welfare benefits. From the perspective of the community, however, these benefits would be defined largely as costs.

Benefit-cost analysis can also be complicated by the difficulty involved in identifying and calculating the secondary costs of programs. Training clients and placing them in gainful employment produces first-order benefits for the individual and presumably for the society. But if, as a result of a program's success in this regard, people already in the job market are displaced and themselves require assistance from governmental services, the net benefit to the community may be much reduced.[85]

The problems associated with benefit-cost analysis have led to an increased interest in a third form of efficiency evaluation, referred to as *cost-outcome,* or *cost-effectiveness, analysis.* A variant of benefit-cost analysis, this approach does not attempt to convert outcomes to monetary equivalents. Instead, programs with common objectives are compared in terms of the costs incurred by each in reaching these objectives. Stated differently, cost-effectiveness is concerned with determining which programs or program strategies produce the greatest results (in relation to their common objective) at the lowest cost.[86] Thus, in a program aimed at reducing the delinquency rate among youths served, the manager might compare the outcomes obtained by two treatment strategies (e.g., individual and group therapy), calculate the costs of delivering these strategies, and determine which produces the most favorable cost-outcome ratio.

Although cost-outcome analysis may be less complex than cost-benefit analysis, the conduct of either is likely to require the expertise of accountants and evaluation researchers with skills and experience in these forms of efficiency evaluation. Perhaps, most importantly, in order to effectively implement these analytic approaches and exploit the potential contribution of external experts, the manager and staff must first establish an internal management information and outcome evaluation capability. This is the foundation upon which efficiency evaluation must be based.

A Note on the Utilization of Assessment

Despite an increased emphasis on assessment as an integral part of program operation, and the tendency to devote more and more program resources to this task, ample evidence suggests that the information generated is often underutilized by managers and their staffs. In recent years, prompted by a concern about the unwillingness or inability of program operatives to make use of assessment, researchers have begun to pay greater attention to the organizational context in which inquiries are conducted, including the needs and values of potential users, the timeliness and usability of the research produced, and improved methods of disseminating information.[87] This is a worthwhile development which should help to create a greater receptivity to, and use of, assessment results by program staff.

At the same time, it is becoming increasingly clear that promoting utilization is not solely the responsibility of researchers. Managers also play an important role in the utilization process by creating organizational conditions that foster appreciation of systematically derived information. Perhaps most important in this regard are the attitudes and behaviors of the managers themselves. Rothman has found that managers who are effective in promoting utilization tend to model self-examination and openness to criticism, place continual stress on finding ways to improve client service, value the acquisition of knowledge to improve performance, involve staff in the consideration of problems facing the agency, and encourage staff participation in decision making.[88]

The manager's posture toward researchers and other specialists directly involved in program assessment is also an important variable in promoting utilization. Public expressions of support for the research function, the provision of personal support to researchers to help offset the marginality that is often associated with this role, efforts to involve specialists in the mainstream of administrative activity and to encourage their ongoing contact with line staff, are critical to facilitating interaction and cooperation between researchers and program operatives.[89]

Finally, some evidence suggests that when information derived from assessment is routinely utilized by managers to evaluate staff performance, reward achievements, and plan for staff development and training, it is likely to have a significant impact on program performance.[90]

In sum, then, the manager is a central actor in the utilization process. He or she must be actively involved in designing and overseeing assessment activities and utilizing the output. The manager who thinks of assessment as something that is done to the program, rather than for it, is likely to find that even the best evaluations are a burden rather than a source of help in the administrative process.

THE CHANGE TASK

The *change task* involves those planned efforts initiated by managers to improve the effectiveness or efficiency of program operations and to increase the satisfaction of those who participate in the program.[91] In addition, managers may find it necessary to change aspects of their programs in order to accommodate the mandates of organizational superiors or external policy and funding bodies. These change efforts may have little to do with program effectiveness, efficiency, or the satisfaction of program participants, but they are important nonetheless.

In one sense it is difficult to disentangle the change task from other managerial tasks that have been discussed in this book. The development of programs is intrinsically a process of change. In this sense, virtually all that the manager does in building, elaborating, refining, and strengthening a program may be thought of as change. In the discussion that follows, however, we shall adapt a somewhat narrower definition. Here we will be concerned with what the manager does to alter or eliminate relatively stable arrangements or conditions that for some reason are considered undesirable, or in need of improvement. The objective of the manager's change effort in this context is to reduce the discrepancy between what currently exists in the program and what he or she or others believe should be.[92]

Defined in this way, the change task becomes particularly salient during the stabilization stage. Although programs may reach the height of their capability during this period, it often happens, as we have previously noted, that internal processes emerge which lead to program rigidity and unresponsiveness. The accretion of past experience, the development of rules and regulations, and a hierarchy to enforce them, while having important functions, sometimes lead to secondary undesirable consequences such as an incapacity to deal with novel situations, to acquire and utilize new information, and to adapt to emerging needs and circumstances. In some instances, methods employed in the program, which were once justified in terms of their contribution to the achievement of program objectives, come to serve other purposes such as the maintenance of power, status, and convenience. These negative, unintended consequences of stabilization sometimes undermine the competence that has been so painstakingly built during the developmental cycle. Under these circumstances, the manager's responsibility for effecting change becomes critical to program renewal and revitalization.

Although change efforts are often directed at correcting problems that impair program performance, they need not be restricted to dysfunctional situations. In many instances, managers initiate such efforts in order to augment the capacity of a program that is already functioning quite adequately. Such things as introducing a new service to reach an unserved population, or promoting an innovative treatment approach that shows promise of being more effective than the one currently used, may have less to do with internal problems or deficiencies than with seizing opportunities for improvement. Change, in short, may be directed at correcting pathology, but it may also be in the service of growth and adaptation.

As the foregoing suggests, the stimuli for change can emanate from several sources, external and internal to the program. These days, in particular, managers are confronted with rapidly changing environmental circumstances that stimulate, if not necessitate, the need for program modifications. Some common examples are: changes in public policy or administrative regulations; new court decisions; declining revenues due to budgetary cutbacks; demographic shifts in the population which alter either the character of social problems or the needs of the population in an area; and changing social values.[93] Another kind of environmental force for change is the emergence of new technology. As promising innovations occur in a field, program personnel are likely to assess their potential for strengthening service delivery and organizational relevance. Some recent examples are adoption subsidies and permanency planning in child welfare, chore services for the frail elderly, and community-based day treatment programs for the mentally ill.

Stimuli for change also emerge from within programs. Front-line staff may push for more discretion and autonomy in the performance of their jobs, or request a greater voice in administrative decision making. In some cases, professionals will advocate for modifications in program policies and procedures that they believe impede service delivery efforts or pose hardships for clients. In yet other instances, they will seek authorization to adopt new treatment approaches, or request a reduction in workload so as to permit more intensive or individualized work with clients. These and a variety of other proposals arise from time to time; and where staff can mobilize around an issue and are willing to press their case, they often serve as important catalysts for change.[94]

Finally, managers often independently undertake change in order to correct such problems as low morale, poor communication, interpersonal or interunit conflict, and ineffective coordination.

This litany of internal and external factors suggests the multiple vectors that impinge upon managers and cue their change efforts. In recent years, both the frequency and intensity of these forces has increased. The combination of rapidly evolving technology; political activism; rising expectations on the part of policy makers, consumers and employees; and fiscal constraints has made change a ubiquitous element of the managerial environment. Many in the social services have become concerned about the increasing energy and resources that managers and staff must devote to keeping abreast of and adapting to these developments. Agencies that have little ability to selectively respond to, or mediate these forces, often find themselves in an almost constant posture of change, with attendant discontinuity and disequilibrium. The costs of unrelenting change in terms of lower morale, inefficiency, and reduced effectiveness are familiar to many experienced managers in the public sector in particular. In some instances, of course, programs seek to maintain stability by adopting the appearance of change but resisting its substance. Recalcitrance in the "bureaucracy," a popular scapegoat of politicians, is often no more than a reflection of the efforts of responsible professionals to ward off, or mitigate, the impact of multiple, sometimes irreconcilable, demands for change which, if implemented, would undermine program coherence and direction. This is not to suggest that managers should be indifferent or unresponsive to problems and new developments. Clearly, to do so (if, indeed, this were possible) would be administratively irresponsible. At the same time, recent experience must alert us to the fact that programs subjected to constant changes in policy, procedure, and technology—all of which may be warranted on their face—often pay a severe price in terms of diminished effectiveness and lowered morale. Thus, the manager who would initiate change in a program should take care to balance the anticipated benefits therefrom against the likely costs to program performance.

Dimensions of Change

Change efforts undertaken by managers may be directed at any number of activities, processes, or conditions. They may range from attempts to correct relatively small, inconsequential problems in day-to-day functioning, to those which seek to transform the fundamental nature of a program. Elsewhere the author has suggested that this array of change efforts might be conceptualized in terms of two dimensions: generality and depth.[95]

Generality refers to the scope or pervasiveness of a proposed change—that is, the extent to which the change affects the program's membership. There are three levels of generality.

1. *Individual:* Those change efforts that seek to modify the behaviors or activities of selected individuals. The manager may, for example, attempt to alter the way a receptionist in an intake unit processes applicants, or increase the

frequency of certain behaviors by individual workers—e.g., submitting reports on time.

2. *Subsystem:* Those change efforts that seek to alter the activities or performance of an entire unit or class of program participants—e.g., a supervisory unit, an outstationed office, or all caseworkers. Examples of change efforts would include: attempts to improve communication among employees in a unit, to increase the productivity of a department, or to introduce a new treatment technology to all practitioners in a program.

3. *System:* Those change efforts aimed at modifying some aspect of the entire program that have operational implications for its entire membership. Introducing or revising personnel policies, adopting new program objectives, or changing the reporting system would be examples.

A second dimension of this scheme concerns the *depth* of the change sought. Again, three levels are suggested.

1. *Procedural:* Those proposed changes that seek to alter structural arrangements, rules, and procedures which guide the day-to-day behavior of employees. The objective here is to facilitate the flow of work activities, or utilize resources more efficiently, not to alter the substance or purpose of the services provided. Examples might be: installing different procedures for interdepartmental referral, developing mechanisms to increase communication among staff, or reorganizing a department.

2. *Programmatic:* Those efforts aimed at modifying the services provided by the program. The focal concern is adding to, eliminating, or significantly modifying services so that the program can more effectively accomplish its objectives. Changes at this level may take the form of introducing new treatment modalities, or adding program elements such as an information and referral unit, a day treatment service, or a job placement unit.

3. *Basic:* Those efforts concerned with changing the core objectives of the program. The intent here is to effect a fundamental shift in the character of the program's mission so that it will address itself to a different set of problems and outcomes. Examples might include: attempts to transform a program concerned with the custody of offenders into one committed to rehabilitation, or changing a recreational program to one that is dedicated to the treatment of emotional disorders.

When these variables of generality and depth are related to one another, a classification of managerial change efforts emerges (see, Table 6-1). Each type of change effort will vary in the time and program resources that must be committed in order to achieve the desired result. Further, the different types of change are likely to involve varying degrees of instability and discontinuity for program operations. Finally, each type of change effort may be assessed in terms of likely staff resistance to manager power ratio—i.e., the extent to which the manager is likely to have the power (influence) necessary to overcome barriers to the acceptance and implementation of the change proposal. The estimates noted in each applicable cell in Table 6-1 are only suggestive and may vary considerably from

TABLE 6-1 Types of Change and Implications for Managers

Generality of Change Effort	Depth of Change		
	Procedural	Programmatic	Basic
Individual	Time: little Resources: minimal Disruption: minimal Resistance/power: favorable	NA	NA
Subsystem	Time: little Resources: minimal Disruption: minimal to moderate Resistance/power: favorable	Time: considerable Resources: moderate Disruption: moderate Resistance/power: equal	NA
System	Time: moderate Resources: minimal to moderate Disruption: minimal to moderate Resistance/power: favorable	Time: considerable Resources: considerable Disruption: moderate to extensive Resistance/power: equal to unfavorable	Time: substantial Resources: substantial Disruption: complete Resistance/power: unfavorable

situation to situation. The more important point is that the manager or change agent should be alert to the demands and problems associated with each type of change initiated.

The Change Process

So far we have identified some of the common stimuli for management-initiated change and the types of changes initiated. Let us turn now to the process of change itself. Management change processes have been variously conceptualized, but for purposes of this discussion we shall address three aspects that appear to be implicit in most such formulations: problem analysis, assessment of resistance and receptivity, and strategy selection.[96]

Problem analysis and goal formulation.   The change process begins with the recognition of a problem. A problem exists when the manager, his or her superiors, or authoritative bodies in the task environment identify a gap between what is presently occurring in the program and some desirable state of functioning. Some problems are largely indigenous to the program. For example, levels of output or outcome may be less than anticipated; the rate of employee absenteeism or turnover disrupts operations; workers fail to comply with policies and procedures; interunit coordination suffers from poor communication or conflict; or employee morale declines and leads to uncooperative behavior. Other kinds of problems are mainly exogenous: the budget for the coming fiscal year is significantly reduced, resulting in the need to reallocate resources; a new law is passed that requires the program to modify its policies and procedures; the agency director or board changes priorities so that some services are to be deemphasized in favor of others. In this case, the discrepancy between current and desirable levels of performance is created by externally imposed demands.

Whether the impetus for change is internal or external, the manager must acquire an understanding of those conditions that stand as barriers to reducing the discrepancy between current and desired levels of performance.

There are several approaches to conducting this analysis, which need not be mutually exclusive. The manager may unilaterally define the problem and its causes, drawing upon whatever data is available and personal observations. Where time is of the essence and change must be quickly accomplished, the manager may have little choice but to proceed in this fashion, but there is some risk that other relevant participants may later find this analysis wanting. Moreover, when subordinates have had little or no role in diagnosing the situation at hand, they will often have little investment in implementing the solutions decided upon. The reader may wish to refer back to the case example earlier in this chapter in which the coordinator of a social service program in a public school district had sought to change the service priorities of her program. The resistance she encountered among social workers was probably due, in large part, to the fact that they had little opportunity to participate in the assessment of the problem originally proposed to her by the director of pupil personnel services.

Second, where the problem is of some magnitude and its solution has major ramifications for the program, the manager may resort to a more formal analytic approach to problem analysis. One such approach, *operations analysis,* involves the use of quantitative techniques for understanding and finding solutions to such organizational problems as the optimal allocation of resources, the assignment of personnel, the sequencing and coordinating of activities, improved decision making, and the like. This technique for problem analysis may be particularly useful when the manager requires a very detailed technical understanding of the reasons for inefficiency, low productivity, and poor coordination.[97]

Another formal approach to problem analysis is the *administrative audit.* According to Tripodi, Fellin, and Epstein, the administrative audit

> ... refers to methods used to evaluate the suitability of program policies and practices directed toward compliance with those policies; to evaluate the adherence of staff practices to designated divisions of responsibility and function; and to evaluate the organizational patterns of work. . . .[98]

An example of an administrative audit might be an evaluation conducted by a legislative budget committee to ascertain whether allegations of child abuse in licensed foster homes are true and to determine their incidence. If abuse is found, the auditors may also analyze existing policies and practices to determine why the agency is not more effective in preventing such abuse or detecting it once it has occurred.

Both operations analysis and the administrative audit are likely to require the use of external experts.

A third approach to problem analysis draws principally upon the information and ideas of program participants, especially subordinates. The manager, sometimes with the assistance of an organizational development consultant, engages the staff in a series of meetings and exercises in order to gain a fuller understanding of the problem from various perspectives and to seek some agreement regarding the issues and preferred solutions. This approach to problem analysis seems particularly indicated when the problem is of an interpersonal or intergroup nature and when the subsequent implementation of change requires the full cooperation and commitment of subordinates. It is important to note, however, that staff participation in this step of the change process should grow out of a real conviction that subordinates have useful information about the nature of the problem and its solutions. When participation is used as a means of gaining compliance with the manager's preconceived notions, it is likely to be counterproductive.[99]

These approaches to problem analysis, which may be used in some combination, will normally generate a fuller understanding of the problem and a decision regarding the course of action to follow.

Assessing receptivity and resistance to change.   A critical aspect of the management change task is the assessment of factors that are likely to impede and facilitate the adoption and implementation of solutions to the problem identified. This assessment serves at least three purposes: First, in considering alternative means for solving a problem, the manager and others must consider not only the intrinsic adequacy of the solutions, but their feasibility as well—i.e., the likelihood of adoption and implementation. Frequently, ideas that are optimal in a technical sense simply cannot be implemented because, variously, of the costs, the resistance of subordinates, or undesirable secondary consequences. Thus, an assessment of the forces that weigh for and against the proposed change will aid the manager in deciding whether it is feasible as well as desirable.

Second, a systematic assessment of resistance often provides valuable insights regarding the limitations or defects in the proposal itself. In this connection, Lawrence comments:

> When resistance *does* appear, it should not be thought of as something to be *overcome*. Instead, it can best be thought of as a useful red flag—a signal that something is going wrong. To use a rough analogy, signs of resistance in a social organization are useful as a signal that some bodily functions are getting out of adjustment.[100]

A manager who is enamored of a particular proposal for organizational change may be inclined to treat resistance as an expression of inertia or a commitment to the status quo. Though this may sometimes be an accurate appraisal, Lawrence's comment suggests that resistance may also contain valuable data about the substance of the proposal itself.

Finally, an assessment of receptivity and resistance can provide the manager with important cues about the strategy of change to be employed, including how long it may take, where to focus his or her energy, and the tactics to be utilized.

An analysis of receptivity and resistance must ultimately be particularized to the organizational unit in question, but let us mention several factors that commonly arise in change situations.

1. History.   Subordinates' perceptions of a proposed change are likely to be influenced by past experience. In programs which have undergone frequent change, particularly of the kind that has been unilaterally imposed by superiors or external agencies, one frequently sees a kind of guardedness, even cynicism among subordinates. Employees who have made repeated, good-faith efforts to implement changes in policies, procedures, or technologies, only to have these efforts short-circuited by new leadership or legislation, are quite naturally hesitant to invest in yet another round of change. One common consequence is the tendency for subordinates to engage in a ritual compliance that masks a deeper going reluctance to commit the change. The merits of a proposal notwithstanding, the manager must be sensitive to the effects of history on subordinates' perceptions of and willingness to cooperate with proposals for program modification.

2. Sunk costs.   *Sunk costs* refer to investments of time, energy, and commitment made by employees to develop and sustain an existing arrangement or pattern of behavior. Generally, the greater the sunk costs in some aspects of the program, the more likely, other things being equal, a change in that arrangement will be resisted. For example, a social worker who has spent some years cultivating relationships with the medical staff on a surgical ward of a hospital might be expected to balk at a proposal which calls for rotating social workers among the wards in that organization. Sunk costs are frequently associated with employees' tenure in an organization. That is, the longer persons have worked in a program, the more likely they are to have a personal stake in its existing structure and processes. There are, of course, conditions that counterbalance sunk costs. Changes which promise to enhance employees' status or power, or allow them to take on more challenging or stimulating assignments, may provide sufficient inducements to outweigh sunk costs.[101]

3. Social relationships.   Employees perform their jobs in a context of social relationships which provide status, group identity, and emotional support. Frequently, these relationships with colleagues are so interwoven with the conduct of job performance that alterations in group composition have the effect, at least temporarily, of reducing personal efficacy. Changes that will interrupt accustomed patterns of interaction are often resisted for this reason. Lawrence has observed this in industry.

> ... management actions leading to what we commonly label change are usually initiated outside the small work group by staff people.... By the very nature of their work, most of our staff specialists in industry do not have the ultimate contact with operating groups that allows them to acquire an intuitive understanding of the complex social arrangements which their ideas may affect.... As a result, all too often [they] behave in a way that threatens and disrupts established social relationships. And the tragedy is that so many of these upsets are inadvertent and unnecessary.[102]

Closely related is the resistance that arises when proposed changes collide with established group norms. Such norms evolve informally in work

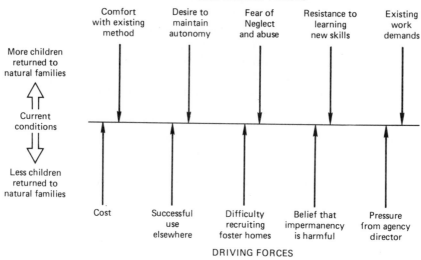

RESTRAINING FORCES

FIGURE 6-3 Force field analysis.

leadership was conceptualized on a continuum. On the one end of the continuum was the centralized, directive style, wherein the manager makes decisions and imposes them on subordinates with the expectations that they will be implemented in accordance with directives. The middle part of the range was characterized as a participative style. The manager here retains the final responsibility for decision making, but relies heavily on the staff to analyze the problem at hand, identify alternatives, and select a course of action. The delegative end of the continuum is one in which the manager defines the parameters of permissible change and the constraints that exist, but otherwise delegates to subordinates authority for problem identification and solution.

Given the range of available styles and strategies, which is likely to be most effective in a change situation? There is no simple answer to this question. Some evidence suggests that change efforts are more likely to be successful when the manager uses a participatory style. For example, Greiner's review of eighteen studies of organizational change indicated that managers who sought the participation of staff in defining the problem and choosing among alternative solutions were more likely to be successful (that is, to achieve the desired result) than those who either imposed the decision or delegated responsibility for it to subordinates.[107]

Increasingly, however, there appears to be agreement among management theorists that the strategy of change selected should depend largely on the prevailing circumstances. A number of situational variables could be considered here, but several seem to be particularly important.

1. The force field. The force field, discussed above, often provides an important clue to the appropriate strategy. If the driving forces in a situation are more powerful than the restraining ones, and especially if these forces come from both within and without the program, a range of styles can be used successfully. The manager's choice in this instance may be determined by a combination of the factors discussed below. However, if the restraining forces outweigh driving forces, the manager will usually find a participative style more effective, since this approach is likely to build understanding and commitment and simultaneously reduce or neutralize resistance.[108]

2. Time. When the program manager is confronted with a problem that requires immediate resolution, a directive style may be the only feasible alternative. For example, crises that pose a danger to clients and require immediate action, or a mandate from a superior that must be implemented in a given period, often leave the manager little option but to act unilaterally, or with minimal input from subordinates. The meaningful involvement of staff in analyzing the problem and weighing alternatives is necessarily time consuming, and under these circumstances it may not be possible to do justice to the participatory process and still accomplish the change required. If the manager has a philosophical preference for participatory change, but urgency or time constraints makes a unilateral approach necessary, it is important that he or she make the reasons for the use of a directive style clear to subordinates.

3. Nature of the problem. In some situations the problem at hand is easily defined and understood and the solutions readily apparent. The manager has sufficient information to make an informed decision. The extensive participation of staff under these circumstances would seem to be both unnecessary and artificial. Conversely, if the problem is ambiguous and good information is lacking, the participation of subordinates with relevant experience and expertise is usually indicated.

4. Experience and expectations of staff. Administrative subordinates will vary in the degree to which they expect to be involved in deciding upon change and how it is to be implemented.[109] If there has been a tradition of participatory management in a program, the use of a directive strategy may be seen as a violation of previously established administrative norms and may provoke anger and distrust. On the other hand, if subordinates have had little previous opportunity to participate in change decisions, if they are accustomed to having change imposed from above, they may be reluctant to assume the risk and responsibility that a participatory strategy requires.[110] Moreover, unless it is clear that the manager intends to promote a new set of norms regarding staff involvement, the sudden adoption of a participatory style may be viewed with suspicion and distrust.

5. The manager's power.   Managers who lack control over rewards and sanctions often find it difficult to impose change on their subordinates. Even when these sources of power are available, the manager who consistently employs a directive change style should probably have the support of superiors. Over time, a style that depends on coercive power to enforce compliance tends to evoke alienation among subordinates and accompanying passive resistance, ritual compliance, and criticism. Managers who lack the support of superiors are likely to become quite vulnerable to staff reprisals under these circumstances.

6. Reliance on staff for implementation.   Where implementation of a change requires the voluntary, informed cooperation of subordinates, a participatory style is usually preferred. Participation tends to build commitment to and ownership of the change. In situations where staff exercise control over their work (i.e., how it is to be done and when), where monitoring of performance and the enforcement of policies and procedures is not practical, the manager must rely on the motivation of participants. There is considerable evidence to suggest that this is the most likely to occur when staff have had a hand in fashioning the change adopted.[111]

In sum, then, the selection of strategy for change should be informed by the manager's consideration of the situational variables. Ultimately, no formula permits precise calculation. The significance a manager attaches to these and other variables will be greatly influenced by his or her philosophy of management, personal characteristics, and long-term goals. Most managers in social welfare give the greatest weight to factors that suggest a participatory style. Still, in the last analysis, the way in which a manager attempts to change an organization, whether it be directive, participative, or delegative, is not an end in itself but only a means. A blind attachment to one or another style of change, for its own sake, often blurs the primary purpose of change—namely, to improve program effectiveness.

SUMMARY

Although programs in the stabilization stage are likely to reach the peak of their potential for effective performance, the actualization of this potential is by no means a fait accompli. Frequently, as we pointed out in this chapter, conditions and processes arise in internal operations or in the program environment that threaten this capability and require that it be redirected.

Three developmental goals take on special importance in this context: (1) the creation of an organizational climate that supports professional growth and self-renewal among program personnel; (2) the development of a capacity for program assessment that generates a continuous source of feedback regarding what s done and with what effect; and (3) an ability to adapt and change in response to problems and emerging realities.

The bulk of this chapter is devoted to the management tasks that must be performed to achieve these developmental goals. The staff maintenance and development task in the stabilization stage is concerned with the kinds of supervisory and leadership practices that are thought to promote staff performance and job satisfaction, as well as concrete working conditions that are conducive to these ends. The assessment task requires that the manager establish systematic procedures for determining if the program is performing in accordance with standards and expectations. Finally, the change task involves the manager in efforts to modify the program in order to enhance its effectiveness or efficiency or the satisfaction of its participants.

NOTES

[1]There are, of course, exceptions to this scenario. A major funding cutback or agency reorganization can threaten the survival of even the most secure programs. Programs that have been supported largely by grant monies often find themselves vulnerable when grants are terminated. Death, curtailment, or absorption by other units of the parent organization are not uncommon under these circumstances. See Chapter 4 for a discussion of the hazards of relying on a grant to start a program.

[2]William Rosengren, "The Careers of Clients and Organizations," in *Organizations and Clients,* William Rosengren and Mark Lefton, eds. (Columbus, Ohio: Charles E. Merrill, 1970), pp. 122-25; and Felice Perlmutter, "A Model of Social Agency Development," *Social Casework,* 50, No. 8 (October, 1969), 471.

[3]Thomas J. Kiresuk and Sander H. Lund, "Program Evaluation and the Management of Organizations," in *Managing Human Services,* Wayne E. Anderson, Bernard J. Frieden, and Michael J. Murphy, eds. (Washington, D.C.: International City Management Association, 1977), pp. 305-6.

[4]George Hoshino, "Social Services: The Problem of Accountability," in *Social Administration,* Simon Slavin, ed. (New York: Haworth Press, 1978), pp. 306-7.

[5]Hoshino, "Social Services," p. 306; and Peter H. Rossi, "Some Issues in the Evaluation of Human Services Delivery," in *The Management of Human Services,* Rosemary C. Saari and Yeheskel Hasenfeld, eds. (New York: Columbia University Press, 1978), p. 243.

[6]Jerald Hage and Michael Aiken, *Social Change in Complex Organizations* (New York: Random House, 1969), pp. 104-6.

[7]Anthony Downs, *Inside Bureaucracy* (Boston: Little, Brown, 1967), pp. 19-20.

[8]*Ibid.,* p. 19.

[9]Donald Klein, "Some Notes on the Dynamics of Resistance to Change: The Defender Role," in *Concepts for Social Change,* Goodwin Watson, ed. (Washington, D.C.: National Training Laboratories, 1967), pp. 26-36.

[10] For a discussion of this and related phenomena, see Peter Blau and Richard Scott, *Formal Organizations* (San Francisco: Chandler Publishing Co., 1962), pp. 228–32.

[11] Gordon L. Lippitt and Warren H. Schmidt, "Crises in a Developing Organization," *Harvard Business Review*, 45, No. 6 (November-December, 1967), 107–8.

[12] Tony Tripodi, Phillip Fellin, and Irwin Epstein, *Social Program Evaluation* (Itasca, Ill.: F. E. Peacock Publishers, 1971), pp. 49–50.

[13] This is similar to what Miringoff has called the worker's *possession of technology*—i.e., the extent to which practitioners are able to effectively implement interventions that, based on theory or empirical evidence, are believed to be able to produce desirable outcomes. Marc L. Miringoff, *Management in Human Service Organizations* (New York: Macmillan, 1980), pp. 20–26.

[14] Kiresuk and Lund, "Program Evaluation," p. 294.

[15] See, for example, Rona Levy and Srinika Jayaratne, *The Clinical-Research Model of Intervention* (New York: Columbia University Press, 1978).

[16] Delbert C. Miller, *Handbook of Research Design and Social Movement*, 3rd ed. (New York: Longmans, 1969).

[17] See, for example, Edward E. Schwartz and William C. Sample, *The Midway Office* (New York: National Association of Social Workers, 1972); and Joseph Olmstead and Harold Christensen, *Effects of Agency Work Contexts: An Intensive Field Study*, Vol. I (Washington, D.C.: U.S. Department of Health, Education, and Welfare, 1973).

[18] William C. Howell, *Essentials of Industrial and Organizational Psychology* (Homewood, Ill.: Dorsey Press, 1976), p. 62–63.

[19] *Ibid.*, p. 62.

[20] Olmstead and Christensen, *Effects of Agency Work Contexts*, pp. 122–25.

[21] Ayala Pines and Ditsa Kafry, "Occupational Tedium in the Social Services," *Social Work*, 23, No. 6 (November, 1978), 499–507.

[22] Part of the problem is that how workers react to organizational conditions and managerial processes is very much affected by individual characteristics such as personal values, past experience, and career aspirations. The same reality is often experienced quite differently by two workers.

[23] Alfred Kadushin, *Supervision in Social Work* (New York: Columbia University Press, 1976), pp. 125–271.

[24] Alfred Kadushin, "Supervisor-Supervisee: A Survey," *Social Work*, 19, No. 3 (May, 1974), 291.

[25] Alice Ullman, Mary Gross, Milton Davis, and Margaret Mushinski, "Activities, Satisfaction, and Problems of Social Workers in Hospital Settings: A Comparative Study," *Social Service Review*, 45, No. 1 (March, 1971), 22–26; and Jerald Hage and Michael Aiken, "Organizational Alienation: A Comparative Analysis," in *The Sociology of Organizations*, Oscar Grusky and George A. Miller, eds. (New York: Free Press, 1970), pp. 517–26.

[26] Hage and Aiken, "Organizational Alienation," pp. 522–25.

[27] Christensen and Olmstead, *Effects of Agency Work Contexts*, pp. 197–204 and 109–15.

[28] Kadushin, "Superviser-Supervisee," p. 291.

[29] *Ibid.*, p. 291.

[30] Kafry and Pines, "Occupational Tedium," p. 505.

[31] Karen S. Haynes, "Job Satisfaction of Mid-Management Social Workers," *Administration in Social Work*, 3, No. 2 (Summer, 1979), 207–18.

[32] Herman Stein, "Administrative Leadership in Complex Service Organizations," in *Social Work Administration*, Harry A. Schatz, ed. (New York: Council on Social Work Education, 1970), pp. 288–98.

[33] Harry A. Schatz, "Staff Involvement in Agency Administration," in *Social Work Administration*, Harry A. Schatz, ed. (New York: Council on Social Work Education, 1970), pp. 279–87.

[34] Harleigh B. Trecker, *Social Work Administration* (New York: Association Press, 1977), pp. 162–64.

[35] Kenneth P. Fallon, "Participatory Management: An Alternative in Human Service Delivery Systems," in *Social Administration*, Simon Slavin, ed. (New York: Haworth Press, 1978), p. 170.

[36] Robert Tannenbaum and Warren H. Schmidt, "How to Choose a Leadership Pattern," *Harvard Business Review Reprint Series*, No. 21072, 176–85.

[37] Hage and Aiken, "Organizational Alienation," p. 523.

[38] Maryanne L. Vandervelde, "Participative and Influenced-based Decision Making, Performance, and Effectiveness: An Analysis of Their Relationship in Human Service Organizations." University of Washington, 1979.

[39] Thomas P. Holland, "Organizational Structure and Institutional Care," *Journal of Health and Social Behavior*, 14, No. 3 (September, 1973), 241–51.

[40] Patricia Y. Martin and Brian Segal, "Bureaucracy Size and Staff Expectations for Client Independence in Halfway Houses," *Journal of Health and Social Behavior*, 18, No. 4 (December, 1977), 376–90.

[41] Vandervelde, "Participative and Influenced-based Decision Making."

[42] A similar conclusion has been reached by several investigators who have examined the relationship between these variables in business concerns. See Howell, *Essentials*, pp. 84–85. A major exception is the work of Likert in which organizations with participatory management systems were found to be more productive than those that were less participatory. See *The Human Organization: Its Management and Value* (New York: McGraw-Hill, 1967).

[43] Charles Glisson and Patricia Y. Martin, "Productivity and Efficiency in Human Service Organizations as Related to Structure, Size, and Age," *Academy of Management Journal*, 23, No. 1 (March, 1980), 21–37.

[44] Howell, *Essentials*, p. 85.

[45] Glisson and Martin, "Productivity and Efficiency," p. 34.

[46] Martin and Segal, pp. 384–86; and Holland, "Organizational Structure," pp. 241–51.

[47] Edward E. Schwartz and William C. Sample, "First Findings from Midway," *Social Service Review*, 41, No. 2 (June, 1967), 143–44; Linn, "State Hospital Environment and Rates of Patient Discharge," *Archives of General Psychiatry*, 23, No. 3 (September, 1970), 346–51.

[48] Kafry and Pines, "Occupational Tedium," pp. 503–5.

[49] Schwartz and Sample, "First Findings," p. 131.

[50] Paul Weinberger, "Job Satisfaction and Staff Retention in Social Work," in *Perspectives on Social Welfare*, Paul Weinberger, ed. (New York: Macmillan, 1974), p. 478.

[51] Ullman, Gross, Davis, and Mushinski, "Activities, Satisfaction, and Problems," pp. 23–26.

[52]Schwartz and Sample, "First Findings," pp. 132–36.

[53]Thomas W. Weirich, "The Design of Information Systems," in *Leadership in Social Administration* (Philadelphia: Temple University Press, 1980), p. 153. A similar conclusion is presented by Cox and Osborne in their study of how human service administrators employ evaluative data in their decision processes. Gary B. Cox and Phillip S. Osborne, "Relationships Among Problem Characteristics, Decision Processes, and Evaluation Activity: A Preliminary Study of Mental Health Center Directors" (unpublished paper), University of Washington, n.d., p. 22.

[54]Indeed, some experts argue that elaborate information systems should be delayed until program stability has been achieved. See Weirich, "The Design of Information Systems," p. 152.

[55]Grover Starling, *Managing the Public Sector.* (Homewood, Ill.: Dorsey Press, 1977), pp. 291–93.

[56]Tripodi, Fellin, and Epstein, *Social Program Evaluation,* p. 25–40.

[57]For a more detailed discussion of methods and techniques, see *Ibid.,* Peter H. Rossi, Howard E. Freeman, and Sonia R. Wright, *Evaluation: A Systematic Approach* (Beverly Hills, Calif.: Sage Publications, 1979); Irwin Epstein and Tony Tripodi, *Research Techniques for Program Planning, Monitoring, and Evaluation* (New York: Columbia University Press, 1977).

[58]Jack Rothman, *Using Research in Organizations* (Beverly Hills, Calif.: Sage Publications, 1980), p. 132.

[59]Holland has argued that an information search requires the existence of a problem. What we propose here is that certain "problems" can be largely anticipated and that information collection can begin before such problems actually occur. Thomas P. Holland, "Information and Decision Making in Human Services," *Administration in Mental Health,* 4, No. 1, (Fall, 1976), 26–35.

[60]Stephen P. Robbins, *The Administrative Process,* 2nd ed. (Englewood Cliffs, N.J.: Prentice-Hall, Inc., 1980), pp. 376–77.

[61]Under the best of circumstances the information sought will be much the same as that collected for internal purposes, but this is often not the case.

[62]Tripodi, Fellin, and Epstein, *Social Program Evaluation,* pp. 45–50.

[63]*Ibid.,* p. 45. Also see Kiresuk and Lund, "Program Evaluation," p. 287.

[64]Rossi, Freeman, and Wright, *Evaluation,* pp. 124–25.

[65]Tripodi, Fellin, and Epstein, *Social Program Evaluation,* pp. 47–49.

[66]Kiresuk and Lund, "Program Evaluation," pp. 294–95.

[67]*Ibid.,* pp. 287–94.

[68]Fremont Kast and James Rosenzweig, *Organization and Management: A Systems Approach* (New York: McGraw-Hill, 1970), pp. 372–75.

[69]*Ibid.,* pp. 372–79; and William King and David Clelland, "The Design of Management Information Systems: An Information Analysis Approach," in *Management Systems in the Human Services,* Murray Gruber, ed. (Philadelphia: Temple University Press, 1981), pp. 276–86.

[70]Theodore D. Sterling, "People and Machines: Humanizing Computerized Information Systems," in *Management Systems in the Human Services,* Murray Gruber, ed. (Philadelphia: Temple University Press, 1981), pp. 287–99; and Weirich, "The Design of Information Systems," pp. 149–50.

[71]P. Bruce Landon and Marion Merchant, "Treatment Information for Feedback and Evaluation in a Mental Health Setting," in *Management Systems in Social Welfare,* Murray Gruber, ed. (Philadelphia: Temple University Press, 1981);

Jack M. Donahue et al., "The Social Service Information System," in *Social Administration*, Simon Slavin, ed. (New York: Haworth Press, 1978), pp. 481–92.

[72] Weirich, "Design of Information Systems," pp. 142–56; Holland, "Information and Decision Making," pp. 26–35.

[73] Weirich, "Design of Information Systems," pp. 144–46.

[74] *Ibid.*, pp. 149–50.

[75] *Ibid.*, p. 146.

[76] *Ibid.*, pp. 146–48.

[77] Rossi, Freeman, and Wright, *Evaluation*, p. 163.

[78] *Ibid.*, pp. 227–40.

[79] *Ibid.*, pp. 194–224; and Epstein and Tripodi, *Research Techniques*, pp. 111–70.

[80] Rossi, Freeman, and Wright, *Evaluation*, pp. 161–71.

[81] Kiresuk and Lund, "Program Evaluation," p. 295.

[82] *Ibid.*, pp. 294–96; and Tripodi, Fellin, and Epstein, *Social Program Evaluation*, pp. 96–107.

[83] *Ibid.*, p. 101.

[84] Rossi, Freeman, and Wright, *Evaluation*, pp. 254–63.

[85] *Ibid.*, p. 267.

[86] *Ibid.*, pp. 273–77.

[87] Kiresuk and Lund, "Program Evaluation," pp. 310–13.

[88] Jack Rothman, *Using Research in Organizations* (Beverly Hills, Calif.: Sage Publications, 1980), pp. 120–22.

[89] *Ibid.*, pp. 122–24.

[90] Kiresuk and Lund, "Program Evaluation," p. 313.

[91] Kast and Rosenweig, *Organization and Management*, p. 578.

[92] Paul Hershey and Kenneth H. Blanchard, *Management of Organizational Behavior*, 3rd ed. (Englewood Cliffs, N.J.: Prentice-Hall, Inc., 1977), p. 275.

[93] Theodore Caplow, *How to Run Any Organization* (Homewood, Ill.: Dryden Press, 1976), p. 192.

[94] Herman Resnick and Rino J. Patti, eds., *Change from Within: Humanizing Social Welfare Organizations* (Philadelphia: Temple University Press, 1980).

[95] Rino J. Patti, "Organizational Resistance and Change: The View from Below," in *Change from Within: Humanizing Social Welfare Organizations*, Herman Resnick and Rino J. Patti, eds. (Philadelphia: Temple University Press, 1980), pp. 116–118.

[96] See, for example, Hershey and Blanchard, *Management of Organizational Behavior*, pp. 273–306; Chris Argyris, "The Primary Tasks of Intervention Activities," in *Perspectives on Behavior in Organizations*, J. Richard Hackman, Edward E. Lawler, and Lyman W. Porter, eds. (New York: McGraw-Hill, 1977), pp. 439–51; and Larry E. Greiner, "Patterns of Organizational Change," *Harvard Business Review Reprint Series*, No. 21072, pp. 154–63.

[97] Walter H. Ehlers, Michael J. Austin, and Jon C. Prothero, *Administration for the Human Services* (New York: Harper & Row, 1976).

[98] Tripodi, Fellin, and Epstein, *Social Program Administration*, p. 70.

[99] Paul R. Lawrence, "How to Deal with Resistance to Change," *Harvard Business Review Reprint Series*, No. 21072, pp. 145–53.

[100] *Ibid.*, p. 152.

[101]Patti, "Organizational Resistance," pp. 125–26.

[102]Lawrence, "Understanding Resistance," p. 150.

[103]E. A. Johns, *The Sociology of Organizational Change* (Oxford, Eng.: Pergamon Press, 1973), pp. 56–60.

[104]Lawrence, "How to Deal with Resistance," pp. 145–53; and Kast and Rosenweig, *Organization and Management*, p. 284.

[105]Hershey and Blanchard, *Management of Organizational Behavior*, pp. 277–80.

[106]Victor Vroom, "Can Leaders Learn to Lead?" in *Perspectives on Behavior in Organizations*, J. Richard Hackman, Edward E. Lawler, and Lyman W. Porter, eds. (New York: McGraw-Hill, 1977), p. 399.

[107]Greiner, "Patterns of Organizational Change," pp. 157–58.

[108]Hershey and Blanchard, *Management of Organizational Behavior*, p. 284.

[109]Joseph A. Alutto and James A. Belasco, "A Typology for Participation in Organizational Decision Making," *Administrative Science Quarterly*, 17, No. 1 (March, 1972), 117–25.

[110]Hershey and Blanchard, *Management of Organizational Behavior*, p. 283.

[111]*Ibid.*, pp. 282–85. Also see Vroom, "Can Leaders Learn?" pp. 398–402.

CHAPTER SEVEN

From Direct Service to Administration: Problems and Prospects for Social Workers in Transition

As noted in Chapter 1, the challenge to social work leadership in the field of social welfare in the 1970s and early 1980s prompted a substantial effort in the profession to develop educational programs that would prepare a cadre of administrative specialists for direct entry to management positions. Unlike their predecessors who were trained in direct services and worked themselves gradually into positions of managerial authority, this new generation of social workers, it was hoped, would be specifically prepared to assume administrative posts in social agencies, without benefit of advanced clinical training or prolonged apprenticeship in direct services.

This significant development raised a number of issues and problems with which social work has struggled, and will continue to struggle in the years ahead. Unfortunately, however, this preoccupation with the preparation of administrative specialists has obscured the equally important and even more pervasive problem of preparing clinicians for management practice in social welfare. It is to this group of social workers—their significance in the management manpower pool, the problems they encounter in making the transition from clinical to administrative roles, and the strategies that might be employed to facilitate their development as administrators—that we turn in this chapter.

THE CLINICIAN-ADMINISTRATOR
AND THE MANAGEMENT WORKFORCE
IN SOCIAL WELFARE

Despite the growing availability of administrative specialists trained in schools of social work, as well as schools of business and public administration, it seems quite likely that in the foreseeable future most of the lower- and middle-management jobs in social welfare organizations will be filled from the ranks of direct practice.

There are several reasons for this assumption. First, movement into administration continues to be one of the few options open to practitioners seeking increased status and salaries.[1] Promotions to positions of administrative responsibility are often based on a prior record of successful clinical performance, so it is understandable that many practitioners view their selection for such positions as an affirmation of their competence as clinicians. Second, despite recent criticisms of clinician-administrators, pointing variously to their lack of organizational knowledge and management skill, there persists a belief in social work that education and experience in direct services are a necessary, if not sufficient, preparation for middle-level administration.[2] Moreover, it appears that this view is shared by a good many agency employers. A recent study of hiring preferences among directors of public welfare agencies indicated that applicants with extensive direct service experience or clinical education were more often preferred for lower- and middle-management jobs than those with more formal administrative training, but less extensive clinical and program experience.[3]

Third, though there is evidence that both public and voluntary agencies may be reappraising the emphasis they place on direct practice experience as a qualification for management, it remains true that most lower- and middle-management jobs require such experience as a matter of agency policy.[4] Finally, the combination of a stabilized labor force in many sectors of social welfare and the growth of unions, will increasingly require agencies to promote from within rather than seek new managerial talent from without. Emphasis will no doubt continue to be placed on selecting from the pool of existing practitioners and attempting through in-service training and continuing education to prepare them for management positions.

Given the important role that clinically trained social workers are likely to play in social welfare administration then, it is vital that we have a better understanding of the problems and potentialities associated with the career transition process, as well as the manpower development strategies that might be employed by schools and agencies in facilitating the development of this management resource.

FROM DIRECT SERVICE
TO MANAGEMENT

It is now widely recognized that a sizeable proportion of social workers whose professional training is in direct services, move into positions of managerial responsibility at some point in their careers. One widely quoted study of members of the National Association of Social Workers (NASW), reported in 1969, found that 50 percent of the members responding listed general administration as their primary job function.[6] Since it is unlikely that more than a minute percentage of the NASW membership had been trained for administration, this finding suggested the magnitude and prevalence of the career transition phenomenon. More recent studies conducted by individual schools of social work have also indicated that direct service workers move into managerial responsibilities in significant numbers. For example, several follow-up surveys of graduates at the University of Washington School of Social Work have shown that shortly after graduation a sizeable percentage are engaged in jobs where administrative responsibilities are among the first or second most time-consuming aspects of their work.[7]

Until recently, this pattern of career mobility from direct service to administration drew little concern, since it conformed nicely with the long-standing and widespread assumption in social work that clinical education and experience were essential preparation for management (see Chapter 1). In the last decade, however, as social agencies came under criticism for ineffective or inefficient administration, there has been a growing sentiment that persons trained and experienced in direct service are often ill prepared for management responsibility.[8] The stereotypical notion that social workers did not make good managers, increasingly prevalent in the 1970s, probably drew some of its rationale from the observation that many clinicians' habits of mind, attitudes, and interpersonal skills did not translate easily to the world of management. Indeed, Saari went so far as to suggest that "knowledge and skill in clinical practice may be antithetical to, or dysfunctional for, sound administration and policy development."[9] Among other things, social work administrators were variously criticized for lacking analytic skills being indecisive, being more concerned with internal processes than organizational effectiveness, and being guided more by compassion than by intellect.[10]

The following appraisal of social service managers (among whom one assumes the author includes social workers) reflects a view that has gained considerable currency.

> ... we shall find that a majority of social service functionaries are simply not technically qualified for the demands their positions exert. That is, they lack the necessary training in management science, have little comprehension of the economic constraints on their operations, and generally also tend to be

confused about the relationship between the social service sector and other segments of the society. In many cases, the neglect of the technological aspect of their positions stems from their belief that a good heart or benevolent intentions are sufficient for social service management.[11]

At this point little can be gained from polemics about the dysfunctional consequences of clinical training for subsequent managerial performance. If most lower- and middle-management jobs in social welfare will be filled by persons from direct practice, it would be more productive to understand the nature of the social and psychological discontinuities that clinicians are likely to encounter as they assume administrative roles.

Making the Transition

The fragmentary evidence available suggests that many clinicians who move into administration experience some degree of role discontinuity, identity confusion, and concomitant personal stress.[12] To some extent these problems are associated with any new job or practice role,[13] but for the clinician-administrator they appear to be more prolonged and intense. Elbow, writing of her experience in becoming the executive of a small social agency, comments on the problems she experienced:

> The major source of internal stress arises from a change in identity and role, a situation not unlike the developmental crises of life. The new executive must revise his self-concept in relation to the position change and must also cope with the perceptions of others, particularly those who have been fellow staff members.[14]

Similar observations made by others suggests that this is not an isolated phenomenon.[15] Clinicians who have planned and prepared themselves to assume an administrative role, or those who are not heavily invested in their identity as clinicians, may find the transition less problematic.[16] However, the more common case appears to be that of the practitioner who has spent years in training and practice to achieve competence, and experienced some success and a sense of accomplishment in this capacity. A career in administration, if it was ever seriously considered, was likely to have been perceived as a distant and future prospect that would somehow be contended with, when and if it occurred. Finally, confronted with an opportunity to become a manager, and most likely attracted by a new professional challenge and the lure of status, money, and power, the practitioner takes on the administrative position only to find that the knowledge and skills so assiduously cultivated and applied in direct service, are not adequate to meet the expectations of the new position. Some components of professional armamentarium can be adapted to the new situation, but the clinician-turned-administrator is likely to discover that there are significant gaps. Perhaps more important, the neophyte manager often finds that assumptions, values, and ways of looking at and relating to people and processes, which had been an integral part of his or her clinical style, must now be questioned and even altered in significant ways. It is not a question of right replacing wrong, for neither clinician nor administrator can lay claim to an ultimate truth. It is, rather, a question of how organizational location and role condition the perception of events, the value placed on them, and the manner in which they are to be addressed. The developmental task confronting the clinician-administrator, then, is not simply one of superimposing additional information and managerial technique on an intact clinical foundation, as social work educators have for so long assumed. The task, rather, is assessing whether the knowledge, skills, and values appropriate to the clinical role are suitable to the organizational realities and role expectations associated with administration.

In what follows we focus upon several areas in which the perspectives acquired in clinical training and practice differ from and sometimes conflict with those that assume importance in administrative roles. In presenting these divergent orientations, it is important to bear in mind that they represent tendencies found in the worlds of direct practice and management, respectively, and may not reflect the views or attitudes of individual practitioners. Our purpose is simply to illustrate some of the transitional problems with which clinician-administrators must frequently contend as they seek to traverse these distinctive practice arenas.

Conceptions of administration.   The vast majority of social workers are employed in formal organizations characterized by a graded system of administrative authority. Social workers in training learn early that much of what they do as clinicians is vitally affected by the policies, rules, resources, and direction provided by administrative superiors. Indeed, as semiprofessionals, social workers derive much of their legitimacy from the organizations that employ them.[17]

Yet, despite the centrality of organizations, and thus administrative superiors, to the lives of social work practitioners, there is a marked tendency in professional circles to view administrative work in largely negative terms. On the one hand, management is often equated with routine, detail, inflexibility, and red tape: functions that require little in the way of professional creativity or skill, that ultimately reduce the incumbent to a mindless functionary, more concerned with rules and procedures than with the provision of service. No less invidious is a characterization of administrators as power-grabbing, manipulating, political creatures, who feel little or no allegiance to professional values, and who are bent on control and personal success for their own sake. Related to both of these conceptions is a tendency to view administrators as purveyors of organizational standards and expectations that conflict with professional norms and prerogatives such as autonomy, intensive high-quality service, and peer evaluation.[18]

To the extent that the clinician comes to accept these views of administration, the task of becoming a manager becomes enormously complicated. First, against this background, a move into administration implies, in some sense, an abandonment of what one has come to believe in and act upon as a professional. The monetary rewards and increased status notwithstanding, the career transition is likely to be perceived as a threat to one's professional integrity. Second, the negative characterizations of management and managers implicitly devalues the skill and knowledge required to perform these roles effectively. If, indeed, "anyone can do administration," the prospective manager must contemplate his or her promotion with some dread, at least insofar as the opportunities it affords for continued growth, development, and membership in the professional community.

If all this is so, why does any self-respecting practitioner choose to become an administrator? We've already mentioned the more obvious inducements that can themselves be compelling. Perhaps equally important is the incentive that comes from the belief that one needn't fall prey to the "pathologies" of management: that one can bring to the new task all the insight, skill, and credibility that existing managers seem to lack. A recent study conducted by the author and several colleagues found, for example, that one of the major motivating factors in clinicians' decisions to become administrators was the feeling that they could "do better" than their superiors.[19] Evidence in this study and the observations of others[20] suggests that "doing better" often means deemphasizing the exercise of authority in relations with subordinates, maintaining informal relationships with former colleagues, and remaining heavily involved in direct service activities. In short, this approach to administration, which some have referred to as the "superclinician" model, is inspired by the belief that the best administration occurs when supervisors and subordinates are performing similar functions and when differences in authority and power are minimized.

This posture is problematic for several reasons. First, it implies a reluctance to embrace the managerial role and thus contend with its demands, requirements, and problems. Second and relatedly, it postpones the task of assessing the knowledge and skills that must ultimately be acquired if managerial functions are to be carried out effectively. Finally, it is likely to generate expectations among subordinates that will at some point come into conflict with the manager's responsibilities.

This is not to say that the skills and organizational perspectives acquired in clinical training and experience are inherently dysfunctional in the management role. Many administrators, especially those in small programs, continue to provide direct services, and the skills previously acquired are indispensable to this task. In addition, an intimate understanding of service delivery processes, the needs and problems of clients, and the conditions that impede or facilitate practitioner performance, can be quite useful to the manager in program planning, personnel management, and supervision. The manager with proven clinical competence, moreover, has a kind of credibility with subordinates that is likely to bolster his or her legitimate authority.[21] These and other advantages accrue to the manager with a clinical background. There is nothing to be gained by "cleansing" oneself of these attributes. On the other hand, the new manager does need to understand the differences between clinical and administrative work, and to recognize the unique skills and perspectives needed in each of these roles. The person should be particularly aware that administration is itself a professional activity that requires at least the same level of expertise and dedication required of clinical practitioners. Attempting to make the transition to management by remaining a *de facto* clinician, who happens incidentally to manage, is to avoid coming to terms with this reality.

Understanding organizations.   Clinical training in social work focuses the direct service practitioner's attention on understanding why individuals think, feel, and behave as they do; the myriad psychological and social factors that give rise to dysfunctions in one or more of these spheres; and how these manifestations can be corrected when they are harmful to self or others. The individual is in most instances the object of social workers' concern. Intervention strategies are largely particularized to dyadic relationships in which the practitioner exercises some control over the selection and implementation of techniques. There is, of course, attention given to the effects of environment on individuals; and some training programs give greater or lesser attention to the practitioner's role in changing social systems that impinge upon clients. But the focal point of the educational process and the core expertise imparted is likely to be what the worker does for and with the client.

Subsequent experience in social agencies tends to reinforce this orientation to analysis and intervention. The practitioner carries responsibility for "cases," each of which has a distinct configuration of needs and problems requiring a highly individualized response. The organizational context, as we noted earlier, influences the nature of these responses, so some effort must be made to understand and accommodate these conditions and forces. But the practitioner who seeks to gain a broader and deeper understanding of organizational processes or attempts to change them is not likely to get reinforced or rewarded for these efforts. Rather, the organization expects and rewards practitioners for "attending to business," and in this case "business" means providing service to clients.

The practitioner who comes into management from this experience normally brings a reasonably good understanding of individual dynamics and some confidence in the ability to apply diagnostic skills and interpersonal techniques to working with subordinates. If the clinician-administrator can avoid the pitfall of relating to workers as clients, he or she can use much from prior training and experience to advantage in this new role—e.g., eliciting ideas and information, identifying strengths and weaknesses of staff, structuring opportunities to facilitate professional development, and facilitating the resolution of interpersonal conflicts among subordinates.

The problem frequently encountered by practitioners-turned-administrators is in assuming that these analytic and intervention skills are a sufficient basis for management. Early on they learn that what transpires in the organization is more than the sum total of the individual personalities that comprise it. Knowledge of individual dynamics is important, but the new manager needs, as well, an appreciation of the organization as a functioning system.[22] Among other things this perspective involves an understanding of the interdependency of processes and events occurring in the agency: the exchange relationships that must occur between the organization and its task environment; the effects of organization structure and climate on such things as communication, worker satisfaction, and performance; the importance of ideological and occupational commitments and professional vested interests as determinants of individual and group behavior; and the dynamics underlying various problems like goal displacement, ritualism, and intergroup conflict.

Unfortunately, though clinician-administrators may become aware of the need for an organizational perspective, many continue to rely heavily on analytic frameworks that stress individual motivation or dysfunctions to explain organizational processes. This is understandable since these tools are acquired early in the course of professional development and tend to become deeply internalized. Equally important perhaps is the fact that much of the theory and research on organizations that might inform the development of a system-oriented perspective consists of fragments of abstract knowledge that are difficult to access, let along apply to specific problem areas. Moreover, where potentially useful knowledge about organizations is available, it has often not been particularized to social welfare agencies, nor have its implications for management practice in these settings been drawn.[23]

Despite the difficulties involved, this aspect of the developmental task facing clinician-administrators is crucial. For without the analytic skills needed to understand organizations as functioning systems, the new manager will fail to see and appreciate much that requires his or her managerial attention.

Orientations to authority.   Central to the training of social work clinicians is the notion that a practitioner's authority in relations with clients inheres primarily in the special knowledge and skill that he or she brings to the service delivery process. Other factors such as tradition, personal charisma, and position may buttress this authority, but it is the clinician's expertise in helping the clients resolve their problems that is likely to be perceived as the principle source of professional authority.[24] There are, of course, situations where the social worker's exercise of authority is not contingent upon the client's acknowledgment of his or her expertise—e.g., protective services and correctional settings. But most practitioners subscribe to the view that rehabilitative goals can be most effectively achieved when clients believe that the practitioner has knowledge and skill that is particularly pertinent to the resolution of their problems.

Authority based on problem-specific expertise does not, however, confer on the practitioner the right to impose solutions on the client. Some would argue that the power of the worker in this relationship often leaves the client relatively little choice in accepting the therapist's conception of desirable change. Nevertheless, the practitioner's posture in the typical scenario is to help the client clarify problems and goals, consider alternatives, and better understand him- or herself, all in the context of a supportive relationship that permits experimentation, risk, and failure.[25] In general, the practitioner's expertise and corresponding influence are used to facilitate the client's ability to problem-solve, but the choice of appropriate courses of action is thought to be the client's prerogative.

Under the best of circumstances, the manager also seeks to build authority on the basis of situation-specific knowledge and skill. The importance given to a manager's demonstrated clinical competence is one expression of the widely held view that, whenever possible, supervisors should base their decisions on professional and technical considerations. Unlike the service relationship, however, when a subordinate fails to accept the direction of the administrator, the latter must be prepared to press for compliance, even in the face of appearing to be arbitrary. Certainly there are times when it is appropriate to defer to subordinates or engage in collaborative decision making, but inevitably there are occasions in which the manager must take courses of action that may not be agreed to or supported by staff. Efforts should be made to build commitment and elicit cooperation from subordinates, but when these fail the manager is often faced with the necessity of using the power of the position to elicit the desired behaviors. This may involve the use of direct tactics like rewards, disciplinary action, and withholding of resources, or more indirect measures such as group pressure. In any case, the manager who consistently shrinks from using the authority of the office when there is disagreement with subordinates ultimately loses the ability to coordinate activities toward the achievement of organizational objectives.

There is some indication that clinicians making the transition to management experience difficulty in assuming and exercising administrative authority. For example, a recent study of social work managers found that one of the most troublesome areas they encountered in their first administrative jobs was relating to subordinates. This difficulty was variously manifested in a discomfort with supervising former colleagues, "difficulty in keeping professional distance from staff," and "being thought of as the answer person." A number of respondents in this study also expressed frustration at the limitations of their authority. The problems cited here included eliciting support and cooperation from subordinates in moving toward the goals of the agency, motivating people to change behavior or improve performance, and gaining cooperation with changes proposed by superiors. Interestingly, when confronted with resistance from subordinates, some of the respondents found themselves tempted to resort to clinical tactics they had previously employed in their treatment of clients.[26]

In much the same vein, Elbow, commenting on her reaction when confronted with the responsibility for decision making as a new agency administrator, remarks:

> In addition to wanting to share the burden, I had a desire to share the responsibilities in order to avoid total accountability. Previously, if a decision was a joint one but unpopular or not workable, they [the staff] could not have blamed me: we would have to share the responsibility. Now I wanted confirmation: we are in this thing together.[27]

Exercising the authority of administrative office does not require that one be insensitive to the needs of subordinates nor reject the belief that workers should have a say in the decision-making process. At the same time, the clinician in transition to management must contend with the fact that authority is intrinsic to the new role: that its constructive use is indispensable to both the manager's performance and that of the organizational unit for which he or she is responsible.

Relations with colleagues.   The practitioner's transition to management inexorably affects the nature of relationships that he or she has had with colleagues. While still a practitioner, the new manager was likely to have participated in a normative system that valued mutuality and cooperation. With some colleagues, at least, he or she probably enjoyed opportunities to ventilate frustration, gain support, exchange ideas and information. Colleagues may also have served as a reference group whose standards of conduct provided guidelines against which to measure performance.

The move into management very often brings changes in these relationships. The understanding and trust that had previously grown out of common experience and interests are likely to suffer as expectations are adjusted, contacts diminish, and organizational perspectives become disparate. Relationships that had once served broadly expressive needs are now likely to be more functionally specific and instrumental. Ideally the manager will work to maintain openness and trust in relationships with subordinates (former colleagues), but there is now likely to be a critical difference. Where such relationships had previously served the mutual personal and professional needs of colleagues, they now become purposefully directed at facilitating subordinates' development and maximizing their contribution to organizational goals. Since, in addition both worker and manager know that the information acquired in this relationship may be used for some evaluative purpose at a later date, a degree of restraint becomes both necessary and functional. Finally, the manager's ability to respond freely to the individual needs of subordinates is limited by the overriding necessity to ensure a modicum of equity in relationships with all staff. In some instances, indeed, the well-being of individual subordinate members cannot be the manager's paramount concern, especially when the effectiveness of the organization is at stake.[28] In short, the manager's new status makes it increasingly difficult for him or her to maintain primary group relationships with colleagues who have now become subordinates. The change in structural arrangements push both superior and subordinate toward an impersonal and neutral level of interaction that is much more characteristic of secondary systems. Efforts on the part of the manager to mix these levels of interaction will almost certainly produce ambiguity, confusion, and dissension.[29]

Many clinician-administrators experience this altered pattern of interaction with colleagues as a reduction in the quality of relationships, a loss of support, isolation, and loneliness. Understandably, new managers often react to this situation with ambivalence and confusion. Some strive to maintain the status quo in relationships with colleagues. While this stance may postpone necessary interpersonal adjustments, it is also likely to hamper the manager's ability to carry out his or her responsibilities, thus compounding the problems associated with the transition.

The resolution of this conflict is seldom accomplished without pain, but the process appears to be greatly facilitated if the manager has access to an informal support system. In the study of career transitions of clinician-administrators, mentioned earlier, new managers often dealt with the strain by turning to administrative colleagues for advice and support. This new informal support system served in many cases not only to buffer some of the isolation they experienced, but also became a new reference group around which managers could begin to forge new professional identities.[30] Elbow observed a similar process in her own development:

> Alleviation of feelings of aloneness and self-doubt comes from the development and acceptance of new, appropriate, and available support systems. Administrators of other agencies, board members, consultation from regional and national organizations . . . provide a variety of resources to meet the need for sharing and reflecting upon experience, ideas, and plans.[31]

Although these relationships can be an important aid in the transitional process, the clinician-administrator must also recognize the constraints that frequently exist in relations with administrative colleagues. The manager is responsible for maximizing the performance of his or her unit. Colleagues who head other comparable units are, in fact, often in competition for resources, personnel, and program jurisdiction. Therefore, it sometimes becomes dysfunctional to share information and ideas openly. When one considers that the manager's credibility with his or her staff often depends on how well he or she protects and advances their interests, the constraints to establishing supportive and collaborative relationships between administrative colleagues become apparent.

This is not to deny the importance of mutual assistance derived from associations with fellow managers, but rather to suggest that the norms and realities that permeate the world of administration, particularly at higher levels, are frequently different from those that obtain among clinicians. One important difference is the need for managers to gain and exercise power in order to be effective in their roles.[32] Frequently, power is won at the expense of others, particularly those seeking to lay claim to the same pool of resources. This prospect of power gain or loss often introduces an element of strategic calculation in relationships between administrative colleagues that makes it difficult to obtain the same level of intimacy and trust that is sometimes possible among fellow practitioners.

Modes of decision making.   Direct service practitioners are taught to treat each client unit as an entity unto itself with its own needs and requirements. While other clients in a clinician's caseload may make competing demands on time and energy, workers tend to be strongly imbued with the notion that it is their professional responsibility to provide those services that will maximize benefits in any given case situation. Oppressive time and agency resource limitations may require the practitioner to do less than might be optimally desired in a particular case, but this is likely to be strongly resisted as an undesirable state of affairs. The continual demands of clinicians for lower caseloads is one effort to minimize the necessity for making such choices.

In contrast, the manager is seldom in a position to consider each worker unit or department under his or her charge an entity unto itself. Each organizational component competes against a resource pool that is nearly always insufficient to satisfy the needs. The manager, therefore, can seldom afford to think in terms of optimal solutions for each of these components. Rather, he or she is forced to consider the best alternatives available under the circumstances. The decision mode for the manager is one of *satisficing* rather than *optimizing;* and while this may be considered unfortunate, in given instances the managerial culture recognizes this as both a necessary and ethical approach to decision making.

This shift in decision-making orientation is often resisted by new clinician-administrators, particularly if they maintain a strong commitment to the program in which they formally worked as direct service practitioners. In addition, it is not uncommon for former colleagues to assume that the recently promoted manager will understand the special needs of that program and advocate for or decide in its favor. The manager who disappoints this expectation is likely to incur some disfavor and even disrupt valued relationships. For the new manager who seeks at once to maintain credibility with former associates and also build relationships with new constituencies, both internal and external to the agency, this can pose a dilemma of both personal and organizational dimensions.[33]

Ultimately, however, the manager must give balanced and equitable consideration to the needs and desires of all units in his or her charge as they relate to a conception of organizational effectiveness and the resources available. The compromises required may not always be consistent with the preferences of subordinates. To this extent, the managerial decision mode engenders some distance from and conflict with staff.

DEVELOPING CLINICIAN-ADMINISTRATORS: SOME WORKFORCE STRATEGIES FOR SCHOOLS AND AGENCIES

The previous discussion has indicated the prevalence of clinician-to-manager career transitions in social work and some of the problems associated with this phenomenon. We turn now to several strategies that might be useful for identifying clinicians with administrative interests and systematically supporting the development of their potential for this field of practice. Very little empirical attention has been given to how direct service practitioners can be assisted to bridge the gap between clinical and administrative roles. What follows, therefore, must be considered tentative until further research and development has been done in this critical workforce area.[34]

The Role of Social Work Education

Schools of social work must assume some responsibility for helping direct service practitioners in training anticipate and prepare for the transition to management at later points in their careers. While degree programs cannot realistically bear this responsibility alone, at the very least they can initiate the process of anticipatory socialization in order to provide a foundation for subsequent career development.

Having asserted the desirability of schools becoming involved in this task, it is important to recognize the educational dilemmas posed by such an undertaking. That is, how to identify and initiate the processes of training selected social workers for career transitions to administration, even while they are immersed in the difficult task of becoming competent direct service practitioners? This problem is more difficult than it may appear at first glance. First, training for direct practice seems, if anything, to require more intense and prolonged preparation than is now provided. The proliferation of theoretical and technical bodies of knowledge generates pressure for increased specialization. There is simply more than can be taught in the time available. The tightening job market, due variously to slow growth in the social welfare sector, declassification of positions that formerly required social work training, and other factors, place graduates in an increasingly competitive job situation and thus force their attention to the acquisition of clinical skills that will make them attractive to prospective employers in the near term.

Second, many students who matriculate in direct service concentrations in schools of social work give little thought to an eventual career in administration. Whatever latent interest or capability they may have in this kind of practice is likely to be submerged in a preoccupation with preparing for the immediate prospect of clinical work. If as well, they are exposed to instructors who implicitly if not explicitly devalue administration as an appropriate professional pursuit, this content is almost certainly to be given low priority on their educational agendas.[35] Under these circumstances, many clinicians in training choose not to devote substantial time and energy to preparing for an eventual transition to management. Even in the face of these constraints some schools have introduced a significant component of administration into the training of direct services workers.[36] However, additional course work in this subject matter, though desirable, will not resolve the dilemma posed earlier. Several additional complementary strategies are necessary.

Curriculum Planning

Too little is yet known to allow us to predict with any certainty those clinical students who are likely to move into administration at later points in their careers. The interplay of personal motivation, education, and job experience, and the fortuities of the job market preclude the development of any good predictive instruments at this point. In the meantime, schools of social work and other professional organizations might initiate programs of research to develop or adapt instruments suited to assessing the management aptitudes of students in direct services. Such a program of research might include the conduct of long-term follow-up studies to determine the predictive validity of such tests, the contingencies that influence career transitions to management, and the relationship of these factors to later administrative performance.[37] In the short run, however, it would be useful for schools to make deliberate efforts to identify students who have already formulated an interest in administrative work and see that they are given active curriculum counseling to prepare them for this eventuality.

For those students who have not yet considered the possibility of an eventual career transition, it is important that schools make them aware of the high probability that they will someday join the ranks of administration. This can be done by presenting available information on career progression at student orientations or in introductory classes, or perhaps more dramatically, by inviting social work administrators to address students on how their own careers have evolved. Since there is some evidence to suggest that women, due to prior socialization, may have difficulty visualizing themselves in administrative roles at later points in their careers, it can be particularly useful for these students to be exposed to women managers who discuss how they were awakened to their own potential for this kind of practice.[38]

The main point is that schools should take some responsibility for stimulating students to plan for long-term career development as well as immediate job prospects. Additional research on career transitions is needed to inform this effort, but the data currently available indicate that professionals must look beyond their immediate developmental goals and at least begin to conjure with what they may need to know and do in subsequent stages of their careers.

Clinical Curriculum

Most curriculum recommendations regarding the preparation of clinicians for managerial work focus on providing more administration classes in the curriculum. This is desirable but hardly sufficient. To paraphrase a familiar quotation, preparation for administration is too important to leave to administration instructors alone. The core of the educational experience for clinically oriented students is, after all, the cluster of courses and field experiences that aim at preparation for direct practice. Understandably, clinical students invest a disproportionate share of their intellectual and emotional energy in this area, so it would seem advisable to use these experiences as an arena for introductory training in administration. Several strategies are possible. First, and perhaps most critical, is to engage the clinical faculty regarding their perceptions of administration as a field of practice. Their ideas and feelings about administrators, managers, and others in positions of authority will be conveyed to students, however subtly. If the message being communicated by such faculty is an anti-administration one ("administration is dull, boring work," "poor clinicians become administrators," "administration is not social work,"), students' receptivity to management as a career option may be diminished.

Second, there should be some time set aside in the basic direct services curriculum to address career transition issues. Questions like, "To what extent can the skills I am learning for direct work with individuals and groups be adapted to the administrative context?"; "How can interviewing skills be used in personnel recruitment?"; "How can group leadership skills be employed in working with committees and task forces?"; "How functional or dysfunctional are psychosocial diagnostic assessments when used in work with subordinates?"; and "How is authority applied in clinical work with clients similar to or different from that used with administrative subordinates?" These and a myriad of similar questions can profitably be addressed by both class and field instructors in the clinical area, perhaps in joint teaching arrangements with administration faculty.

Direct service classes might also address the conditions necessary to support and maintain effective service delivery in agencies. The contrasting views of administrators and direct service workers in agencies could be used in class to suggest the sometimes divergent perspectives on this issue and the rationale underlying each. The loneliness, isolation, and loss of peer support frequently experienced when a practitioner moves into an administrative position can, as we have seen, be matters of some difficulty. Case presentations and roleplays would illustrate and sensitize students to these potential problems and present ways of dealing with them.

Third, field placements tend not to be used as opportunities to sensitize students to organizational and administrative issues. Yet data from a recent study indicate that worker involvement in some aspect of agency administration shortly after graduation is frequently a stimulus to considering management as a career option.[39] Agency field instructors have long struggled with how best to provide administrative experiences to students, given their inexperience and the frequently sensitive nature of management tasks. However, it would seem that if students are to have an opportunity to assess their interest and capability for administration, some exposure in field placements would be essential. Ideally, these experiences should extend beyond mere study and analysis of agency structure and processes to include actual involvement in administrative work. Providing staff support for board committees, supervising undergraduates in field placement, planning for staff meetings or retreats, program development, and grant writing are just a few examples of the experiences that might become an integral component of the field practicum.

In the final analysis, we are not suggesting that clinical content be substantially sacrificed. Students' primary purpose at this stage of their development is to build competency in direct service. To divert a substantial portion of their clinical training to administration would violate the students' expectations and undermine the efforts of clinical faculty. Still, it seems well within the realm of feasibility to weave administrative content into the fabric of education for direct service without diverting students and faculty from their principal educational goal. This would serve to provide a foundation for those who will make a later career transition and provide a better understanding of the administrative context of service delivery for those who will remain practitioners throughout their careers.

Administration for Clinicians

Findings from a recent study indicate that clinician-administrators perceive the administration content to which they were exposed as students as generally too abstract, too unrelated to practice problems, and poorly taught. Such courses were viewed as having little utility, either as a stimulant to thinking about administrative practice or as preparation for these roles.[40] We suspect that such classes, limited in number as they will inevitably be, will never provide a sufficient foundation for later career transitions. At the same time, there is no reason why they cannot be more engaging. Part of the problem may lay in the traditional notion that students should first be immersed in theory and then gradually exposed to practice. For a full course of specialized study, this approach may have something to recommend it. In the context of one or two courses in administration, however, it would seem much wiser to start with specific and concrete practice illustrations involving situations not too dissimilar from what students can observe in field placement. Moreover, there may be some value in focusing on areas of administrative practice that deal with interpersonal issues—e.g., conflicts between departments, providing negative feedback to subordinates, or managing task group interaction—so that students can draw from their repository of clinical knowledge and skill. Such an approach would not only draw parallels between clinical and administrative practice but would also underscore some of the marked differences. Finally, an increasing number of instructional aids for teaching administration (tapes, simulations, program manuals) can be used to simulate "real practice" and provide students with a hands-on practice experience.[41] If such courses are viewed as an early testing ground for students to identify their motivation and aptitude for administrative work, this experiential focus seems more suitable than one that is primarily oriented to providing a theoretical background on organizational and administrative theory.[42]

The Role of Social Agencies

However important social work training may be in alerting students to their managerial potential, administrative experience and working relationships with superiors in agencies after graduation are likely to serve as the immediate catalysts for a transition to management. Many social workers, it seems, must first achieve a sense of mastery in clinical work before they are prepared to become invovled in a new practice arena.

Having acquired a sense of competence in one role, many then seem able to formulate a new set of career development goals. Thus, it appears that the social worker's personal readiness for a role change combined with an opportunity provided in the agency serves as the initial impetus toward management. There are several recommendations that agencies might consider in order to better identify and develop clinicians with managerial potential.

Career Planning

It is perhaps too obvious to suggest the need for a deliberate process of career planning. Yet the experience of many clinicians would indicate that their interest in, and aptitude for, administrative work is often discovered and supported through largely informal, ad hoc mechanisms. A chance relationship with a supportive superior, the unplanned assumption of administrative responsibility due to the absence of an administrator, the fortuitous involvement of a clinician in management tasks—these and similar occurrences are often the ways in which the managerial potential of direct service workers comes to an agency's attention. These informal processes for identifying promising clinicians will no doubt continue to be important in the selection of managers. It would also seem advisable, however, for agencies to formalize the process to ensure that the identification of future administrators is not left solely to the vagaries of chance. One simple procedure would be to institute periodic career-planning conferences with each member of a clinical staff in order to discuss future professional development, including the desire to become involved in administration. There would seem to be some advantages to having such conferences conducted by someone other than the immediate superior (e.g., a staff development specialist) in order to minimize the negative or positive biases that may color the assessment of a clinician's capability. In any case, such conferences could provide an opportunity for the worker and agency to arrive at some agreed-upon goals for professional development and the means that will be employed to achieve them—e.g., continuing education, special assignments, job rotation, and the like. A behavioral contract similar to the one suggested by Mayadas and Duehn, wherein worker and agency arrive at some developmental benchmarks to be assessed after an agreed-upon interval, might also aid this planning process.[43]

Executive Assessment Centers

Industry has long made use of executive assessment centers where aspiring managers are exposed to a period of intensive observation in order to identify their strengths and weaknesses for administrative work.

Such centers, focusing on social welfare management, could be established in universities or operated by national organizations to perform similar assessment functions for social agencies. Agencies could utilize such centers for clinicians who, in the course of their career planning conferences, have been identified as potential future managers. There is a great deal to be learned from the operation of already established centers serving industry,[44] but a period of research and development would be needed to adapt the available tools and procedures to the distinctive needs of the social welfare sector.

In-Service Preparation

A complaint frequently voiced by social work administrators is the suddenness with which they find themselves thrust into management roles. Many have spent years carefully preparing themselves for clinical practice only to find themselves precipitously put into positions of responsibility for which they have had little advance training. Assuming the existence of a career-planning mechanism, it would seem useful to provide would-be managers with supervised administrative experiences before they assume full responsibility for such positions. There are several ways in which this might be done. First, selected clinicians could be chosen for administrative internships in which they would be rotated through the management divisions of an agency—e.g., fiscal management, research and planning, or personnel. In each area they could be provided a thorough orientation and supervised work assignments. A second mechanism, perhaps more suitable to smaller agencies, would be to assign workers to serve as administrative assistants to the executive or major department heads. The executives, in this instance, could act as preceptors, defining skill and knowledge objectives with the clinician and designing learning experiences to achieve these ends.

Both of the above recommendations would require that the clinician be relieved of his or her case responsibilities for a period of time. A third suggestion, not requiring sustained absence from case responsibilities, would involve assigning clinicians to undertake certain ad hoc administrative tasks such as program planning, information system development, or program evaluation. Social work managers are frequently introduced to administration in this way; however, only infrequently are such assignments given with the explicit intent of aiding the clinician's development as a manager, and seldom is there provision for systematic supervision that would enable the clinician to extract principles of practice that might later be applied in managerial roles. In essence, what is being suggested is a kind of minifield practicum, consciously employed by the agency to cultivate the managerial talents of selected clinicians.

Transitional Support

The transition from clinical to administrative roles, as we have previously discussed, is often experienced as a period of considerable stress. Managers frequently seek the support and counsel of other administrators to help them adjust to this new role. However, access to these informal networks is often quite unpredictable. There would appear to be some utility in formalizing these support networks by providing debriefing seminars for new managers where administrative problems, personal reactions to the management role, and tactical issues could be periodically discussed. Such groups could serve both the emotional and cognitive needs of new managers and perhaps widen the base of information from which they could draw in developing their administrative styles. These groups should probably be led by someone who has no ongoing administrative relationship with the participants so that they can freely exchange ideas and feelings. For neophyte women managers, such groups may be particularly critical, since there is some reason to believe that women managers are not as readily received in informal networks as their male counterparts.

Continuing Education

In recent years much has been said of the need for universities to develop more management content in continuing education programs. Indeed, schools of social work as well as schools of business and public administration have significantly extended their offerings in response to this demand. The supply of timely, easily accessed continuing education offerings for clinicians is, of course, essential, but perhaps the more critical problem is the structural arrangements under which continuing education courses are offered to agency employees. It appears increasingly evident, based on recent experience, that such courses should be designed in conjunction with agency personnel so that they are more likely to address problems that are actually being confronted by managerial personnel. Too many courses offer general principles and guidelines, on the assumption that practitioners will make the necessary translation to their work. What seems needed, on the other hand, are courses that grow out of some contractual arrangement between the educational institution and agency where the problems and issues confronting administrators in these agencies become the focal point of the educational experience. Without this kind of mutual definition and collaborative problem solving, continuing education seems frequently to miss the mark.

Equally important is the need to systematically link the continuing education programs offered by universities with agency career development systems. Too often courses in management taken by agency employees have no relationship to career goals that have been mutually identified by the employee and his or her agency. Agencies often fail, therefore, to formally acknowledge continuing education in evaluating or promoting employees.

SUMMARY

This chapter has dealt with the problems encountered by professionals trained and experienced in direct services who, at some point in their careers, move into management positions. Five problem areas are identified, including (1) how direct service practitioners perceive administration as a practice, (2) their perspectives on organizational behavior, (3) their orientations to authority, (4) the changing nature of collegial relations in the managerial arena, and (5) the different modes of decision making required. The last half of the chapter presents recommendations to schools of social work and social agencies that would enable these institutions to better identify clinicians with management interests and potential, and to assist them in preparing for an eventual transition into administration.

NOTES

[1] David Macarov, "Management in the Social Work Curriculum," *Administration in Social Work,* 1, No. 2 (Summer, 1977), 140–41.

[2] *Ibid.,* p. 144.

[3] Rino J. Patti and Ronald Rauch, "Social Work Administration Graduates in the Job Market: An Analysis of Managers' Hiring Preferences," *Social Service Review,* 52, No. 4 (December, 1978), 567–83.

[4] Rino J. Patti and Charles Maynard, "Qualifying for Managerial Jobs in Public Welfare," *Social Work,* 23, No. 4 (July, 1978), 288–95.

[5] Rino J. Patti and others, *Educating for Management in Social Welfare* (unpublished monograph), University of Washington, 1976, pp. 13–14.

[6] Alfred J. Stamm, "NASW Membership: Characteristics, Deployment, and Salaries," *Personnel Information,* 12, No. 3 (May, 1969).

[7] Linda Wachter, "Summary of Reports Concerning Graduates of the School of Social Work" (unpublished paper), University of Washington, 1977, p. 6.

[8] See, for example, "The Manager vs. the Social Worker," *Public Welfare,* 36, No. 3 (Summer, 1978), 5–10; and Burton Gummer, "Is the Social Worker in Public Welfare an Endangered Species?" *Public Welfare,* 37, No. 4 (Fall, 1979), 17.

[9] Rosemary C. Saari, "Effective Social Work Intervention in Administrative and Planning Roles: Implications for Education," in *Facing the Challenge: Plenary Session Papers* (New York: Council on Social Work Education, 1973), p. 43.

[10] Gummer, "Is the Social Worker in Public Welfare an Endangered Species?" pp. 15–17; Jerry Sturem, "The Call for a Management Stance," *Social Work,* 19, No. 5 (September, 1974), 615–24.

[11] John W. Sutherland, *Managing Social Service Systems,* (New York: P.B.I. 1977) p. 1.

[12] See, for example, Rino J. Patti, Elenore Diedrick, Dennis Olsen, and Jill Crowell,

"From Direct Service to Administration: Part I: Analysis," *Administration in Social Work,* 3, No. 2 (Summer, 1979), 131–51; and Raymond M. Scurfield, "Social Work Administrators: Their Educational Preparation, Role Transition, and Job Satisfaction," *Administration in Social Work,* 4, No. 2 (Summer, 1980), pp. 47–60.

[13]Norma Radin, *A Follow-up Study of Social Work Graduates with Implications for Social Work Education* (New York: Council on Social Work Education, 1974), p. 106.

[14]Margaret Elbow, "On Becoming an Executive Director," *Social Casework,* 56, No. 9 (November, 1975), 525.

[15]See, for example, Rino J. Patti and Michael J. Austin, "Socializing the Direct Service Practitioner in the Ways of Supervisory Management," *Administration in Social Work,* 1, No. 3 (Fall, 1977), 268–80; and Daniel Levinson and Gerald Klerman, "The Clinician-Executive," *Administration in Mental Health* (Winter, 1972), 53–67.

[16]Levinson and Klerman, pp. 53–67.

[17]Nina Toren, "Semi-Professionalism and Social Work: A Theoretical Perspective," in *The Semi-Professions and Their Organization,* Amitai Etzioni, ed. (New York: Free Press, 1969), pp. 150–60.

[18]*Ibid.,* p. 151; and Ralph Dolgoff, "The Organization, the Administrator, and the Mental Health Professional," *Administration in Mental Health,* 2, No. 2 (Spring, 1975), pp. 47–55.

[19]Patti, Diedrick, Olsen, and Crowell, "From Direct Service to Administration," p. 142.

[20]Elbow, "On Becoming an Executive Director," pp. 525–26; and John R. Ryan, "Social Work Executive: Generalist or Specialist?" *Social Work,* 8, No. 2 (April, 1963), 26–29.

[21]Ryan, "Social Work Executive," p. 27. Also Rino J. Patti, "Patterns of Management Activity in Social Welfare Agencies," *Administration in Social Work,* 1, No. 1 (Spring, 1977), 5–18.

[22]Levinson and Klerman, "Clinician-Executive," p. 56.

[23]Some recent efforts to move in this direction are Jack Rothman, *Planning and Organizing for Social Change* (New York: Columbia University Press, 1974); Rosemary C. Saari and Yeheskel Hasenfeld, eds., *The Management of Human Services* (New York: Columbia University Press, 1978); and Burton Gummer, "Organization Theory for Social Administration," in *Leadership in Social Administration,* Felice D. Perlmutter and Simon Slavin, eds. (Philadelphia: Temple University Press, 1980).

[24]Toren, "Semi-Professionalism," pp. 152–53.

[25]Levinson and Klerman, "Clinician-Executive," p. 59.

[26]Patti, Diedrick, Olson, and Crowell, "From Direct Service to Administration," p. 24.

[27]Elbow, "On Becoming an Executive Director," p. 527.

[28]Levinson and Klerman, "Clinician-Executive," p. 62.

[29]Herman Resnick, "A Social System View of Strain," in *Change from Within: Humanizing Social Welfare Organizations,* Herman Resnick and Rino J. Patti, eds. (Philadelphia: Temple University Press, 1980), pp. 28–45.

[30]Patti, Diedrick, Olsen, and Crowell, "From Direct Service to Administration," p. 29.

[31]Elbow, "On Becoming an Executive Director," p. 527.

[32]Levinson and Klerman, "Clinician-Executive," p. 63.

[33]Ryan, "Social Work Executive," pp. 27–29.

[34]The following discussion is drawn from Rino J. Patti, Elenore Diedrick, Dennis Olsen, and Jill Crowell, "From Direct Service to Administration: Part II: Recommendations," *Administration in Social Work,* 3, No. 3 (Fall, 1979), 265–75.

[35]Patti, Diedrick, Olsen, and Crowell, "From Direct Service to Administration: Part I," p. 140.

[36]Rex Skidmore, "Administration Content for All Social Work Graduate Students," *Administration in Social Work,* 2, No. 1 (Spring, 1978), 59–74.

[37]See Edwin Ghiselli, *Explorations on Managerial Talent* (Pacific Palisades, Calif.: Goodyear Publishing Co., 1971), for a discussion of similar programs in industry.

[38]Patti, Diedrick, Olsen, and Crowell, "From Direct Service to Administration: Part I," p. 137.

[39]*Ibid.,* p. 142.

[40]*Ibid.,* p. 139.

[41]See, for example, Michael J. Austin, *Management Simulations for Mental Health and Human Services Administration* (New York: Haworth Press, 1978).

[42]Patti, Diedrick, Olsen, and Crowell, "From Direct Service to Administration: Part I," pp. 141–42.

[43]Nazneen S. Mayadas and Wayne D. Duehn, "Performance Contracts in the Administration of Social Work Education," *Administration in Social Work,* 1, No. 4 (Winter, 1977), 443–452.

[44]Richard Steiner, *Managing the Human Service Organization* (Beverly Hills, Calif.: Sage Publications, 1977), pp. 45–47.

CHAPTER EIGHT

Developing Social Welfare Administration: Issues for the Social Work Profession

In the first chapter we noted that the social work profession was, by the 1970s, engaged in an intensive effort to create a theoretical and educational infrastructure that would sustain the development of administration as a method of practice and produce a cadre of practitioners who would be equal to the rapidly rising performance expectations facing managerial personnel in social welfare agencies. Although much has been accomplished in this respect in the intervening years, a number of remaining critical issues must be addressed if social work is to reestablish itself as a major source of administrative leadership in the field of social welfare. In this chapter we focus on several of those issues that will present a continuing challenge to the profession in the 1980s and beyond.

DEFINING THE DISTINCTIVE ELEMENTS OF SOCIAL WELFARE ADMINISTRATION

As the core profession in the field of social welfare, social work carries a particular responsibility for formulating an approach to administration that grows out of the substantive concerns and special attributes of social agencies, and one that is consonant with the values and purposes the profession seeks to promote in these organizations.

In the first chapter we observed that social work's historic inattention to management had left the profession woefully unprepared to respond to the rapidly escalating administrative expectations that confronted social agencies in the 1960s and 1970s. Lacking their own theory and research, a body of literature, and professional forums from which administrators could derive support and guidance, social workers looked to the established management professions, most particularly business administration, for the knowledge and skill needed to meet the new demands placed on them. Faced with the necessity to quickly buttress an inadequate skill repertoire, it was not surprising that social workers in both agency management and educational programs adopted a wide variety of managerial technologies developed primarily in business and military settings, often without sufficient attention to their possible long-term effects on the nature and mission of social agencies, or their congruence with professional values.[1]

In the intervening years, many of the concepts and tools from general administration have been incorporated into the practice and education of social welfare managers. Management information systems, MBO, program budgeting, cost accounting, cost effectiveness, and a host of other technologies have become integral to the language, if not always the substance, of administrative practice in social welfare.

Abetted by a policy environment that greatly emphasizes efficiency and productivity, this transfer of concepts and techniques into the social welfare sector proceeds apace and shows no signs of slackening. Yet even as this occurs, there is a growing sense of disquiet in some quarters about the potential tyranny of managerial technologies: a concern that the indiscriminate use of these techniques may be subtly, but nonetheless fundamentally, altering the character and purpose of social agencies.[2] This transformation is characterized by a displacement of previously paramount values such as individualization, mutuality, and social change, with such values as productivity, efficiency, and compliance.

In response to these concerns a social welfare management perspective has begun to emerge that takes as its point of departure the distinctive characteristics of social welfare organizations, the ideological nature of social services, and the values of the social work profession. This perspective holds that it is necessary to fashion a model of management that is indigenous to social welfare and committed to preserving its integrity: one that reaffirms and maintains the progressive agenda that has traditionally been sought by this institutional sector.

If this model of administrative practice is to be developed, social work must play a central role in its formulation because it, to a far greater extent than any of the other human service or managerial professions, has molded the character of the social welfare field. No other professional group is as closely associated with this field, nor as heavily invested in its philosophical underpinnings or its future development.

The outlines of this model of social welfare management have begun to emerge. One aspect has been the effort to identify the attributes and processes of human service organizations in general, and social welfare organizations in particular, how they differ from other kinds of nonprofit and for-profit organizations, and the ways in which these differences condition managerial behavior. Some of these points are highlighted in Chapter 2. A second dimension of this model is beginning to be addressed in the as yet small, but growing volume of literature that seeks to determine the effects of various administrative practices and structural arrangements on the quality and effectiveness of social services. Some of these findings and observations are summarized in Chapter 5 in the sections on design and staff development. A third dimension of this model is concerned with the normative and ethical components of social welfare management practice. What is required here is a consolidation of principles and precepts to guide social work managers as they inevitably confront an array of difficult choices and dilemmas. A number of sensitive and important questions face practitioners: the maintenance of client confidentiality and privacy in the context of increasingly centralized information systems; advocacy on behalf of unserved or oppressed populations in a time of conservative political sentiment; tradeoffs between productivity and efficiency and the quality of service; the extent and nature of consumer participation in agency decision making; and the reconciliation of client interests with those of external policy and funding groups. These and related issues are increasingly the object of attention in social work, but the posture of the profession has yet to crystallize sufficiently to provide a framework of choice for administrators on the line.[3]

This may well be the most critical aspect of an emerging model of social welfare administration; because without a clear sense of social mission and a set of ethical prescripts it seems quite probable that "methods of expediency," which Scott and Hart argue have permeated the modern organization,[4] will come to dominate the management scene in social welfare as well. These methods are:

> ... largely a practical exercise in puzzle solving. The rational requirements of technology, the coordination requirements of job specialization, and the productivity expectations of society require that managers direct their energies and talents to finding solutions for the immediate, practical, and material problems that confront them. So pressures for solving concrete problems have overriden any propensity for thinking about values.[5]

A similar fate may await social welfare administration unless it is firmly embedded in a sense of social responsibility.

Thus, although we are beginning to perceive the distinctive elements of social welfare administration, the task of explicating these elements and articulating them into a coherent model of practice lies largely ahead. This model will draw heavily upon the knowledge and technology of the managerial professions, but the selection and adoption of these techniques should be informed by a keen awareness of how they contribute to the realization of the values and goals sought by the social work profession.

RESEARCH ON MANAGEMENT
PRACTICE IN SOCIAL WELFARE

Although a substantial proportion of trained social workers hold administrative positions (perhaps as much as 50 percent), very little is known about the nature of their practice. Such practice research that is done is almost entirely concerned with direct services, and while this is important, the dearth of empirical work on administration is a major obstacle to the advancement of this practice.

Systematic investigation is sorely needed in at least two areas. The first has to do with the nature and characteristics of management practice in social welfare: what managers do and how they do it. Some descriptive research is available (see discussion in Chapter 2), but it is far from adequate. Little is known, for example, about how social welfare managers allocate their time among various tasks, activities, and roles; whether the activity configurations found among this population of managers differs significantly from those of managers in other types of organizations; the strategies and tactics employed by managers to deal with commonly recurring problems like frequent changes in legislative policy, budget reductions, impediments to interagency coordination, and multiple funding sources; and the methods used to install and maintain technologies like MBO and computerized management information systems, and the effects of such technologies on service delivery. In short, what social welfare managers do, how they solve problems, and the like, remains largely a black box. This kind of information is needed to ground theory in practice reality and to inform the development of educational programs. It will also help retrieve the practice wisdom that has been acquired and begin the process of systematically testing its efficacy.

The assessment of managerial effectiveness in social welfare is a second critical area of inquiry. A recent study of education for social welfare administration in social work concluded that a priority need in this field was to:

> organize knowledge around the concept of effectiveness and efficiency within the context of the question: what qualities increase or decrease the probability of effective and efficient administrative practice?"[6]

With the exception of a few scattered studies, scant attention has been given to the relationship between managerial behavior and indices of program performance and worker satisfaction.[7] The discussion in Chapter 5 suggests some of the dimensions of managerial effectiveness, but additional research is necessary to refine and test what is still an embryonic knowledge base. For example, there is still considerable uncertainty as to whether managers can simultaneously act in ways to maximize productivity and efficiency among subordinates and at the same time maintain job satisfaction and quality service delivery. Are some of these outcomes necessarily achieved at the expense of others? We still know very little about the relationship between worker satisfaction and quality of work. Is satisfaction a means for promoting quality work, or is it a consequence of worker performance? Perhaps more fundamental is the matter of whether managerial behavior accounts for any substantial amount of the variance in indices of program performance or to what extent might these performance outcomes be explained by organizational or environmental conditions over which managers have little or no control? To what extent is managerial performance ultimately determined by the personal attributes or past experience of subordinates or their technical abilities?

These and related questions regarding managerial effectiveness will not be easily or quickly answered.[8] Nevertheless, progress in this area is essential to the advancement of management practice. Without this empirical base, the profession will have little basis for justifying its practice prescriptions or for asserting its claim to management leadership in social welfare.

THE JOB MARKET

Ironically, even as social work has begun to devote substantial attention to the development of theory and practice in social welfare administration and to the preparation of practitioners for this field, there is a concern that the number of such positions going to social workers may be declining.[9] Several interrelated factors appear to account for this trend.

First, a view persists among many policy makers, governmental executives, and top-level agency managers (social workers among them) that "social work" is somehow antithetical to good management. The training and personal predispositions of social workers, in this view, makes them particularly ill suited for managerial positions that require, among other things, rational analyses, a willingness to ferret out inefficient practices and force compliance with policies and procedures, and a capacity for making hard, politically unpopular decisions. The title of a recent feature in a professional journal, "Social Workers *versus* Management," (emphasis added) which contains the commentaries of a number of officials in the public social services, suggests that the orientation of the profession is at cross-purposes with the imperatives of social welfare management.[10] The fact that there are thousands of social workers who function ably as administrators and executives in the public social services seemingly does little to modify this assumption. Social workers in such positions often lose their professional identity in the eyes of superiors and policy makers. One often hears it said that when social workers succeed in high-level administrative positions, they do so in spite of, not because of, their professional background. The explanation for social workers' success in administration seems a version of "pull yourself up by your own boot straps"—i.e., social workers surmount the odds against becoming good administrators by overcoming the liabilities of their professional training.

A concomitant and not unrelated development has been the declassification of positions in public social agencies. *Declassification* is a process that reduces or liberalizes the educational and experiential requirements necessary to qualify for such positions. Although declassification has been most pronounced at direct service levels, there is some evidence that it is directed at administrative positions as well. For example, a recent study of job specifications for administrative positions in state public social agencies found that the MSW was exclusively required as an educational degree in only one-third of the job specifications. Master's degrees in the social sciences or other human service professions were considered equivalent to the Master of Social Work degree in about 30 percent of the job specifications. Finally, in 30 percent of the job specifications for administrative positions in social services and mental health, no master's degree requirement of any kind was specified.[11] The findings of this study led the authors to conclude:

> ... that graduate social work education is not widely perceived as a unique qualification for supervisory or administrative responsibility in public agencies. ... The authors' information indicates that personnel systems are making efforts to remove what many regard as arbitrary obstacles to jobs at every level, and the managerial level is no exception.[12]

A third development that has affected the competitive position of social workers in the managerial job market is the rapidly expanding number of graduates from the nation's schools of business administration. At this writing 50,000 masters of business administration (MBA) students are being graduated each year.[13] There is some concern that not all of these persons will be absorbed in the for-profit sector. Assuming this is the case, it seems reasonable to expect that an increasing number of MBAs will seek employment in the public sector, and not a few of these in social welfare. Even though the training received by MBAs is being criticized within business circles,[14] business managers continue to enjoy the status in our society of what some have referred to as a "secular priesthood."[15] Given the broad concern about waste, fraud, and mismanagement in social welfare, it seems likely that business-trained managers will be looked to as a source of expertise to "clean up the welfare mess."

Taken together, these developments pose a significant challenge to the social work profession as it seeks to hold and increase its share of the management job market in social welfare. Clearly the profession can no longer assume that simply because it produces competent administrators, that such persons will be absorbed in this job market. Several strategies seem warranted. We have already commented on the importance of defining the distinctive elements of social welfare administration and launching a program of research that will enable the profession to develop an empirically based practice. These efforts will form the cornerstone of social work's attempts to build credibility in this job market. Beyond this, other initiatives are called for.

Professional schools and associations must make a concerted effort to inform policy makers, personnel boards, and governmental executives about the development of administrative training programs in social work. Despite the number of such programs initiated in recent years, it appears that few outside the profession are aware of this undertaking. Job specifications in public welfare continue to reflect the view that the Master of Social Work is a generalist or clinical degree.[16] Personnel policies, in particular, must be modified to incorporate a recognition that social work, like business and public administration, is involved in preparing people for management practice.

In the years ahead, social work should also seek to extend opportunities for graduate study in administration to the large pool of persons without advanced degrees already employed in social welfare. This will require extended degree programs, which enable persons to pursue graduate work even while they remain employed full time. In a time when the labor force in social welfare is leveling off, or even declining, social agencies will increasingly fill management positions from within. It would seem desirable, then, to recruit to the profession persons within the existing labor force, particularly those already in supervisory or administrative positions. Since schools of business and public administration also increasingly look upon this population as a source of student recruitment, schools of social work will need to accommodate the special needs and circumstances of this group in order to make a case for the marginal value of education in social welfare management as contrasted to more general management preparation. Among other things, the ability of schools of social work to attract this kind of student will depend on the depth, specificity, and practice relevance of the educational content. Specializations in social welfare administration must be equal to those of other management fields in theoretical rigor and technical sophistication, and at the same time particularize these learnings to the problems, organizational structures, and policies encountered by practitioners.

SEXISM IN SOCIAL WORK

Despite the fact that social work is a field numerically dominated by women, there is evidence that both educational institutions and social agencies engage in policies and practices that discourage women from moving into management.[17] Invidious stereotypes that characterize women as incapable of or unsuited to the demands of administrative leadership, though not as strong and pervasive in social work as elsewhere, have nevertheless permeated the institutional fabric of the profession. Not only has this undermined a professional ethos that places high value on egalitarianism, it has also deprived the profession of a managerial talen pool that it can ill afford to overlook. If we assume that managerial aptitude is randomly distributed among men and women in social work, then it follows that the profession has done itself a great disservice by failing to nurture the administrative capabilities of women.

There is another facet to this problem. We mentioned earlier that one of the obstacles to managerial access for social workers is the belief by some, external to the field, that the qualities of social work professionals do not lend themselves to effective management. This external perception may grow out of the sexist attitudes that pervade society. This is to say that the negative characterization of social work as a source of administrative leadership may be partly a function of an implicit logic that goes as follows: Since social work is a woman's profession, and women do not generally possess the attributes necessary for good management, then social work must not be a promising source of recruitment for administrators. One can only speculate, but it appears that the profession has acquiesced in this logic and, in an effort to maintain control over institutions with which it is associated, has sought to "masculinize" its image by selectively promoting and developing men for positions of leadership. The failure to develop women for administration may, in part, be a strategy for building credibility with powerful external publics. This is not to absolve the profession of responsibility, but merely to observe that such sexist practices may be a partial result of an adaptive maneuver by the profession to win the approval of gatekeepers and resource controllers and thereby retain a leadership role in an institutional sector upon which it is vitally dependent. To the extent that this is true, the profession's strategy of "masculinizing" its leadership appears to have been shortsighted. The profession's status is inextricably intertwined with how society values women. To implicitly reaffirm these negative stereotypes is ultimately to perpetuate society's view of social work.

At the same time, under current conditions, the profession is exploiting only a fraction of the managerial potential available within its ranks. How much better to challenge prevailing societal attitudes by offering the very best *men and women* that social work has for administrative leadership. In the last analysis, the profession would seem better served by promoting its most competent managers, whatever their sex, and thereby attempt to alter societal attitudes.

The task of cultivating this latent pool of managerial talent will not be an easy one. This effort, now substantially underway, must proceed on a number of fronts, including those aimed at changing how women view themselves in relation to management, as well as those concerned with removing interpersonal, organizational, and policy barriers that have blocked access to administrative opportunity. There is a literature which details the nature of the programs that will be required,[18] and there is no need to repeat that here. Suffice it to say that much remains to be done in order to insure that women are properly represented in the ranks of social welfare administration.

LOOKING TO THE FUTURE

At this writing it appears that the 1980s will be a decade of curtailment and retrenchment in social welfare: a period in which conservative, even reactionary, ideology will dominate the political scene. Social work, along with other professions and institutions rooted in the liberal tradition, will face a struggle to preserve the humanitarian character of social welfare policies and programs. In part this struggle will be waged at state and federal legislative levels, in part at the level of direct service delivery. But perhaps the most critical arena will be the middle and upper echelons of social welfare organizations, where managers and technical specialists, using the authority and discretion at their command, give shape and substance to the programs implemented. Within the constraints of policy and funding, this discretion can be employed to maximize the opportunities for and improving the circumstances of the poor and disadvantaged. The extent to which this occurs will depend on the philosophic commitments and technical expertise of those who provide adminsitrative leadership. Let us hope that social workers are counted significantly in this cadre.

NOTES

[1]Murray Gruber, "Total Administration," *Social Work,* 19, No. 5 (September, 1974), 625–36; and Rino J. Patti, "The New Scientific Management: Systems Management for Social Welfare," *Public Welfare,* 33, No. 2 (Spring, 1975), 23–31.

[2]For a discussion of this issue, see Rosemary C. Saari and Yeheskel Hasenfeld, "The

Management of Human Services: A Challenging Opportunity"; and Arnold Gurin, "Conceptual and Technical Issues in the Management of Human Services," in *The Management of Human Services*, Rosemary C. Saari and Yeheskel Hasenfeld, eds. (New York: Columbia University Press, 1978), pp. 8–11 and 297–304.

[3]Some important beginning works on this matter are: Charles S. Levy, "The Ethics of Management," *Administration in Social Work*, 3, No. 3 (Fall, 1979), 277–89; Burton Gummer, "Is the Social Worker in Public Welfare an Endangered Species?" *Public Welfare*, 37, No. 4 (Fall, 1979), 12–21; Harold Lewis, "Management in the Non-profit Social Service Organization," in *Social Administration*, Simon Slavin, ed. (New York: Haworth Press, 1978), pp. 7–13; Willard C. Richan, "The Administrator as Advocate," in *Leadership in Social Administration*, Felice D. Perlmutter and Simon Slavin, eds. (Philadelphia: Temple University Press, 1980), pp. 72–85; Scott M. Wilson, "Values and Technology: Foundations for Practice," in *Leadership in Social Administration*, Felice D. Perlmutter and Simon Slavin, eds. (Philadelphia: Temple University Press, 1980), pp. 105–22.

[4]William G. Scott and David K. Hart, *Organizational America* (Boston: Houghton Mifflin, 1979), pp. 38–40.

[5]*Ibid.*, p. 39.

[6]James R. Dumpson, Edward J. Mullen, and Richard J. First, *Toward Education for Effective Social Welfare Administrative Practice* (New York: Council on Social Work Education, 1978).

[7]Joseph A. Steger, Richard Woodhouse, and Robert Goocey, "The Clinical Manager: Performance and Management Characteristics," *Administration in Mental Health*, 1, No. 2 (Fall, 1973), 76–81; Joseph A. Steger, George Manners, and Richard Woodhouse, "Clinical Management: A Descriptive Model," *Administration in Mental Health*, 4, No. 1 (Fall, 1976), 83–90; and Jon P. Howell, "The Characteristics of Administrators and the Effectiveness of Community Mental Health Centers," *Administration in Mental Health*, 3, No. 2 (Fall, 1975), 125–32.

[8]There is a sizeable literature in business administration on the subject of managerial effectiveness, which can provide a point of departure for similar efforts in our field, but it cannot substitute for intramural efforts. See, for example, John L. Morse and Frances R. Wagner, "Measuring the Process of Managerial Effectiveness," *Academy of Management Journal* 21, No. 1 (March, 1978), 23–35; and L. L. Larson, J. G. Hunt, and R. N. Osborne, "The Great Hi-Hi Leader Behavior Myth: A Lesson from Occam's Razor," *Academy of Management Journal*, 19, No. 4 (December, 1976), 628–41.

[9]Gummer, "Are Social Workers in Public Welfare an Endangered Species?" p. 14.

[10]"Social Workers Versus Management," *Public Welfare*, 36, No. 5 (Summer, 1978), 5–10.

[11]Rino J. Patti and Charles Maynard, "Qualifying for Managerial Jobs in Public Welfare, *Social Work*, 23, No. 4 (July, 1978), 290–91.

[12]*Ibid.*, p. 293.

[13]Fred M. Hechinger, "The M.B.A. Losing Some of Its Luster," *New York Times Magazine* (January 4, 1981), Education Section, p. 19.

[14]See, for example, Steve Lohr, "Overhauling America's Business Management," *New York Times Magazine* (January 4, 1981), pp. 14–17, 42–45, 51–53, 58, 62; and David Vogel, "America's Management Crisis," *The New Republic* (February 7, 1981), pp. 21–23.

[15]Scott and Hart, *Organizational America,* p. 26.

[16]Patti and Maynard, "Qualifying for Managerial Jobs," p. 294.

[17]Leslie B. Alexander and Toba S. Kerson, "Room at the Top: Women in Social Administration," in *Leadership in Social Administration,* Felice D. Perlmutter and Simon Slavin, eds. (Philadelphia: Temple University Press, 1980), pp. 195–215.

[18]*Ibid.* Also, Esther Wattenberg, ed., *Room at the Top: Moving Women into Administrative Positions in Social Welfare* (Minneapolis: Center for Urban and Regional Studies, University of Minnesota, 1978); Martha William, June S. Oliver, and Meg Gerrard, *Women in Management: A Bibliography* (Austin: University of Texas, 1977); Rosabeth Kantor, *Men and Women of the Corporation* (New York: Basic Books, 1977).

APPENDIX

Social Service Reporting Form

INTAKE FORM
CHILD PROTECTIVE SERVICES

WASHINGTON STATE
DEPARTMENT OF
SOCIAL & HEALTH
SERVICES

1. FORM'S UNIQUE NO. **26694**

2. **EMERGENT FAMILY**
5 = Yes
1-4 = No

3. CASE NAME ( )

LAST   FIRST   M.I.

ADDRESSES, PHONES   ZIP CODE

CASE NAME ( )

LAST   FIRST   M.I.

ADDRESSES, PHONE

8. FAMILY CASE NUMBER

9. NUMBER OF CHILDREN IN HOME

10. INAPPROPRIATE FOR CPS
MO   DAY   YR   REASON CODES

11. GUARDIAN'S NAMES *(if not same as case name)*, ADDRESSES, PHONES   ZIP CODE

12. WHO CONTACTED AGENCY
CODE   (DESCRIPTIVE TYPE)   KEEP NAME CONFIDENTIAL YES NO

NAME   ADDRESS   PHONE

13. INFORMATION TAKEN BY   24 HOUR SERVICE

NAME   UNIT   CSO   BRANCH

4. DATE IF REFERRAL TO CRISIS INTERV.
MO   DAY   YR

5. DATE OF REFERRAL TO CPS
MO   DAY   YR

6. COLLAT. DATE
MO. DAY YR.

CIRCLE ALL THAT APPLY
1. O.I.
2. REF.
3. C. INV.
4. OTHER

7. CPS STATUS OF CASE AT TIME OF COMPLAINT
(Please circle applicable No. codes)
1. TRANSFER IN
2. NO CPS RECORD
3. CLOSED CPS RECORD
WORKER _____ DATE _____
4. OPEN CPS _____
WORKER
5. PREVIOUS COMPLAINT AND CASE NOT YET ASSIGNED
6. PREVIOUSLY SCREENED OUT OR PLACED IN CONSULTATION FILE

14. NON-CPS STATUS OF CASE AT TIME OF COMPLAINT
CLOSED _____
OPEN _____
(TYPE OF RECORD)

15. **— CHILDREN IN HOME —**
LAST NAME   FIRST NAME   M.I.

RELATION TO CHILD / ALLEGED PERPETRATORS
FIRST   SECOND

ALLEGATION (CHECK AS MANY AS APPLY)
PA PN MN EX SA MI DE

RESIDES WITH
1. _____ SCHOOL _____ SEX____ AGE____
PA PN MN EX SA MI DE

RESIDES WITH
2. _____ SCHOOL _____ SEX____ AGE____
PA PN MN EX SA MI DE

RESIDES WITH
3. _____ SCHOOL _____ SEX____ AGE____
PA PN MN EX SA MI DE

RESIDES WITH
4. _____ SEX____ AGE____
PA PN MN EX SA MI DE

RESIDES WITH
5. _____ SCHOOL _____ SEX____ AGE____
PA PN MN EX SA MI DE

RESIDES WITH
6. _____ SCHOOL _____ SEX____ AGE____
PA PN MN EX SA MI DE

RESIDES WITH
7. _____ SCHOOL _____ SEX____ AGE____
PA PN MN EX SA MI DE

CODES TO BE USED

WHO CONTACTED AGENCY

AN = Anonymous
AD = Adult Protect.
CI = Crisis Interv.
CP = Child Protect.
CT = Court/Court Staff
HA = Health Agen.
HO = Hospital
LE = Law Enforce.
MH = Mental Health
CW = Child Welfare

NF = Neighbor/Friend
SP = Self: Parent/ Guardian
PO = Parent outside home
PH = Physician
RE = Relative
SC = School
SE = Self: Child
OD = Other DSHS Agen.
OT = Other

ALLEGED PERPETRATORS RELATION TO CHILD

NM Natural Mother
NF Natural Father
SM Stepmother
SF Stepfather
AM Adoptive Mother
AF Adoptive Father

FM Foster Mother
FF Foster Father
RM Receiving Home Mother
RF Receiving Home Father
UP Unrelated Child
IN Institutional Facility

GG Group Care Facility
DC Day Care Facility
SI Sibling
OR Other Relative
PP Parent's Paramour
OT Other

CODE EXPLANATION
Allegation

PA Physical Abuse
PN Physical Neglect (other than medical)
MN Medical Neglect

EX Exploitation (non-sexual)
SA Sexual Abuse
MI Mental Injury
DE Death

16. **DATE CASE ASSIGNED**
MO.   DAY   YR.

17. **CASEWORKER**
NAME   NUMBER

DSHS 4-233 (Rev. 1-80)   3

243

WASHINGTON STATE DEPARTMENT OF SOCIAL & HEALTH SERVICES

1. UNIQUE IDENTIFIER |＿|＿|＿|＿|＿|＿|＿|

2. CASE NAME

|＿|＿|＿|＿|＿|＿|＿|＿|＿|＿|＿|＿|＿|＿|＿|＿|＿|＿|＿|＿|＿|＿|＿|＿|＿|＿|＿| |＿|＿|
LAST NAME ⸱ FIRST NAME ⸱ M.I.

CASE NAME

|＿|＿|＿|＿|＿|＿|＿|＿|＿|＿|＿|＿|＿|＿|＿|＿|＿|＿|＿|＿|＿|＿|＿|＿|＿|＿|＿| |＿|＿|
LAST NAME ⸱ FIRST NAME ⸱ M.I.

3. DATE OF CASE-WORKER'S INITIAL RESPONSE
MO. ＿ DAY ＿ YR. ＿

4. DATE OF CLIENT'S SERV-VICE TERM
MO. ＿ DAY ＿ YR. ＿

5. FAMILY CASE NUMBER |＿|＿|＿|＿|＿|＿|＿| Ø |

6. CHILDREN IN HOME — CHILD'S NAME

	LAST	FIRST	MI	SEX	ETHN.	BIRTHDATE MO. DAY YR.
Oldest						
2nd oldest						
3rd oldest						
4th oldest						
5th oldest						
6th oldest						
7th oldest						

7. ALLEGED PERPETRATORS WHO HAVE BEEN PROVIDED SERVICE:

RELATIONSHIP TO CHILD	NAME	ADDRESS	PHONE
|＿|＿|			
|＿|＿|			

8. NUMBER OF CHILDREN |＿|＿|

9. ALLEGED PERPETRATORS DIRECTLY RESPONSIBLE FOR CHILD'S RISK: RELATION TO CHILD

CHILD	1st Abuser	2nd Abuser
Oldest	|＿|＿|	|＿|＿|
2nd oldest	|＿|＿|	|＿|＿|
3rd oldest	|＿|＿|	|＿|＿|
4th oldest	|＿|＿|	|＿|＿|
5th oldest	|＿|＿|	|＿|＿|
6th oldest	|＿|＿|	|＿|＿|
7th oldest	|＿|＿|	|＿|＿|

CODES TO BE USED

NM=Natural Mother
NF=Natural Father
SM=Stepmother
AM=Stepfather
AM=Adoptive Mother
AF=Adoptive Father
FM=Foster Mother
FF=Foster Father
RM=Receiving Home Mother
RF=Receiving Home Father
UP=Unrelated Child
SI=Sibling
OR=Other Relative
PP=Parent's Paramour
BS=Baby Sitter
SC=School Personnel
GH=Group Home
GC=Group Care Facility
GC=Group Care Facility
HD=In Home Day Care
FD=Family Day Care
DC=Day Care Center
IN=Institutional Facility
OT=Other
UN=Unknown

10. STRESS FACTORS AFFECTING FAMILY
(Please circle all codes that apply to case.)

01 Parent Under 20.
02 Single Parent.
03 Marital Problems.
04 Isolation, Inadequate Family Support.
05 Insufficient Income.
06 Heavy Financial Debt.
07 Lack of Work Skills.
08 Financial Mismanagement.
09 Housing Problems.
10 Unemployment.
11 Physical Illness, Injury and Handicap: Parent.
12 Physical Illness, Injury, and Handicap: Child.
13 Alcohol Problem: Parent.
14 Alcohol Problem: Child.
15 Other Drug Problem: Parent.
16 Other Drug Problem: Child.
17 Mental Health Problems: Parent.
18 Mental Health Problems: Child.
19 Mental Retardation: Parent.
20 Mental Retardation: Child.
21 Pregnancy.
22 Heavy Child Care Responsibility.
23 Lack of Affordable Day Care.
24 Absence of Essential Family Member.
25 Physical Abuse of Spouse.
26 Child Abuse of Parent.
27 Newcomer to Household/New Baby.
28 Recent Relocation.
29 Parent Abused as a Child.
30 Custody Issue.
31 Loss of Control During Discipline.
32 Authoritarian Method of Discipline.
33 Lack of Communication Skills.
34 Parenting Skills Deficiency.
35 Other (Please specify below).

11. PERCEIVED RISK: ASSESSMENT OF RISK AT POINT OF INTERVENTION
(Place a degree of risk code in all applicable cells.)

CHILD	PA	PN	MN	EX	SA	MI	DE
Oldest							
2nd oldest							
3rd oldest							
4th oldest							
5th oldest							
6th oldest							
7th oldest							

ABUSE/NEGLECT CODES EXPLAINED:

PA=Physical Abuse
PN=Physical Neglect (other than medical neglect)
MN=Medical Neglect
EX=Exploitation (Non-sexual exploitation)
SA=Sexual Abuse
MI=Mental Injury
DE=Death

12. PERCEIVED RISK: ASSESSMENT OF RISK AT TERMINATION
(Place a degree of risk code in all applicable cells.)

CHILD	PA	PN	MN	EX	SA	MI	DE
Oldest							
2nd oldest							
3rd oldest							
4th oldest							
5th oldest							
6th oldest							
7th oldest							

DEGREE OF RISK CODES TO BE USED:
(See detailed instructions.)

0=None
1=Very low
2=Low
3=Moderately low
4=Moderate
5=High
6=Very High
9=No Investig.

13. AMOUNT OF DIRECT SERVICE FOR FAMILY
(Please circle a single item number.)

1=Low: 2 or less interviews and/or 5 or less phone calls.

2=Medium: 3-7 interviews and/or 6-19 phone calls, may include brief receiving home placement and/or agreed court wardship.

3=High: 8-19 interviews and/or 20-39 phone calls and/or foster care services and/or court hearing.

4=Very High: 20 or more interviews and/or 40 or more phone calls and/or 3 or more court hearings.

CHILD PROTECTIVE SERVICES

14. DIRECT SERVICES (Please circle all codes that apply.)

	SERVICE		SERVICE
01	Investigation	08	Parent Training
02	Crisis Counseling	09	Family Counseling
03	Placement Service	10	Marital Counseling
04	Referral	11	Individual Counseling
05	Contract/Monitoring	12	Sexual Abuse Counseling
06	Advocacy	13	Group Process
07	Transportation	14	Other (Specify below)

15. OTHER DSHS SERVICES (Please circle all codes that apply **and** enter the number of children provided those services marked with an asterisk.

REFER- RAL	PRO- VIDED	SERVICE	REFER- RAL	PRO- VIDED	SERVICE
01	02	Homemaker	12	13	Parent Aid
03	04	Chore	14	15	Volunteer
05	|__|	*Day Care	16	17	Financial
06	|__|	*Foster Home	18	19	Transportation
07	|__|	*Receiving Home	20	21	Indian Child Welfare Comm.
08	|__|	*Group Home	22	23	E.P.S.D.T.
09	|__|	*Institutions	24	25	Family Plan.
10	11	Crisis Interv.			

16. COMMUNITY SERVICES (Please circle all codes that apply **and** circle alphabetic codes if specified service is needed but unavailable.)

PARENT(S) REFER- RAL	PARENT(S) PRO- VIDED	CHILDREN REFER- RAL	CHILDREN PRO- VIDED	SERVICE	PARENT(S) REFER- RAL	PARENT(S) PRO- VIDED	CHILD(REN) REFER- RAL	CHILD(REN) PRO- VIDED	SERVICE
01	02	03	04	A. Individual Counseling	01	02	03	04	O. Crisis Nursery
05	06	07	08	B. Psychiatric Evaluation	05	06	07	08	P. Inpatient Medical
09	10	11	12	C. Family Counseling	09	10	11	12	Q. Outpatient Medical
13	14	15	16	D. Parent Training	13	14	15	16	R. Shelter
17	18	19	20	E. Marital Counseling	17	18	19	20	S. Food
21	22	23	24	F. Group Counseling	21	22	23	24	T. Transportation
25	26	27	28	G. Inpatient Psychiatric	25	26	27	28	U. Employment
29	30	31	32	H. Drug Treatment	29	30	31	32	V. Parent Aid
33	34	35	36	I. Law Enforcement	33	34	35	36	W. Woman's Infant Child
37	38	39	40	J. Alcoholic Treatment	37	38	39	40	X. Volunteer
41	42	43	44	K. Sexual Abuse Counseling	41	42	43	44	Y. Day Care
45	46	47	48	L. Parent's Anonymous	45	46	47	48	Z. Legal Aid
49	50	51	52	M. Developmental Stimul./Rehabil.	49	50	51	52	1. Criminal Prosecution
53	54	55	56	N. Native American Social Services	53	54	55	56	2. Domestic Violence Shelter
					57	58	59	60	3. Other _____

17. LEGAL STEPS TAKEN BY TERMINATION   (Please circle all codes that apply.)

CHILD	NONE	CONSENT TO PLACE	COURT UNWILLING TO HEAR CASE	PETITION FILED	AGREED DEPEND- ENCY	SHELTER HEAR- ING	FACT FIND- ING	DISCOV- ERY HEAR- ING	SIX MONTH REVIEW HEAR- ING	DEPRIVA- TION	RELIN- QUISH- MENT	DIS- MISSED
Oldest	01	02	03	04	05	06	07	08	09	10	11	12
2nd oldest	13	14	15	16	17	18	19	20	21	22	23	24
3rd oldest	25	26	27	28	29	30	31	32	33	34	35	36
4th oldest	37	38	39	40	41	42	43	44	45	46	47	48
5th oldest	49	50	51	52	53	54	55	56	57	58	59	60
6th oldest	61	62	63	64	65	66	67	68	69	70	71	72
7th oldest	73	74	75	76	77	78	79	80	81	82	83	84

18. LOCATION OF CHILD(REN) AT TERMINATION   (Please circle all codes that apply.)

CHILD	BOTH PAR- ENTS	MOTHER (ONLY)	FATHER (ONLY)	OTHER RELATIONS	RECEIVING HOME	FOSTER HOME	GROUP HOME	INSTIT.	FRIENDS/ UNRELATED	RUNAWAY
Oldest	01	02	03	04	05	06	07	08	09	10
2nd oldest	11	12	13	14	15	16	17	18	19	20
3rd oldest	21	22	23	24	25	26	27	28	29	30
4th oldest	31	32	33	34	35	36	37	38	39	40
5th oldest	41	42	43	44	45	46	47	48	49	50
6th oldest	51	52	53	54	55	56	57	58	59	60
7th oldest	61	62	63	64	65	66	67	68	69	70

DSHS 4-234 p.2 (Rev. 1-80)   3

WASHINGTON STATE
DEPARTMENT OF
SOCIAL & HEALTH
SERVICES

19. LEGAL STATUS OF CHILD(REN) AT TERMINATION
(Please circle all codes that apply.)

CHILD	CUST. WITH PARENT	TEMP. RESP. WITH DEPT.	TEMP. RESP. WITH RELATIVE	TEMP. RESP. WITH LIC. C.P. AGENCY	PERM. CUST. WITH DEPT.	PERM. CUST. WITH RELATIVE	PERM. CUST. WITH LIC. C.P. AGENCY
Oldest	01	02	03	04	05	06	07
2nd oldest	08	09	10	11	12	13	14
3rd oldest	15	16	17	18	19	20	21
4th oldest	22	23	24	25	26	27	28
5th oldest	29	30	31	32	33	34	35
6th oldest	36	37	38	39	40	41	42
7th oldest	43	44	45	46	47	48	49

20. CASE PLAN AT TERMINATION
(Please circle all codes that apply.)

	All Services Termin.	Services To Be Provided by Another CPS Office	Services To Be Provided by CWS	Services To Be Provided by Other DSHS	Non-DSHS Agency Will Continue to Provide Service	Refer to Another Agency or Profess. For Other Services	Notification to Juven. Ct. of CPS Termin.
	01	02	03	04	05	06	07
	08	09	10	11	12	13	14
	15	16	17	18	19	20	21
	22	23	24	25	26	27	28
	29	30	31	32	33	34	35
	36	37	38	39	40	41	42
	43	44	45	46	47	48	49

21. REASONS FOR TERMINATION
(Please circle all codes that apply.)

COMMENTS

INVESTIGATION NOT COMPLETED:

CHILD	Child Unable to Locate	Refused to Cooperate	Moved
Oldest	01	02	03
2nd oldest	04	05	06
3rd oldest	07	08	09
4th oldest	10	11	12
5th oldest	13	14	15
6th oldest	16	17	18
7th oldest	19	20	21

INVESTIGATION COMPLETED AND OTHER SERVICES ATTEMPTED/PROVIDED:

CHILD	No Risk, On-going Services Unnecessary	Risk, On-going Services Refused	Risk, Family Moved	Risk, Family Cooperative, Low Potential For Change	Risk, Needed Services Not Available	Risk Minimized, Family Needs Time to Consolidate Gains	No Addit. CPS Serv. Req'd Bec. Of Improv. Family Situation	Child No Longer Living With Offending Adult	No Addit. CPS Serv. Req'd Bec. Parent Rts. Modified or Terminated	Court Unwilling To Hear Case
Oldest	01	02	03	04	05	06	07	08	09	10
2nd oldest	11	12	13	14	15	16	17	18	19	20
3rd oldest	21	22	23	24	25	26	27	28	29	30
4th oldest	31	32	33	34	35	36	37	38	39	40
5th oldest	41	42	43	44	45	46	47	48	49	50
6th oldest	51	52	53	54	55	56	57	58	59	60
7th oldest	61	62	63	64	65	66	67	68	69	70

22. DATE CENTRAL REG. NOTIFIED	**23.** DATE PROSECUTOR NOTIFIED	**24.** DATE LAW ENFORCEMENT NOTIFIED	**25.** DATE FORM COMPLETED
MO DAY YR	MO DAY YR	MO DAY YEAR	MO DAY YEAR

26. IDENTITY OF ALLEGED PERPETRATOR	**27.** ALLEGATION OF ABUSE/NEGLECT	**28.** CASEWORKER
1. SUBSTANTIATED	1. SUBSTANTIATED	
2. UNSUBSTANTIATED	2. UNSUBSTANTIATED	NAME NUMBER
3. UNDETERMINED	3. UNDETERMINED	

29. OFFICE CASE TRANSFERRED

OFFICE NO.   OFFICE

CASE SUMMARY

Index